MW00443583

Woodturning Today
A Dramatic Evolution

Eternally useful

2004: Seven-piece nest of bowls in western maple by Mike Mahoney, Orem, Utah, from the American Association of Woodturners permanent collection. The collection was created in 2004 on the occasion of the AAW moving into new offices in Saint Paul, Minnesota, with gallery space.

Mike Mahoney, a professional turner, carefully selected this section of tree trunk. His long experience harvesting and turning his own wood led him to anticipate its rich color and figure, accentuated by the first stages of decay. He has deftly excavated and released each bowl in turn from a single block, a traditional production method for making nested sets of salad bowls without losing much wood to chips and shavings.

Although the form is utilitarian and these bowls could be used, it's not likely they will ever see chips or dip. The shift in intent—choosing and working with the material for aesthetic rather than functional reasons—is a mark of the contemporary woodturner. Mahoney is exploring woodturning as a visual art, using an old technique to reveal and repeat a remarkable aspect of the material. The sleek regular bowls, arranged in a graduated succession, set up appealing contrasts with the wild figure and line of their rims. The effect is stunning.

Woodturning Today
A Dramatic Evolution

Celebrating
THE AMERICAN ASSOCIATION OF WOODTURNERS
25th Anniversary
1986–2011

The American Association of Woodturners is an international, nonprofit organization dedicated to the advancement of woodturning. Our mission is to provide education, information, and organization to those interested in turning wood.

Woodturning Today: A Dramatic Evolution
Celebrating the 25th anniversary of the American Association of Woodturners, 1986–2011

Copyright 2011, American Association of Woodturners, Saint Paul, MN. All rights reserved.

Editor: John Kelsey, Lancaster, PA
Design and Layout: Maura J. Zimmer, Warwick, RI

AAW Executive Director: Cindy Bowden

Editorial Advisors:
> Jean LeGwin, Wilmington, NC, publications chair
> Betty Scarpino, editor, *American Woodturner*
> Steve Loar, Indiana, PA
> David Ellsworth, Quakertown, PA

Funding support provided by the Windgate Charitable Foundation, Craft Supplies USA, and Dale Nish.

This activity is made possible in part by a grant from the Minnesota State Arts Board through an appropriation by the Minnesota State Legislature, and a grant from the National Endowment for the Arts.

Printed in China.

978-1-56523-587-8 (paperback edition)

Library of Congress Cataloging-in-Publication Data

Woodturning today : a dramatic evolution : celebrating the American Association
of Woodturners 25th anniversary, 1986-2011 / [editor, John Kelsey]. -- 1st ed.
   p. cm.
Includes index.
ISBN 978-1-56523-587-8
1. Turning (Lathe work)--United States. 2. American Association of Woodturners.
I. Kelsey, John, 1946- II. Title: Dramatic evolution. III. Title: Celebrating the
American Association of Woodturners 25th anniversary, 1986-2011.
TT201.W67 2012
684'.083--dc22

                    2010044667

American Association of Woodturners
222 Landmark Center
75 5th St. W.
Saint Paul, MN 55102
(651) 484-9094
www.woodturner.org

Distributed to the book trade by:
Fox Chapel Publishing, Inc.
1970 Broad Street
East Petersburg PA, 17520
(800) 457-9112
www.foxchapelpublishing.com

Dedication

*This book is dedicated to all the woodturners of yesteryear,
from the ancient civilizations in Europe, Asia, and the Middle East,
to all the bodgers, production turners, shop teachers, and
grandfathers who gave us this wonderful craft. Thank you.*

Table of Contents

Woodturning is an ancient craft known to many cultures worldwide, but as you'll learn from the essays in this section, nobody is quite sure how ancient. During the first half of the 20th century, woodturning was part of the high-school woodshop curriculum, but by mid-century, the craft was being kept alive by industrial pattern makers, turners of architectural detailing, and amateur craftsmen working in garages and basements, along with a few pioneers who somehow gained higher visibility.

Cultural upheaval in the 1960s and '70s created new interest in all traditional crafts. A new wave of woodturning artisans emerged, along with a new market in turning tools, lathes, and materials, and a new interest in getting together to share ideas and techniques.

Between 1975 and 1985, numerous woodturning weekend symposiums had been organized, notably in Philadelphia and Provo, Utah, and there had been ground-breaking exhibitions of turned wood. Many late-night conversations had tossed around the idea of an organization for woodturners, one that could continue to produce symposiums, exhibitions, and events, and become a clearing house for information and ideas. But the concept did not gel until October 1985 during the Woodturning Vision and Concept *conference held at the Arrowmont School of Arts and Crafts in Tennessee.*

What does it look like when a craft organization grows from zero to more than 13,000 members in just 25 years? In this section, five former presidents of the organization write about the time when they were most active. Alongside the budget struggles and the eternal problem of how to manage constituencies of members within a large and diverse organization, the AAW soon began to organize its own exhibitions of turned work. The photographic record of these exhibitions tells a parallel story to the organizational one, a story about the rapid evolution of the woodturning craft itself.

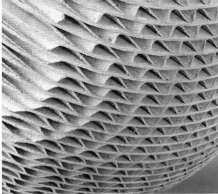

Inspired by nature

2007: Smoke, Wind and Fire by J. D. Mathis, Northeastern Oklahoma Woodturners, box elder, 15.5" tall.

Suggesting a slightly twisted piece of cloth, or the whip of a skirt on the dance floor, or the splash of a pebble in the pond, this vase celebrates the partnership that has recently developed between the lathe and the sculptor. J.D. Mathis roughly formed and hollowed both ends on the lathe and then applied a keen sense of natural movement to inject life and action into this calico-colored chunk of wood.

The box elder is spalted, which means it has been invaded by decay-causing micro-organisms that give it the grey coloring. The red color comes from insect damage. Says Mathis simply, "I turned the wood to the basic shape, then carved the spirals around the vase inside and out." Our eyes know there's more to it than that.

President's Welcome

I began turning wood at about the age of twelve. My Dad was very knowledgeable about American period furniture, built reproductions, and had a lathe in his workshop. My first interests were in turning spindles and I turned quite a few Queen Anne table legs.

College took me away from my Dad's workshop, and after tours of duty in Viet Nam and Europe as an officer in the U.S. Air Force, I traveled extensively over the next 30 years. The lathe in my Dad's workshop became a distant memory, but my fascination with it never left me.

About 15 years ago I found myself living in the Chicago suburb of Hinsdale. The house had a large basement, so I bought a lathe and began turning spindles again. I tried to teach myself new things, but my progress was slow. I knew nothing of the American Association of Woodturners.

Later we moved to Denver and my wife, Melinda, saw an advertisement for the Utah Woodturning Symposium. It sounded interesting so on a whim we went. What an eye opener! While there we had the good fortune to meet Jerry Smith, a PhD educator with a passion for both teaching and woodturning. Jerry encouraged us to join the Denver chapter of the AAW, and we did. That chance meeting with Jerry changed my life. My knowledge of woodturning, my skills, and my creativity skyrocketed, but the thing I love most about the AAW is the camaraderie. I have met thousands of people from all over North America and around the world, and I've become close friends with many. Everyone is so willing to share their knowledge, their skills, and their creative inspirations. The woodturning community is truly unique and wonderful.

Each of us has our own story about how we discovered woodturning and what an important part the AAW played in our development, growth and enjoyment of the craft. Some, like me, tell "regular Joe" stories. Others tell stories of developing into world-renowned artists whose strikingly beautiful

2010: AAW President Tom Wirsing introduces the thick book of information attendees received at the Hartford symposium.

creations demand very high prices. Many diverse stories are included in this volume, reflecting the inclusive nature of the AAW and the many twists and turns in our development over our first 25 years. You will also see, in the beautiful and fascinating photographs, the development of both turning technique and artistic inspiration over those 25 years.

Woodturning Today: A Dramatic Evolution celebrates the 25th anniversary of the American Association of Woodturners. Read on—I promise you will be fascinated by what you see and learn. And if this book is your introduction to our fellowship, I hope you may be intrigued and encouraged to try woodturning, and perhaps to join us.

With warm regards,

Tom Wirsing

Tom Wirsing
President of the Board of Directors
American Association of Woodturners

Editor's Acknowledgments

This book owes everything to the visionaries who, right from the beginning, published a newsletter that became a quarterly journal that became a full-color, bimonthly magazine. In the beginning, these volunteer board members and advisors did the work themselves, then they hired a succession of professional editors (page 176). Members of the American Association of Woodturners built an early Internet bulletin board about turning, and today the organization's sites (www.woodturner.org, www.galleryofwoodart.org) are diverse, extensive, and complete. These decisions reflect the AAW's consistent core mission of sharing information, ideas, events, and good fellowship with everyone interested in woodturning.

Angelo Iafrate championed this 25th anniversary book project during his term as AAW president (page 100). Publications committee chair Jean LeGwin agreed to get it done and has remained on top of it from beginning to end. Alan Lacer and Steve Loar each contributed draft outlines. Larry Sommer, Tom Wirsing, and Bill Haskell offered early encouragement, as did David Ellsworth, Albert LeCoff, and Mark Sfirri.

As the work got under way I have relied on the advice, energy, insight, and labor of *AW Journal* editor Betty Scarpino, plus members Steve Loar, Terry Martin, Ernie Conover, Kevin Wallace, and the tireless David Ellsworth. Dick Gerard, Bill Ramsey, Mark Lindquist, Albert LeCoff, Kevin Wallace, Ed Davidson, Kip Christensen, and Andi Wolfe all contributed important photographs, both new and old. My designer colleague Maura Zimmer created the beautiful layouts. Peter Exton helped me write and edit the many unsigned texts, Monica Day and Katie Weeber chased down caption information, high-res files, and permissions. Malcolm Zander applied his meticulous proofreading eye to everything.

My work on this project also owes deep gratitude to my wife, Tina Fruchter, whose dining-room table has, for months, been heaped with all the paper that supports a major book. Alan Giagnocavo and my colleagues at Fox Chapel Publishing have kindly tolerated my divided attention.

The ultimate acknowledgment has to go to the hundreds and thousands of woodturners, amateur and professional, who have gathered under the AAW banner these past 25 years. Thanks for everything! And keep your tools sharp.

—John Kelsey, Lancaster PA, January 2011

Mission statement, silver anniversary book project

The AAW 25th anniversary book will record the organization's history and recount the role of the AAW and its members in the evolution of woodturning as an art form; the growth of turning as an amateur activity; and the place of woodturning in the context of American and international craft and culture. The book will emphasize personal stories by diverse voices and be illustrated throughout with photographs of turned work, woodturners, and turning events.

ABOVE: **2000: Open bowl with incised bead, spalted big leaf maple, 15" dia.**
This lovely salad bowl with a stable foot was carefully finish-turned after the wood had fully dried, marking Bill Luce's traditional beginnings in the craft. It also reveals his essential reverence for the natural beauty of wood, a shared appreciation that unites turners. Photo by Roger Schrieber.

BELOW: **2002: Selene, round-bottom bowl with raised bead, holly, 6.5" dia.**
Bill Luce has turned his attention to round-bottomed bowls made when the wood is fresh-sawn and wet. In drying, the wood shrinks and the bowl subtly and beautifully changes shape. Says Luce, "The round-bottom vessel can create a statement of elegance and refinement, or serve as a vehicle for a strongly organic statement."

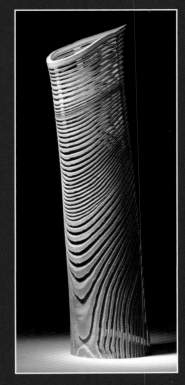

ABOVE: **2009: Skeleton Tube, turned and sand-carved, Douglas fir, 16" tall.**
Bill Luce carefully sandblasted the soft, spring-grown portion of the tree's annual rings, leaving the harder summer growth and the transverse ray cells. The artist has stepped beyond the traditional vessel and spindle forms, revealing in a hollow tube the inner structure of the living tree. AAW permanent collection.

Woodturning evolution

The craft and art of woodturning evolves through the lifelong journeys of thousands of individual woodturners. Since 1986 the field has enjoyed a dramatic acceleration propelled by the exchange of ideas, information, and fellowship made possible by the American Association of Woodturners.

These three unadorned wooden turnings by AAW member Bill Luce, of Renton, WA, illustrate this evolution through the subtle microcosm of one artist's work. All three were turned from local wood Luce himself harvested—a directness of making that is rare among craft media.

Luce's work tends to meditative qualities, generated perhaps by Japanese influences in his youth and enhanced recently by a sensitive use of sand-carving. He has invested years trying to capture the essential power of wood and reveal it in simple forms. In 2000 he produced a highly refined salad bowl that emphasized wood figure and color. In 2002 he was investigating the material more closely through subtle alterations of form and ornament. By 2010 he had stripped the meat from the bone, leaving a delicate remnant exposing the wood's complex structure and its slow, seemingly fluid, growth.

In his ten-year career, the artist has gone ever deeper into the tree's body, finding new ways to express its marvelous nature.

In the beginning

1982: Eucalyptus bowl by Bob Stocksdale of Berkeley, CA, 7" dia.

Bob Stocksdale turned thousands of beautiful wooden bowls during his long career, which spanned from the 1940s until his death in 2003 at age 89. He was renowned for his skill, his eye for exquisite form, and for his ability to see into the log and coax the most gorgeous figure to the surface. His work set a standard many modern woodturners would try to emulate. According to the late furniture maker Sam Maloof (who owned the bowl shown), "Bob Stocksdale was the father of American woodturning." In 1995, the AAW made Stocksdale an honorary lifetime member; there's more about him on page 34.

It Goes Around

The enchantment of woodturning

Betty Scarpino

Enchantment results from the process of making wood shavings—they pile up on shop floors and are the fuel for compost, regeneration, and growth. Our lathes keep us engaged and interested in working wood in a way that other forms of woodworking do not equal.

Instant gratification is part of the lure—a wooden salad bowl can be created in less than a day, from log to dinner table. Chainsaw a log into turning blanks, mount the blanks onto a lathe, apply a turning tool, and shape the wood. Any form from a bowl to a baluster is possible.

Lathes have been around for centuries, way before the advent of electricity. Powered by waterwheels or human beings, lathes have helped woodturners easily shape wood from square to round, as well as simplifying the hollowing of bowls, cups, and other such treenware.

Wood mounted on a lathe can be worked freshly cut (green) or dry, with air-dried wood generally preferable to the kiln-dried variety. And unlike other machines in a shop, the lathe moves the wood, spinning it around. As the wood spins, a woodturner holds a sharp tool, which rests on a toolrest. The turner advances the tool into the spinning wood to remove the unwanted mass inside a bowl. Shavings fly!

There are two basic methods of turning: faceplate turning and spindle turning (see page 16). In faceplate turning, the wood is attached to the lathe with the grain running perpendicular to the bed of the lathe. For spindle turning, the wood is attached so that the grain runs parallel to the bed of the lathe. Wood grain matters.

To attach a piece of wood to the lathe for making a bowl, the turner can screw it to a faceplate, or grab it in a mechanical chuck. For spindle turning an item such as a rung for a chair or a candleholder, the piece of wood would be held between the drive center and the tailstock. For turning a hollow vessel, the wood could be mounted either way—between centers as for spindle turning, or attached to a faceplate or mounted in a chuck.

Live centers go with the tailstock, drive centers go into the headstock, faceplates and chucks thread onto the drive spindle—admittedly, lathe terminology can be various and confusing. But the basic process of woodturning remains straightforward and simple: attach a piece of wood to a lathe so it can rotate around and around, apply a sharp tool to the whirling wood, make shavings until the wood that's left on the lathe has taken the form the turner set out to create in the first place.

Function primarily defines treenware. However, for many contemporary woodturners, function takes backstage to form and beautiful grain patterns found inside the wood. Bragging rights for burls, curl, crotch wood, and flame patterns are what it's all about. Function is simply the excuse...we need reasons and justifications for the thousands of dollars required to set up a proper workshop. Machine and tool manufacturers have taken heed: the offering of lathes, tools, and woodturning supplies has grown exponentially during these past 25 years.

Reflections of self

1986: Self-Portrait by Michelle Holzapfel, Marlboro, VT, wild cherry double burl, turned and carved, 18" tall, from the collection of Bruce Kaiser.

Holzapfel was at the forefront of the movement during the 1980s to elevate the stature of the turned wood bowl, both conceptually and technically. A work such as this leaves the viewer with as many questions as answers. Was it really turned and carved from one piece of wood? Or was the bowl turned as a separate piece, then glued to the carved upraised hand? And what makes it a self-portrait? Is it of the artist herself...or of the wood-art movement?

The field of contemporary wood art is relatively new. Primarily driven by a handful of woodturners, it is enriched by the fascinating combination of hobbyists, amateurs, and professionals. Work from our lathes is expressive and of unimaginable shapes and forms and has spawned sub-categories defined by such words as hollow vessels, multi-axis, eccentric, segmented, therming, lost-wood, reassembly, inside-out, reshaping, carving, and pen making. All are lathe-based, many defy the label of woodturning, but we embrace them all (and you will find them all defined and explained as you turn the pages of this book).

No longer is the thin-walled vessel the line that separates treenware of the past from contemporary works off the lathe. Woodturners make, exhibit, and sell massive pieces, tiny wonders, wavy green-turned nested vessels, hollow forms, teapots, offset-candle holders, and sculpture. Turned pens fetch thousands of dollars. Museums and private collections vie for the best turned-wood objects.

With a very few exceptions, woodturning programs have not appeared in university art departments. Instead, most woodturners are self-taught through woodturning programs at schools like Arrowmont School of Arts and Crafts, the Center for Furniture Craftsmanship, and Anderson Ranch Arts Center. Many professionals offer small group instruction, held in their private studios. National, regional, and mini-symposiums are ongoing, almost weekly.

The woodturning movement spawned several organizations. Or perhaps several organizations were instrumental in causing the woodturning movement. Arguments abound for every version of our recent history. The American Association of Woodturners, the Wood Turning Center, and the Collectors of Wood Art are the major organizational players. Within the AAW, local chapters and their national symposiums are hotbeds of information sharing.

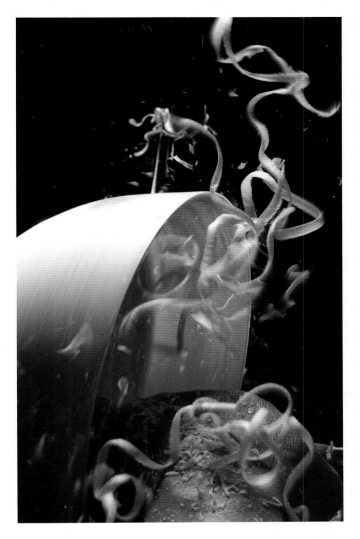

An exciting experience

Moist shavings fly into the air as the turner guides the sharp steel cutting tool across the surface of the whirling wood. The reddish glow inside the bowl is light shining through the thin wall of wood. Compared to all other forms of woodworking, turning is the quickest way to make a beautiful and useful finished object. Building skill at the lathe fully engages the turner, mentally as well as physically. Photo by Binh Pho.

And share we do. The woodturning field is perhaps unique in that there are almost no secrets. Why keep techniques and methods secret when the true ingredient of a successful turned object is the craftsmanship and individual approach infused into the wood?

Betty Scarpino is editor of American Woodturner *magazine, the bimonthly journal of the American Association of Woodturners. Betty's own turned wood art is shown on page 150.*

Not your highschool shop class

How the wood goes 'round and 'round

Treen vessels

Everyone in medieval Europe and colonial America used everyday wooden dishes like these. They were locally made everywhere by craftsmen operating foot-powered, spring-pole lathes (page 26).Wood tableware from Old Sturbridge Village in Massachusetts.

Faceplate turning: bowls, platters

Many contemporary woodturners, like this Colorado cowboy, own or hanker after a modern precision bowl-turning lathe. A machine like this can grasp and whirl a heavy lump of wood without vibration and at high speed, so the skilled turner can shape the workpiece quickly and precisely.

Turning lathe

The 18th-century Dominy workshop, now housed at the Winterthur Museum in Delaware, was organized around its great wheel lathe, here set up to make a round-top table. Such a lathe, powered by a sturdy apprentice, could rotate the workpiece steadily in one direction— a big advance that became widespread early in the 1800s.

Spindle turning: chair legs, peppermills

Many contemporary woodturners, like this Albuquerque kid, enjoy making pens, vases, and bowls on a mini-lathe. These well-engineered and affordable machines descend directly from the lathe you last saw in high school shop class.

Not your momma's salad bowl

Turning hollow

Hollowing a thin-walled form through a small opening. The first time you pick up a contemporary turned pot, you can't believe how thin and light it is. With this technique, woodturners can match the flowing shapes and infinite vocabulary of wheel-thrown pottery.

Barbara Crockett
Rescued Beauty, urban curly box elder, 9" tall

Turning green

The miracle of turning fresh-cut green wood. The wood is soft and alive. The wet shavings fly like apple peelings. It's amazingly quick, from raw piece of tree to completed object. The wood shrinks delightfully unpredictably as it dries out.

Bob Hadley
Let It Be, urban macadamia, 8" dia.

Carving, inlaying, and painting

The artist turns a thin and light wooden shell, then uses it as a canvas to express ideas via carving, inlaying, and painting. The modern power carving tool can be held and used almost like a pen.

Stephen Hatcher
Spring Arrives, urban maple, 7" tall

Malcolm Zander
I Love Yew and I Love Yew Two, Pacific yew, turned and carved, 3.5" tall

Images this page from Turning Green, the AAW juried exhibition held in 2007 in Portland, OR.

Forerunners

1973: Salad bowl by Jerry Glaser, mahogany turned and carved.

During the 1960s and 70s, Jerry Glaser's work took him to London where he was able to purchase whole logs of exotic timber and ship them home to Los Angeles. Glaser shared his wood stash with his close friends, the woodturner Bob Stocksdale and the furniture maker Sam Maloof. After retiring in 1987, Glaser founded a company to make high-quality woodturning tools out of special alloy steels. Long friendships, wood sharing, and technical collaboration have always characterized the field of woodturning. In 2007, the AAW made Glaser an honorary lifetime member.

Woodturning Before 1985

Woodturning is an ancient craft known to many cultures worldwide, but as you'll learn from the essays in this section, nobody is quite sure how ancient. For many hundreds of years leading up to the industrial revolution, the foot-powered woodturning lathe was the only woodworking machine in common use. During the first half of the 20th century, woodturning was part of the high-school woodshop curriculum, but by mid-century, the craft was being kept alive by industrial pattern makers, turners of architectural detailing, and amateur craftsmen working in garages and basements, along with a few pioneers who somehow gained higher visibility.

Cultural upheaval in the 1960s and '70s created new interest in all traditional crafts. A new wave of woodturning artisans emerged, along with a new market in turning tools, lathes, and materials, and a new interest in getting together to share ideas and techniques.

The Useful Wooden Bowl

Everybody had one, for a thousand years

Robin Wood

Throughout medieval Europe, most people had few possessions, but almost everyone would have owned the clothes they stood up in, a knife, a spoon, and a turned wooden bowl. This bowl would be a very personal thing. I have talked with many older people who speak fondly of the wooden bowls they ate from as children. They are always able to describe in intimate detail the shape, size, and particularly the decorative beads and grooves or some other feature in the wood that identified their bowl.

1545: The HMS Mary Rose, which sank off the southern coast of England, held a trove of everyday turned woodenware.

Wooden bowls tend to be incorrectly associated with poverty, but in fact people used them at all social levels. They were often so valued that if one split after many years of use, it was mended by drilling holes on either side of the split and binding the wood together. Many old bowls show signs of years of wear after repair. In the 17th century, the introduction of cheap mass-produced glazed pottery hastened the decline of domestic woodenware.

The historical evidence of wooden bowls is a little like the fossil record, with some periods well represented while others provide little or no evidence at all. Until

Medieval times: Excavations in the old City of London have produced many examples of turned woodenware. This example is partially burnt and may have been used to carry embers for a fire.

1600 AD, nearly every home had a wood fire, and a broken bowl soaked with fats and oils from long use was the perfect kindling. Of the few bowls that were mislaid, only a tiny fraction ended up in an environment that preserved them, either completely desiccated in desert regions or, more commonly in Europe, completely waterlogged, which cuts off the oxygen needed for decomposition. Some of the best finds have been in privies and wells, where a lost bowl was presumably deemed not worth recovering.

Waterlogged wood is fragile and can easily crumble to dust as it dries out. This was the fate of many finds from early excavations, and although conservation techniques have improved it is still difficult to preserve a bowl in its original state. If a bowl has been quickly buried in damp organic waste, preservation over hundreds of years can be exceptional. I was amazed by one bowl from medieval London which told the whole story of its life. It has a patch of bark surface left on its base, showing that the turner had made the biggest bowl possible from a small alder tree. The toolmarks are clearly visible and tell of every turn of the lathe, the sharpness of the tool, the speed of the cut, and the skill of the turner. The bowl was worn and partly rotted before it was discarded, so

perhaps its life ended as a scoop for animal feed. It was also covered with a crusty deposit which, under the microscope, proved to be the pupae of flies. I imagine it lay in a rotting rubbish dump or animal pen before being sealed over and preserved.

Many objects have found their way into what will become archaeological layers only when they have stopped being useful, but shipwrecks are valuable sources. King Henry VIII's warship, the Mary Rose, sank off Portsmouth in 1545 and was recovered from the sea bed in 1982. The cold waters and a layer of oxygen-excluding silt had preserved many wooden artifacts, including bowls and dishes. Such finds can tell us much about how they were used by ordinary people.

The archaeological record often can be filled in using contemporary documents, and it also is possible to draw conclusions about wood from pottery vessels, which survive in great quantities. Cultures tend to use either wood or pottery for tableware, so in a given period if there are few open pottery forms, it's likely that wood was used instead. The Romans were a pottery culture and since about 1600, the English and Americans have been so too. However, for more than one thousand years after the Romans left, the British were primarily a wooden culture.

Medieval bowls were made on a pole lathe very much like the one I use to produce bowls today. This simple machine applies the action of a strong leg and a springy pole to spin a block of wood backward and forward. Depressing the treadle spins the bowl toward the turner for a cut, which appears as a spiral groove. As the process is repeated, the surface of the bowl develops a delightfully varied texture, grooved yet cleanly cut, which is a great part of the essence of traditional bowls. These humble vessels brim with character and life. When I first started studying them, I would have described them as crude or naïve, but I have come to realize they were made with remarkable skill. The roughness is not because the maker was incapable of doing the job well, but because he worked at great speed with simple tools, using green or partly seasoned wood. A bowl made this way twists and shrinks as it dries. From a distance we see a strong but simple form, but looking more closely, we see it is not quite round, and we notice the tooled finish made of hundreds of individual cuts. These subtle details make the bowls feel alive and when I handle them I can feel the touch of the maker from across the years.

Archaeologists have dated turned shale buttons from the late Neolithic period in England, about 2000 BC. In Egypt, wooden stools with legs that probably were turned date from about 1500 BC. The earliest evidence of bowl turning in Britain may be a small disc of wood dated from about 600 BC. It looks like the waste piece cut from the base of a bowl after turning on the lathe. There are several finds of bowls across Europe from this era. A superb bowl from a grave in Bavaria, dated about 600 BC, was uncovered during the 1880s. It is clear from the very fine turning and the captive ring turned around its foot that this was a well developed technology. A collection of Iron Age wood vessels, dated to 350 BC, was found with the Hjortspring Boat in Denmark. The collection includes three turned boxes with lids hollowed

600 BC: A Bavarian grave gave up this fine and very early example of a turned bowl. It was excavated in 1880 and later destroyed. This drawing is from the original archaeological report. It's unclear whether the ridges are intentional decoration or normal tool marks.

through small openings. This also suggests a high level of technical skill.

The golden age of woodturning in Europe began after the fall of the Roman Empire. From around 500 AD until 1500, nearly everyone, from kings to paupers, ate and drank from turned wooden vessels. These ranged from high status cups turned in burr wood with silver gilt rim mounts, to much more utilitarian mass-produced bowls. Wooden tableware and the practice of drinking from wooden bowls can clearly be seen in the Bayeux Tapestry, which depicts the Norman conquest in 1066, and fragments of medieval woodenware have been found throughout Britain.

During the 16th century, living standards rose and those who were well-off could afford pewter plates and dishes. Salt-glazed stoneware jugs from Belgium and Germany gradually replaced wooden bowls as the commonest drinking vessel and potters started making more earthenware dishes. However, the biggest challenge to woodenware came in the late 17th and early 18th centuries, when cheap glazed pottery plates, dishes and bowls became available. This coincided with another rise in disposable income and a great increase in the proportion of households where food was eaten from a table. This change had its effect on tableware designs, so the dishes and bowls of the 16th and 17th centuries gave way to flat plate forms. Wooden eating bowls continued to be used well into the 19th century, particularly in more conservative country districts, but very large orders must have dried up and the turners' market and influence declined.

As the demand for turned wooden tableware gradually dropped, turners had to find new markets, a change that happened across Europe. For example, in Russia, turners started to paint their work and it gradually evolved from functional objects into tourist curios. By the 19th century, painted Russian woodenware was exported all over the world and it still has a significant market today.

In Britain, the most important new market was making parts for frame furniture. Historians have suggested that turned furniture parts have always been common, but in fact before the 17th century turned furniture was restricted to relatively uncommon high-status pieces. In the early medieval period turners made the very special "turneyed" or "throwen" chairs for monarchs and others at the top of the social scale. Three-legged stools with heavy turned legs also appear in illustrations. The earliest turnings in frame furniture were legs for tables and beds, which were turned and then carved. The turners, however, were forbidden by the then-powerful guilds from making joined furniture with square mortise-and-tenon joints. This meant the turners became subcontractors to the joiners. One alternative was to make turned furniture with round joints, which the guilds allowed. The designs of the old massive turned chairs and stools were simplified and lightened, resulting in ladder-back and spindle-back chairs with rush seats, still in production everywhere.

Perhaps the most famous of all turned chairs, the Windsor chair (page 30), started in production in the first quarter of the 18th century. Windsors were made from turned parts socketed into a solid slab seat, and were produced in large numbers in both England and America. Another rising market for turnery was making pulleys and pulley blocks for the rigging of sailing ships. By the early 1800s the Royal Navy alone was ordering 100,000 pulley blocks a year and they were one of the first items to become truly mass-produced by clever machines that replaced hand manufacture.

Some turners continued the tradition of making ceremonial drinking vessels. The most spectacular of these were wassail bowls. By the 17th century, the Anglo-Saxon drinking toast, "Waes Heil" or "good health", had developed into various forms of festive communal drinking. The bowl was filled with warmed ale or sometimes wine with sugar and spices. While early wassail bowls were simple drinking vessels like medieval mazers, in the 17th century, turners made bowls that were too big and heavy to carry. In England, these were commonly turned out of the newly imported lignum vitae, a heavy and dense wood that was thought to have curative properties, notably for treating venereal diseases. These bowls were too large and heavy to be passed around like a communal mazer. Instead, they were filled at the table and small cups were then dipped into

Robin Wood examines an old and well-used dairy bowl.

1600s: A standing cup with finely incised surface engravings, from the Pinto collection, Birmingham.

probably a better indication of their general use in the kitchen. Eventually such new materials as enameled steel and then stainless steel took the last markets for utilitarian woodware. When the last turners approached retirement, there were no apprentices to be found.

For at least a thousand years our ancestors ate and drank every day from wooden bowls and cups. Such vessels are rarely put on show in museums, and photos of medieval wooden bowls rarely appear in print. But especially to woodturners today, these old bowls are an important part of our cultural heritage. They were made as purely utilitarian objects, but they are also objects of great beauty. And they are the direct ancestor of the decorated, thin-walled wooden vessel that sits at the heart of today's woodturning arts.

Robin Wood is a professional bowl turner living in Derbyshire, England. He uses a pole lathe with tools he has forged himself. This essay is excerpted with permission from his recent book, The Wooden Bowl, *published by Stobart-Davies in Britain and distributed by David Brown Book Co., Oakville, CT 06779 in the United States, www.oxbowbooks.com.*

the bowl. Another important group of high-class 17th century drinking vessels is the armorial standing cup—tall, goblet-like vessels with lids decorated with incised patterns representing coats of arms and heraldic beasts.

By the end of the 18th century, bowl turning in Britain and much of industrialized Europe was in serious decline. The tradition continued in less industrialized parts of Europe, such as rural Wales and most of Scandinavia. Larger bowls always remained popular for chopping vegetables and mixing food. In the dairy, they were used for settling milk overnight before skimming the cream and for working churned butter to remove moisture. In grand houses, they were used for washing silver. Invariably, when these bowls appear for sale in antique shops they are called "dairy" or "butter" bowls, even when covered with knife cuts from long kitchen use. In the United States they are called "batter" bowls,

VOICES

Michael Mode: appreciate what was done before

While perusing a book about the nomads of Central Asia, I came across a photo of a man and his wife from Kyrgyzstan making a bowl on a hand-powered, reciprocating lathe. I liked the possibility of making one myself. I called Will Wallace-Gusakov, a young friend and turning enthusiast, and on a morning in May 2005, we put together the lathe shown in the photo. We made one small bowl in the afternoon.

Most of the parts could be made with an axe out of a log and some branches. The mounting spindle or mandrel and the turning tools would be the only things the nomad needed to carry to be capable of making wooden dishware.

I have always thought that knowing the roots of a craft, of how it was done in the old days, is important to my understanding and appreciation of what was done before, without all the technology available today.

2005: Most of the lathe could be made with an axe.

John Kelsey: get the shivers thinking about it

A friend found this turned wooden bowl in a dusty market in Mali in 2004. One of a stack on offer for not much local cash. Every villager owns one, he said, and uses it for scooping, eating, drinking, and washing—for everything. It's 9 in. diameter by 4 in. high with a waxy finish, and holds more than two quarts of water. Small metal staples mend a crack in the wood near the rim.

I can get the shivers studying this bowl and thinking about the unbroken and universal tradition it represents in human culture.

2004: Turned and carved in Mali, a bowl like this would be used for everything.

Colonial era: Dressed in period costume, Ernie Conover demonstrates turning on a foot-powered pole lathe.

Turning Between Centers

Spindles for furniture, chairs, spinning wheels, and stair rails

Ernie Conover

The lathe is amongst the oldest of machines. At its simplest, all that is required is a set of centers, a sharp tool, and some means of revolving the work. A piece of twine can do the revolving part. While most turners today envision wrapping the twine around the work and tying a bowline into which the turner inserts his foot, it was actually attached to a long stick that greatly multiplied the short stroke possible with the foot alone. Once at the bottom of the stroke, a spring pulls the twine back to the starting position. A readily available spring is a tree branch, either still on the tree or mounted above (or in some cases below) the lathe in the shop, hence the name "spring pole lathe." By medieval times, the pole was often replaced by a longbow with halves of the string going through off-center holes in a spool. The rigging was arranged so that turning the spool compressed the bow. When the force was eased, the bow would turn the spool in the opposite direction to the starting place. The whole affair worked much like a modern window shade without click stops.

Early turners did not have the luxury of a table saw or band saw, and so had to reduce their billets by splitting the wood from a clear log of suitable length—a process called riving. The turner first pounds wedges into the end of the log to split it into usable segments and then further rives these pieces with a froe before further reducing the riven piece to something approaching round with a drawknife. A great advantage to riven stock is that all grain fibers are parallel, so a very strong finished turning results. The dainty proportions of Windsor chairs are the results of riving. The entire process, bucking the log, riving, and turning, is done with the wood green. The wood works much more easily green, and as long

16th century: The turner in his workshop in a medieval woodcut from Holland. Note the rack of tools on the wall, and the work-in-progress in the background.

as a complete annular ring is not encompassed in the billet, checking will not be a problem. Once dry, the turning will be slightly oval due to the differences in tangential and radial shrinkage, but not noticeably so to the eye. Ovalness can only be discerned by touch or mechanical measurement.

21st century: A Moroccan artisan demonstrated spindle turning during a conference in Germany. He sits on a low stool, powers his lathe with a strung bow, and guides the tool with one hand and the opposite foot. Photo by Terry Martin.

I have turned a fair amount on a pole lathe, and the exercise brings much understanding of turning itself. First and foremost, your tools have to be razor sharp or you do not get much work done. Since one or the other foot has to be treadling, you have to stand on the other leg, but your hands are in contact with the tool rest, either directly or through the tool. Because of the hand contact, I find balance not to be a problem, though I do switch feet frequently. Most who know a little about human powered lathes will tell you that you have to back the tool away on the reverse stroke. In fact, on normal cuts with a gouge or a planing cut with a skew, you do not. For other cuts, such as incising a groove with the toe of a skew chisel, you do. You do not really withdraw the tool so much as ease up the pressure. It is a matter of timing, and once you set up a rhythm it becomes second nature.

A second type of lathe was the great wheel lathe where an assistant (likely a serf in Europe or a slave in southern America) turned the wheel, which delivers constant rotary motion. I have turned on the great wheel lathe at Colonial Williamsburg with volunteers from the audience providing the locomotion, and there is no essential difference from turning on a modern lathe. A nicety of the Williamsburg great wheel is a sort of bench connected to the lathe frame just behind the turner. You sit or lean on it and it is a very comfortable way to turn. I have wondered if this would be a good scheme for a modern lathe, especially if the turner possessed physical handicaps. You take some of the weight off your feet and you can slide readily left or right to control the tool.

The treadle lathe also provides constant rotary motion at the spindle, but lacks much power. Therefore, treadles were the province of metal and ornamental lathes where diameters were small. Ornamental turning is a cross between metal turning and woodturning and dates to the 17th century, becoming a well-established hobby for the wealthy aristocrat during the 18th century. Ornamental turning is a whole subculture of turning (see page 146) and one can devote a lifetime to this fascinating pastime.

A well established trade

An important thing for the modern turner to realize is that by 1600 turning was a well established trade. By this time turning lathes (and their accoutrements) were quite sophisticated. Lathes with live spindles are documented in Joseph Moxon's *Mechanick Exercises*, published in numerous editions between 1627 and 1700. Various ornamental lathes with advancing spindles and eccentrics to actuate them are also detailed. The art of hand-chasing threads on the lathe had been perfected. Turners worked extensively with materials other than wood, including bone, ivory, horn, tortoise shell, and brass. This is all to say that turning was completely figured out by 1750, and Charles Plumier's *The Art of Turning*, published in 1749, has more information than most modern turning books.

Even with crude lathes, the turner's output was very sophisticated. Mannerist furniture of the 1600s was heavily embellished with turnings of robust proportions and great variation in diameter. Turned elements included complicated legs, bun feet, supporting columns, and split turnings. Interestingly, split turnings appear to have been done by paper-joining the two halves to a thin strip of wood. The reason for this was probably that the turner could chuck the resulting glue-up between dead centers without the paper joint prematurely splitting. Many of these decorative half-turnings were ebonized

James Prestini

James Prestini's exploration of woodturning was directly influenced by the wave of European artists, architects, and craftsmen who moved to the U.S. during World War II. Among these were the founders of Germany's Bauhaus, a school that sought to unify art, craft, and technology. Unlike the proponents of the Arts & Crafts Movement, these individuals viewed the machine in a positive light, and industrial design and product development were pursued. The New Bauhaus was established in Chicago, and it was here that Prestini came to know and be influenced by Mies van der Rohe, Laszlo Moholy-Nagy, and Herbert Bayer. Though these individuals were often at odds with each other, they all embraced the Bauhaus aesthetic of accomplishing the most with the least—an approach that Prestini took to heart in turning wood bowls.

Prestini's exploration of woodturning was short-lived, from 1933 to 1953, while he also created sculptural work in wood, and before he moved on to other mediums including marble and metal. Nevertheless he set a standard for excellence in woodturning and, with the presentation of his work in a major exhibition at the Museum of Modern Art in 1949, established the validity of the wood bowl as an art object.

1940s: Prestini worked with a metal lathe. Its gear-driven tool post gave him mechanical control of the forms he created.

1948: Thin and light turned wooden bowl and napkin rings by James Prestini.

Bob Stocksdale

World War II impacted Bob Stocksdale's life differently. Following the bombing of Pearl Harbor, he was drafted. In an environment of fervent patriotism, Stocksdale chose to be a conscientious objector and was sent to work at a camp in Michigan under the auspices of the United States Forest Service. After the Forest Service learned that he was a woodworker, he was taken to the Service headquarters and shown what he later described as "the most beautiful woodworking shop that you could imagine, with all kinds of tools and everything, and nobody to run them."

Stocksdale was put in charge of the facility and one day tried turning a bowl on the lathe. The results led him to make more, and he eventually began to market bowls through a small shop in Ohio, being given only the condition that he "keep up the quality." Ultimately, Stocksdale created a new approach to woodturning by simply replacing the glaze of ceramic tea bowls from Japan and other Asian countries with the pattern and figure of wood. The path of anti-war sentiments leading to a life as a woodturner would ultimately play out among the next generation of pioneering woodturners.

1970s: Natural edge bowl by Bob Stocksdale, walnut burl, 13" diameter.

Along with his unerring eye for form and wood figure, Bob Stocksdale was first to perfect the method of retaining the natural surface of the log as the rim of his turned bowl. This required perfectly sharp tools, and impeccable technique.

1980s: Rosewood vessel by Bob Stocksdale. Like Prestini, Stocksdale was renowned for his ability to turn bowls with coin-thin walls, the inside perfectly echoing the outside.

Living with Wood Art

1970s: Ed Moulthrop, an architect in Atlanta, perfected a process for replacing the water in fresh-sawn wood with a waxy chemical called polyethylene glycol. This permitted him to turn hollow wooden forms of unprecedented size that did not crack and break.

The orbs flanking the chair are by Ed Moulthrop and his son Philip; the three forms in the background were all made by Philip. The angular turning in the left foreground is by Stoney Lamar. This is the living room of Arthur and Jane Mason, major collectors of turned wood art and leading members of the Collectors of Wood Art, and AAW honorary lifetime members, 2005. More about the CWA on page 196.

Studio Movement

The stories of these five woodturners reflect the currents that shaped the field during these pivotal years: the impact of World War II on the individuals and the influx of artists from Europe, a modernist embrace of the machine in creating work, the legacy of the Arts & Crafts movement, the impact of Asian design, folk craft traditions handed down by early settlers, industrial arts, craft guilds, Scandinavian design, engineering, publications such as Popular Mechanics, and architecture. It was all thrown into the mix during a period of economic recovery following the war when individuals sought out their destinies in an ever-changing landscape where any path could show promise.

Of course, woodworking was just one of many material disciplines redefining itself. What has become known as the American studio craft movement grew out of earlier European craft movements and indigenous arts and ritual objects. Prior to the Industrial Revolution, craft objects had been part of daily life. Following it, artists working in craft media worked in reaction, either by offering an antidote to mass-produced objects or by commenting upon modern life.

During the Great Depression, the federal Works Progress Administration and the GI Bill allowed crafts to flourish at the local and national level. Following the war, the US experienced an economic boom that made it possible for individuals to pursue the life of an independent craftsperson, working as designer makers and building cottage industries. When Bob Stocksdale and Rude Osolnik began their careers as woodturners they did so with the intention of making a living, as did hundreds of potters, metalsmiths, and others in the post-war environment. Artists from the Bauhaus and other European disciplines taught craft processes at the School of Design in Chicago, Black Mountain College in North Carolina, Cranbrook Academy of Art in Michigan, and other schools across the country. In retrospect, it's of interest to note that Germany and Japan, the countries defeated in World War II, were the greatest aesthetic influences in the emerging field of contemporary craft.

In 1968, the Beatles released yet another hit single, the words echoing the spirit of the time: "You say you want a revolution—well, you know, we all want to change the world." The first generation of creative

1980s: Unsung Bowl Ascending #3 by Mark Lindquist, spalted maple burl, 17" high.

Mark combined the lathe with the chain saw (page 63), creating expressive, rough-hewn turned sculptures that won acceptance in the downtown art world.

woodturners had developed markets for their functional work, having no idea that the revolution of the lathe would soon provide a means of challenging the status quo and living for a new generation. The Vietnam War had driven individuals to rethink and reinvent contemporary culture. The ensuing 'back to the earth' movement led many to consider traditional craft media such as clay, metal, and wood as a means to live life as they chose. Yet, the spirit of the work was changing.

Mark Lindquist grew up with the lathe, watching and learning from his father, Melvin. In the late 1960s, Mark studied art at a small New Hampshire college and completed a two-year apprenticeship to a Zen potter. "In late 1960s New Hampshire," he recalls, "opposition to the war and disillusionment with what society viewed as 'progress' led to professors leaving the establishment and going to live in the mountains, kids from the city going into farming, and people eking out a living selling useful items they made with their own hands. There was honesty in growing your own food and making things yourself, and the craft movement grew out of this environment. It was also a time of seeking for deeper meaning in simple activities and objects. I began applying the Zen ideals I learned as a potter's apprentice to the woodturning I learned as a child, and turning away from the time-honored traditions of woodturning, I set out to create a market for wooden vessels as art."

Stephen Hogbin saw a relationship between the two wars and the impact on artists working in craft media: "The second World War had a similar impact on the USA and people like Jackson Pollock expressed a new freedom of approach. Soon after, Peter Volkous punctured the plate in a similarly violent and confrontational manner. Yet, the turners like Prestini and Stocksdale had continued to politely make their wonderful bowls in an Arts and Crafts manner."

As a young designer living in London, Hogbin experienced Carnaby Street in full swing as the spirit of the 1960s transformed the environment. He viewed the conservative nature of design in relation to the previous generation's experiences.

"My training started in the 1950s, and a number of my instructors had experienced the Second World War," Hogbin says. "There is no doubt that war takes a huge toll on the individual and how they see the world. They looked for order in the chaos and felt a responsibility to articulate the need for the designer to bring a new vision. It was very moving to watch their struggle with intentions and creativity. In the late '60s, there was a revolutionary air in the arts. Expressionism was giving way to conceptualism. The captains of industry were leading the way into a cynical world or a place where every one could afford good design."

Giles Gilson saw something else in the concerns of the previous generation:

"I grew up hearing my father and his friends complain that things weren't as good as they used to be…that things weren't as well made. My father would point out one of the new cars and talk about design flaws or how a part wasn't fitted properly. Later, in my studies of both the arts and industrial design, I learned the how and why of quality."

1974: Cedar Chair by Stephen Hogbin, from a suite of two chairs, and a table made from a single 76" dia. turning cut and reassembled. Chair, collection of Yale University Art Gallery; chair and table, collection of Minneapolis Institute for the Arts.

Stephen Hogbin demonstrated the lathe's capacity to produce visually intriguing parts that could be cut apart and recombined into unexpected forms, such as these full-sized chairs with table, sawn and reassembled from a single turned disk of red cedar.

1985: Hollow form by David Ellsworth, figured koa, 8" dia.

1980: Hollow form by David Ellsworth, Sonora Desert ironwood, 10" dia. Collection of Bruce Kaiser.

David Ellsworth was first to solve the problem of hollowing a form through a tiny opening. This technique allowed him to work with wild figure of highly distressed wood.

David Ellsworth puts it this way: "What probably characterized this era for creative persons like myself was a sense of personal empowerment that emerged from the political and cultural turmoil of the '60s. Making money, owning property, and cultivating a future were not our primary objectives. The concept of 'retirement' was so foreign and remote that only our parents could appreciate our lack of foresight. That said, those of us who pursued our art with the intensity that I had engaged probably thought as I did that 18-hour days were commonplace. We played all the roles, including acquiring raw materials, learning techniques, the skills of advertising, photography and marketing, traveling to exhibitions, bookkeeping, taxes, boxing and shipping, writing articles, giving lectures…any and all elements to further expose, promote, and distribute our artwork. Most of all, we became part of a very supportive community of wonderfully creative people, all of whom were entrepreneurs in their own right, and all living on the edge. It was a vital time with vital people."

William Hunter graduated from Santa Monica City College with an associate arts degree in fire science in 1968, passed the exams to become a firefighter, and was called to begin training. However, this career path would not protect him from the draft and being sent to fight in Vietnam. He considered joining the Navy reserve,

but his mind was made up after discussing his options with a college professor. He would continue his college education and take a deferment, leaving open the option to go into firefighting.

While studying philosophy and sociology at California State University, Dominguez Hills, he began working in wood with a couple of friends, eventually creating and selling their wares at local craft shows. He and his friend Harvey Holland named their endeavor the "Global Village Wood Shop," inspired by Marshall McLuhan's vision of the world becoming one unified village with a free exchange of ideas.

As part of the new counter-culture movement, Hunter embraced independence, protested the Vietnam War, and promoted social change. Being an artist allowed him to operate outside the norms of society, take charge of his life, and avoid being part of corporate culture. To

1980s: Twelve Cycles (Calendar Piece) by Giles Gilson, various exotic woods, curly maple, mahogany, 12"

Giles Gilson perfected the intricacies of pictorial inlay in turned work, and went on to craft a large body of sculpture that featured finely wrought wooden surfaces alongside the glowing colors of automobile lacquer (page 141).

realize this vision of a contemplative and self-sufficient life, one guided by a deeper commitment to self-exploration and expression, Hunter and his friends began to search California for a rural property they could buy and settle on. This led him to settle on a piece of land near Yosemite National Park, where he ultimately built his home and studio, and established himself as a wood artist.

Pragmatic Idealism

In the 1970s, the idealism of the late 1960s became increasingly pragmatic.

"Many of the post-World War II artists formed strong university art departments and some, like Alfred University, the College of Arts & Craft in Oakland, the Kansas City Art Institute, and the School for American Crafts at R.I.T., developed programs where crafts were

taught," David Ellsworth recalls. "Private craft schools like Archie Brae, Black Mountain, Penland, Haystack, Arrowmont, and the Anderson Ranch gained strength by picking up teachers from both university and private studios. These schools became the training ground for a new generation of artists working in a craft medium."

As bigger and better organized craft fairs began appearing across the continent, craftspeople maintained a simple approach to display and selling, and many looked on the concept of "marketing" as being part of "the establishment" they were rebelling against.

Mel Lindquist had been creating bowls and vases out of spalted wood for over a decade, though he marketed his work only locally. In the late '60s, at his son Mark's urging, he had begun to exhibit at craft fairs, and when Mark began creating work to sell in 1971, the two looked to regional craft fairs, especially the Rhinebeck craft fairs, which offered an upscale clientele, and to galleries in the Northeast and New York City. In the midst of the rustic simplicity of the craft fairs of the time, Mark created booths that were small galleries, complete with track lighting and sculpture stands. His presentation of the work, as well as his nontraditional approach to woodturning, showing bowls with irregular grain, natural edges, and flaws, opened a new market for woodturning, culminating in the acquisition in 1978 of two of Mark's pieces and two of Mel's by the Metropolitan Museum of Art in New York City. This pioneering work by Mark Lindquist certainly can be seen in retrospect as the "big bang" for the field of woodturning, which had previously seemed to lie dormant in the woodshops of high schools throughout the country with little to no market existing for serious artistic wood turnings.

"Rhinebeck was important because it was close to New York City and they would get curators, department store buyers and Madison Avenue people," Lindquist recalls. "The New York Times began covering 'serious work' in galleries exhibiting work in craft media, including The Elements, Fairtree Gallery and Florence Duhl."

As Ellsworth explains: "The craft shows—particularly the Renaissance craft shows in California, the Pacific States Show in San Francisco, and the Stowe, Vermont, craft show (which later become the Northeast Craft Show at Rhinebeck, New York), both sponsored by the American Craft Enterprises, the marketing entity of the American Craft Council—became the marketplace for crafts by offering direct public sales and a resource for galleries to view and stock up on new work by established and emerging artists. Craft, and the Movement of Modern Craft was in full swing when I came into the field."

"During the mid 1970s, the streets of Southern California were lined on weekends with aspiring young crafters choosing an alternative and creative means to make their way in the world," recalls Hap Sakwa, who was supporting himself by creating small bud vases and bowls. "Handmade houses, granola, tofu, bell-bottoms, Buddhism, and *The Whole Earth Catalog* were a lot more appealing than, say, suburban ideals promoted at the time."

"During the early 70s, I was broke and decided that I wanted to make stuff," Giles Gilson says. "We were all

1986: Perfect Reflection by Hap Sakwa, poplar with resin and lacquer, 19" wide. Wood Turning Center Museum Collection, photo by Eric Mitchell.

Sakwa was among the first woodturners to forsake craft and devote his attention to "art." He later became a photographer.

TOP: 1988: Flutes in palo santo by William Hunter, 10" dia., photo by Barry Blau.

ABOVE: 1997: Flying Loose by William Hunter, cocobolo, 10" high, photo by George Post.

1980s: William Hunter of Los Angeles carved spiral shapes into turned bowls, ultimately piercing the vessel walls and reducing the form to a sequence of curved ribs.

finding ourselves and looking for freedom. We didn't want to go to work for someone else. Some of the people who went on to become leading figures in the field made pipes and other items for sale in head shops. I made weed pots and honey dippers. True freedom was being able to do things for yourself, even if it was humble. In the 70s, a woodturner was a woodworker…thought of as a carpenter. There wasn't a separate category. But when the craft fairs started and Jimmy Carter was elected and his vice president's wife, Joan Mondale, was interested in handmade crafts, it brought an amount of validity to what we were doing."

"I left London, England, to teach in Canada," Stephen Hogbin recalls. "The Vietnam War was taking its toll and Americans were moving to Canada…some to study crafts at the newly formed Sheridan College. The students had a huge impact on my life because they had confronted the big questions in their lives about what is right and wrong."

One of the artists who impressed Hogbin was a young woodturner named Michael Brolly.

"He was interested in the idea of fragmentation and took the concept in a totally different direction to what had interested me," Hogbin recalls. "I was interested in deconstructionism, but that was a concept coming from architecture and unfamiliar to Michael, whose interest in 'other world images' seemed significant."

Michael Brolly says, "I did not plan on going to college. I wanted to be a really great carpenter like my favorite uncle. Since I was not signed up for either college or the Army, in my senior year of high school I had to take a test to see where I stood with all of the other graduating seniors that year, and I scored in the top 2 percentile. The government sent around evaluators to try to guide us into what they deemed the proper slots. It was right after the Tet Offensive in Vietnam. The evaluator freaked out when he saw my scores and said, 'You have to go to college, they are going to make cannon fodder out of you. There is a war going on out there, you will be drafted before the end of summer.' He said, 'I'll get you in college' and he did. I went to Philadelphia Community College and got to take a couple of introductory art classes there. I was self-taught up till then."

Brolly went on to study art at Kutztown University and to expand the language of artistic woodturning with his unique approach to the field.

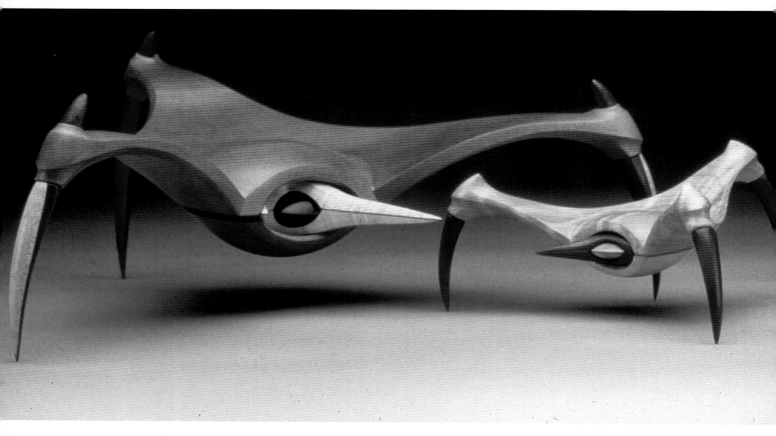

1992: Mother/Daughter, Hunter/Prey II, by Michael Brolly, mahogany, maple, bubinga and ebony, 13" wide and 6"wide, the Lipton Collection. Photo by David Haas.

Michael Brolly, building on Stephen Hogbin's work, discovered that he could create startling images by turning wooden forms and sawing them, then recombining the pieces.

As the 1970s segued into the 80s, the new breed of woodturners exhibiting alongside Stocksdale, Osolnik, and Moulthrop in the emerging craft galleries took a hands-on approach to both their careers and the field itself.

"Our goal was not only to sell the work for our own personal survival, but more importantly to legitimize our craft in the eyes of the art hierarchy that included galleries, collectors, museums, and critics," David Ellsworth says. "It was this challenge that led to the struggle in understanding the balance between traditional and contemporary crafts and, of course, the ongoing debate between Art and Craft. I saw my personal role during this period as both maker and teacher, each sharing the responsibility to 'do good work'. My early involvement in teaching was a natural avenue for me, and it allowed me to help expand a greater awareness of my work to a much broader audience and, therefore, help legitimize the entire field of woodturning as it continued to grow. At that time, my feelings were that to have more and more people doing good work in woodturning meant that all of our standards would rise and that our individual efforts would eventually broaden into a representative 'field' not unlike ceramics, glass, metals, and jewelry. I feel that the formation of the American Association of Woodturners has proven those early projections to be correct."

Kevin Wallace writes frequently on wood art and contemporary craft. He is director of the Beatrice Woods Arts Center in Ojai, California.

1970s

The American Craft Council shows, especially Rhinebeck (New York), serve as important vehicles for nascent stars like Mel and Mark Lindquist, David Ellsworth, and others. The rural ambience draws shoppers, galleries, and museums from the metropolis. The Southern Highland Craft Guild shows serve as a similar venue for Rude Osolnik.

1974

Stephen Hogbin's solo exhibition at the Aggregation Gallery in Toronto forever shatters the circularity of turned work. Coinciding with the World Craft Conference, Hogbin serves official notice that something new is happening in the musty field of woodturning.

Cover photo, Creative Woodturning *by Dale Nish, BYU press, 1975. Nish shows how to turn in black-and-white photos, with a color section of excellent, traditionally styled woodturnings. His book sells many thousands of copies world wide, and turners often cite it when asked how they got started.*

1975

Creative Woodturning, by Dale Nish, introduces working unseasoned wood. Dale lets us know that there is more going on than hobby work in the basement.

1976/1980

Albert LeCoff organizes nine informal workshops at the George School in Newtown, Pennsylvania. These are melting pots for networking and the free exchange of ideas, skills, and techniques. The George School Symposiums shows there is mass and created inertia.

1978

The Art of the Turned Bowl, the first major national museum exhibition of woodturners, is held at the Renwick Gallery of the Smithsonian. It features the works of Melvin and Mark Lindquist, Ed Moulthrop, and Bob Stocksdale. Whether art or craft, woodturning has been granted credibility.

1979

After publishing his book *Creative Woodturning* and attending the early George School symposiums, Dale Nish initiates the Utah Woodturning Symposium which he directs for 18 years. These yearly workshops expose a zealous and faithful following to a wide and continuing variety of contemporary talent.

1980

Wood Turning: The Purpose of the Object, by Stephen Hogbin, explores the lathe as a starting point rather than as an end in itself. Hogbin dramatically and permanently changes how we perceive the lathe and its potential.

1981

A Gallery of Turned Objects catalogs the first *North American Turned Object Show*, organized by Albert LeCoff and the Amaranth Gallery/Workshop. The accompanying exhibition and conference, held at Bucks County Community College, is a Who's Who gathering—Hogbin, Ellsworth, Nish, Stubbs, Gilson, Key, Hosaluk, Sfirri, Raffan, Stocksdale, and many more.

1982

Arrowmont School of Arts and Crafts offers its first woodturning classes, taught by Mel and Mark Lindquist. Arrowmont sets the bar high with excellent teachers in a dedicated though modest wood turning facility, making the big jump to a modern new shop in 1997. This focus is eventually followed by Brookfield Craft Center, Anderson Ranch for the Arts, and the Center for Furniture Craftsmanship.

1985

Art Of Wood-Turned Bowls, by Edward Jacobson is published. Wooden bowls are collectible and their makers are now artists. Envy begins here.

Albert LeCoff: woodturning in my life

My life-long career in the woodturning field began because I was exposed to woodworking in junior and senior high schools in Philadelphia from 1963 through 1968. However, during my teens I also struggled with two choices: dedicating my life to a gymnastic career or to woodworking. I chose woodturning. Here, then, are some key moments that shaped my life up to the formation of the American Association of Woodturners:

1964: I shock my shop teacher

In eighth grade, I made a French provincial side table for my grandmother who lived with us. I painted the maple table white with gold trim so it would match my grandmother's furniture. My shop teacher, who saw the piece as well-designed and crafted, was shocked that I insisted on painting it.

1966–1968: Mr. Acker teaches me something

My high school shop teacher, Bob Acker, was a great influence because he taught us not to copy. There was a table full of how-to and design publications, and he told us that we could use these books for ideas, but we could not completely copy anything from them. We could let the books guide us, but we had to change at least one design element.

1968–1973: I struggle with gymnastics and turning

Having been a competitive gymnast throughout high school, I received a gymnastic scholarship to college. Winding up at the Philadelphia branch of Antioch College, I negotiated an agreement that I could earn a degree in arts and crafts if I completed a course in visual design and an apprenticeship. This was good news, but I was still drawn to gymnastics and wanting to coach.

1973: Skip Spiller helps me get an apprenticeship

To satisfy Antioch's terms and learn woodworking from a master, I followed through with Skip Spiller, a friend of my parents who had already introduced me to Manny Erez, a master spindle turner from Israel. He must have been 60 years old at the time and I was 23. Manny worked in a furniture factory where he made all the prototypes for the turned parts in rock maple. He also had his own well equipped shop where he worked after hours to fill orders for balusters, newel posts, and turned patterns.

1973–1975: Manny Erez takes me under his wing

Manny was planning to return to Israel to retire, and he wanted to be sure that his clients would have a turner who "peeled the wood." He decided to train someone, and that someone was me. Manny proposed that I become his student for one year. The best part was that after the year was up, I would own Manny's complete woodworking shop and all his tools. After watching Manny turn a newel post in less than 15 minutes completely by eye that exactly matched a dozen earlier newel posts, I realized the art in the craft of wood turning.

1974: Manny makes a wood turner out of me

That discovery set me to working with Manny in earnest to learn the skills I needed. At one point, he bought a book, *The Practical Wood Turner* by F. Pain, to show me details to supplement his mediocre English. We ended up working together for two years, and we even moved the shop and expanded it. This became my business, called Amaranth Gallery and Workshop, which I ran from 1974 to 1986. I also taught woodworking at a community center; a school for the emotionally challenged, Ashbourne School; and a small private school, Chestnut Hill Academy.

1975: My first wood-turning workshop

I visited Rochester Institute of Technology where I considered applying for a graduate assistantship. I knew a student there, and as we were going through the wood studio the other students discovered I was a turner and asked me questions about how to use the lathe and the turning tools. That turned into a three-day weekend workshop. The same year, since I had my apprenticeship, Antioch College granted me a degree in arts and crafts with a minor in math, which pleased my parents. I dropped my gymnastics dream cold turkey.

1975: The first of many symposiums takes shape

At the end of that weekend workshop, I decided to look for a school that would be suitable for a hands-on symposium. I visited Palmer Sharpless at the George School in the winter of 1975. Palmer was a skilled turner, and the school shop had plenty of lathes. On a handshake agreement that same day,

Albert LeCoff created the first woodturning symposium in Newtown, PA, in 1976. He went on to help found the AAW and the Wood Turning Center in 1986. In 2008, the AAW made him an honorary lifetime member.

Palmer and my brother Alan and I decided to organize a symposium at the school.

March 1976: We hold the first symposium

The symposium format in March 1976 was simple: hands-on instruction, five very different instructors, and enrollment limited to fifty people divided into five manageable groups. The groups rotated to each instructor to experience that instructor's approach to lathe turning. At night, people returned to the shop to practice what they learned, and the instructors gave them pointers.

July 1976: The idea gets a boost

A story about the symposium was published in the third edition of *Fine Woodworking* magazine in the summer of 1976. The article led to phone calls, requests for notes, and requests for more workshops. That led to nine symposiums—two a year through 1980. We held the number to fifty to accommodate the unbelievable demand. I insisted on visiting every instructor in their home shop before they came—to see how they worked and to make sure they would be a good instructor.

September 1981: I'm launched

After the nine symposiums, Palmer wanted to cut back on his activities, and the symposiums had to come to a halt. We realized that the three of us were the only ones who got to experience all the instructors in action along with their diverse work. We agreed to organize the tenth and final symposium in September 1981 at the Bucks County Community College. The size of this venue allowed us to get 30 of the past instructors to come back, and 100 people registered to take instruction. The list of instructors and attendees reads like a list of the Who's Who in woodturning as of 1981. We also organized the exhibition called the *Turned Object Show.* The exhibit was documented in a publication called *Gallery of Turned Objects.* Through my connections with Dale Nish, the Brigham Young University Press published the book that year. Organizing this exhibition at the same time as the symposium essentially launched me into organizing wood turning shows and publications for the next 25 years.

October 1985: The American Association of Woodturners is born

In 1985, I was asked by the Arrowmont School of Arts and Crafts to give the keynote address at its *Woodturning: Vision & Concept* symposium exhibition in October at the school in Gatlinburg, Tennessee. I concluded by saying it was time for the wood turning field to have its own organization, like the other craft fields. Dick Gerard, a part-time wood turner, immediately stood up, saying that he agreed and that he had a stack of questionnaires that would survey the realities of forming a wood turning organization. This was the birth of the AAW, and I was elected as the first vice president and the chair of the conference committee. It would be formally incorporated in April 1986.

1986: I receive a grant to start the Wood Turning Center

While on the AAW board in 1986, I received a $5,000 challenge grant from a friend. The matching grant was to help me establish the nonprofit Wood Turning Center, which I did later in 1986. My vision was to establish a place full of lathes, with a library and an exhibition space. The Center's first major exhibition and publication, supported by private funders, was *Lathe-Turned Objects: An International Exhibition,* which ran from September to November, 1988, at the Port of History Museum in Philadelphia before a three-year tour.

1976: Albert LeCoff, blue plaid shirt, watches the woodturners watching Manny Erez at an early woodturning symposium held at the George School.

Ron Roszkiewicz: I was a tool merchant

The roots, I believe, for the emergence and flourishing of the craft in the 1980s were established 15 years earlier when one of the most popular publications of the time, the *Whole Earth Catalog*, featured a review by J. Baldwin that highlighted quality imported tools from Woodcraft Supply. At the time, imported tools were exotic. Unlike Britain, the United States did not have an unbroken legacy of apprentice training in the turning trades, nor the tool-making to support it. Imported tools served a very small niche market of artists, tradesmen, and students.

In the upheavals of the 1960s, many people felt an overwhelming desire to return to hand trades and the land as an alternative to grey-flannel anonymity. In support of this movement, the *Whole Earth Catalog* appeared in 1968 with practical reviews that fanned sparks of interest into a blaze. Every home and every college dorm room seemed to have a copy.

The catalog's woodworking section opened with an impressive full page devoted to Woodcraft Supply (established in 1928). Visiting the lone Woodcraft store at the time in Woburn, Massachusetts, was like riding a time machine to the past. The tools were made of rosewood, brass, and oil-coated blued steel. For some of us it was a gateway, we believed, to a more natural place. The cranky old Yankees who worked there had special knowledge they would dispense to those they believed were truly interested. I bought the turning tools and books and went home to figure out the secrets of the craft.

Then in November 1974, I noticed a "help wanted" sign at the Woodcraft store and got the job. Little did I realize that I had arrived at the beginning of the re-emergence of the woodturning craft in the United States. I remained at Woodcraft for the next eight years.

I quickly learned that I was not alone in my enthusiasm. The Whole Earth display brought thousands of inquiries from all over the country, and our subsequent aggressive direct mail campaigns pushed us kicking and screaming into exponential growth.

As a result, more tools, books, and gadgets were needed to feed the retail beast. This was easier said than done, since at the time many hand processes went into the making of a gouge and scraper. Typically made of high carbon steel, woodturning blades were forged and formed with machines driven by countershafts and straps, by workers dressed in leather aprons straddling wide sanding-belt wheels. Add a water wheel for power, and it could be 1850. The shapes of these tools were inconsistent and so was the tempering. There were good batches and bad. We could guess which tools had been made on Monday morning or Friday afternoon.

At the time, most of our turning tools came from Robert Sorby of Sheffield, England, who continued to manufacture them as a courtesy to long-time customers. Their principal business was Martin ice-skate blades for serious skaters and Olympians, but Sorby yielded to our interest for new tools and higher quantities, and began experimenting with new materials and methods. Eventually they replaced freehand-ground carbon steel with machine-ground high

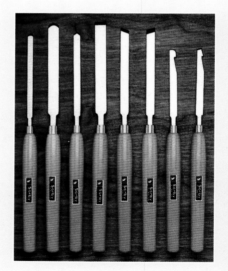

1970s: Long-and-strong turning tools, and deep bowl gouges, first appeared on the U.S. market during the 1970s. They were the first wave in what has become an avalanche of new tool designs and signature lines of tools for the amateur turner.

speed steel, resulting in a better, long-lasting blade. The new tools were easier to sharpen, the edges lasted longer, and they were available in big quantities. Sorby also took on machining the Peter Child chuck, the first of many specialty chucks now available.

With its growing market, Woodcraft was able to sell more and more books, and that too encouraged publishers to focus on woodworking and woodturning craft books. At the time of the *Whole Earth Catalog*, only turning books by Peter Child and Frank Pain were available, and only from British publishers. Neither was useful for teaching beginners. Dale Nish's how-to book arrived in the nick of time, and articles about turners and turning began to appear in *Fine Woodworking* magazine, *Woodworker's Journal* and even *Popular Mechanics*. By the beginning of the 1980s, the conditions were set for the American Association of Woodturners to organize this eager audience. In 1968, Woodcraft had been sending out a couple thousand catalogs and flyers a year. By 1982, we were sending out 300,000 copies of a 128-page catalog, and had grown from revenues of under $1 million to nearly $6 million. By then new competition from Garret-Wade, Lee Valley, and the now-defunct discounter, Trendlines, had entered the field.

Along with this vast increase in the availability of tools and equipment came a flood of grassroots information by way of the many woodturning symposiums that Albert LeCoff organized, and the subsequent formation of the American Association of Woodturners.

Today there are many choices for tools, books, and suppliers. High quality tools are available online and from local specialty stores. In the early 1970s, the choices for lathes were between Delta 14-inch swing home hobbyist machines and 2-ton patternmaker's lathes bought at auction from the local Navy yard. Today woodturners don't have to make compromises and adapt metalworking miniature lathes or full-size metal lathe accessories. The rudimentary four- or six-piece set of turning tools has been supplemented with specialty tools, signature artist tools, and common shapes made out of exotic materials. And there are innumerable books, DVDs, and television shows dedicated to teaching the fundamentals and exhibiting extraordinary skills. In looking back over 30 years, it's certainly possible to think that the tipping point may well have been a good review for a dusty, 50-year-old tool store.

A self-centering scroll chuck, here used in combination with a tailstock cone, offers a variety of secure methods for mounting the workpiece on the lathe. Chucks like these are a huge improvement over earlier methods. Photo courtesy Fox Chapel Publishing.

Turners made a market for tools

One of the most significant things the formation of the AAW helped create was a large market of woodturners who needed tools. Trade shows were quickly becoming a major part of the annual symposium, where attendees could purchase any type of basic tool as well as the latest gadgetry. Additionally, demonstrators brought and used their own specialty tools at the symposiums, only to find woodturners asking about the possibility of buying them. Other professionals established schools to teach the expanding membership basic and advanced techniques, often marketing tools of their own design to the students. I believe it is the symbiotic relationship of the innovator, the expanding marketplace created by the AAW, and the willing buyer that fueled much of the technical innovations we see today. It is not uncommon to see advertising about a new tool use the phrase "designed and used by a woodturner for the woodturner.... "

There were many technical problems confronting woodturners 20 years ago that have been resolved now and hardly given a second thought by present-day woodturners. For example, it was not uncommon to see wood plugs covering up screw holes on the bottom of bowls, whereas now this method of attachment is unacceptable because it can be alleviated by technique and/or equipment.

Innovative developments included devices for mounting wood onto the lathe, highly wear-resistant steel for tools, and ease of changing lathe speeds and direction.

—*J. Paul Fennell, Turning 20 catalog essay, 2006*

John Jordan: lathes—a quarter-century of change

The lathe we use and sometimes take for granted today has roots dating back to at least the ancient Egyptians. While the basic function is still the same, the lathe is much different here in the early 21st century, and the equipment advances in the 25 years that the AAW has been in existence are significant, in particular for the individual studio or amateur turner.

When the AAW's first gathering of woodturners took place in Lexington, Kentucky, in 1987, the choices in equipment were limited. While specialized industrial equipment was being made, geared largely to the patternmaking trade, these big lathes were expensive, and many required 3-phase power. They were out of reach of most turners. A modest number did end up in the shops and studios of enterprising turners, and I know that some are still in use for sculptural turning.

Most of us at the time were using industrial arts or high school shop lathes made by the larger woodworking machinery manufacturers including Delta, Powermatic, and General, or hobby type equipment. Indeed, if not for Sears and Shopsmith and their home shop machines, a number of well-known turners may never have gotten their start. While most of these lathes were capable of good work, they were less than ideal for what is by far the most popular area of woodturning—bowls, vessels, and sculptural work.

The state-of-the-art lathe was the Canadian-made General 260, used by many professional turners (though a fair number also used the pedestal-type Union Graduate lathe produced in the UK). Ernie Conover introduced a lathe that used a cast iron headstock, tailstock, and toolrest, based on lathes from the 1800s, but with modern tapered bearings. It was basically a kit that could be fitted to one's own wooden bed. Delta had a new variable speed lathe using a DC motor drive system that was a sign of things to come, although the lathe itself was less than successful. Jim Thompson built and sold a small number of large custom lathes geared toward the studio/professional turner. Denver Ulery made available parts for shop-built bowl lathes, typically using concrete as a lathe base/stand. Later, John Nichols, who had made parts for Denver, produced fabricated lathes and parts. These custom lathes could be tailored for specific work, particularly large work, which previously would have been difficult. Bonnie Klein introduced a small tabletop mini-lathe that was easy to transport, allowing

turners to make (and demonstrate) small projects anywhere there was a power outlet.

John Jordan

The early 1990s saw the introduction of several lathes that got away from the industrial arts type machines with their limited swing and other compromises. The Australian Woodfast and Vicmarc lathes were very popular. These were heavy, simple machines well suited to bowl turning. Countless numbers of bowls, vessels, and other projects have been produced on these lathes by their happy owners. DC variable speed motors became more widely available on these lathes, a big improvement over the step pulleys or clunky mechanisms of older variable speed lathes.

Shopsmith Mark V five-function combination machine

Oneway lathe

Vicmarc lathe

Stubby 750 lathe

As the popularity of woodturning grew, the lathe manufacturers took the wants and needs of the woodturners into consideration. In the mid-1990s, lathes took what many feel to be the most significant advance in technology—the variable speed AC drive. While DC drives were quite an improvement over step pulleys, the AC drives provided silent, smooth, and trouble-free power. Combined with modern precision bearings and drive pulleys/belts, lathes were now quiet. Smooth and quiet, and a joy to work on.

Oneway Manufacturing in Canada brought their new Oneway 2036 lathe to the North Carolina symposium in 1995. To say it was a hit would be an understatement. A number of other lathe companies have come and gone—some produced good machines, others not so much. Most of the advances in equipment have come from smaller companies and individuals, rather than the large woodworking machinery manufacturers, although these major companies have adopted many outside ideas and improvements into their own product lines.

It is difficult to mention all of these companies and advancements in equipment, but looking back at two and a half decades of the AAW, I don't know many turners that would want to go back. As turners, our input and ideas are valued and often implemented. The mini-lathe that Bonnie Klein introduced has resulted in mini-lathes from many companies. The mini-lathe has become a significant segment of woodturning, and indeed, they are the Sears/Shopsmith machine of today, allowing an inexpensive entry into woodturning. They are also very popular as a way of introducing young people to woodturning.

Specialized bowl/vessel lathes have grown into high quality, state-of-the art offerings from a number of different companies, including the Robust lathe, the Serious lathe, the Stubby lathe, and improvements and new models from Oneway. Powermatic and JET have very popular models in several price ranges. Delta has been less active, but has introduced some new models recently. If your interests or needs are very specific, there are likely lathes made just for you. There are modern, high-tech versions of the 19th century ornamental lathes. Many companies are adapting their lathes for ever-growing special interest turning. Such special features as sliding/swiveling heads, sliding beds, vacuum ports, and sophisticated indexing have become commonplace, all geared toward meeting the needs of today's woodturners.

Yes, the lathe is a simple machine that still provides the same basic function it always has, but we've come a long way since the AAW started, and it will be interesting to see what changes the next 25 years bring.

Wood Stock

How turning changed the timber trade

Stan Wellborn

Prior to the soaring growth of woodturning in the 1970s and 80s, the availability of diverse wood stocks—in species, forms, and sizes attractive to turners—was sparse. Most lumber dealers had limited inventories of hardwoods, usually walnut, cherry, maple, and ash, all sawn into planks and stickered to air dry. Turners often found themselves limited to making spindleware or thin platters and bowls, or gluing up slabs to make larger blanks.

Some of the pioneer masters of course—Prestini and Stocksdale, among others—did scout out importers of exotics and produced iconic bowls from ebony, cocobolo, Cambodian boxwood, amboyna, wenge, and bubinga. Those pieces attracted the eye of collectors, and more and more casual turners began to demand that wood dealers add to their inventories rare species not available to most consumers. In the book *To Turn the Perfect Wooden Bowl*, Bob Stocksdale describes the difficulties he encountered in the early 1960s as he began to see the possibilities in turning wood harvested from around the world, particularly in tropical forests. "I had a good connection in Los Angeles with a place called Tropical Hardwoods. You'd go there, and if you wanted the middle of that timber there, they'd just cut it up for you. It never bothered them in the least to cut up a section, a circle, or anything like that out of a log."

In addition to exotics, by the early 1980s woodturners also saw the possibilities of wood harvesting in their own neighborhoods. Gary Roux, a woodturner in Illinois and also president of the International Wood Collectors Society (IWCS), recalls two big trends.

"Strangely, the first was the availability of safe and relatively inexpensive chain saws—which allowed the average person to cut chunks of green wood and put them right on the lathe or seal them for future use," says Roux. "Now, most turners prefer to use domestic woods they find in their yards or salvage from piles of firewood."

Woodturners scrutinize the turning squares and spindle blanks on sale at a recent AAW symposium.

Turners want colorful, richly figured wood species and unusual natural formations such as these burls.

"The second was a tremendous growth in knowledge about wood itself. The average person might know five species of wood, but a veteran turner today can probably identify 50 to 75 and may have turned many of them," Roux says.

With the surge into the U.S. of imported and exotic species came other concerns. One was health. Many a turner found that certain woods produced skin rashes, irritated eyes and nose, and other allergic reactions. Those sensitive souls have learned to avoid toxic woods or use measures that protect from inhaled dust or skin contact.

Another issue among some turners was biodiversity. Was turning contributing to the demise of rare or endangered species? Were they responsible in some way for deforestation in the tropics?

"Worry that turners are endangering the rain forest is clearly out of proportion to the problem," said Bill Hibdon, who has purchased tropical woods at Hibdon Hardwoods in St. Louis for more than 30 years. "More exotic species get veneered for car dashboards and fancy furniture than are ever used by the turning community. No turner should feel guilty that turning a chunk of imported wood is contributing to clear-cutting in the tropics."

Exotic wood dealers now operate under CITES (Convention on International Trade in Endangered Species) regulations that restrict some imports and forbid commerce in endangered domestic species. It is rare to find a lignum vitae or rosewood log in a warehouse today, and Roux notes that wood scavengers can be prosecuted in Florida for picking up crabwood or oysterwood, even if the trees were fallen and on the ground. Such woods, he notes, still find their way to eBay or club auctions, however.

A California company named Forgotten Woods is an importer that works closely with Amazon basin farmers in Peru, near Brazil and Bolivia, on lands legally designated by the government to be cleared for mining or agriculture. "In today's world, the question is not whether trees will be cut, but rather what will happen to them afterward," says Lance Peck, who runs the operation. "Forests are cut to plant food crops, raise animals, and serve commercial timber companies, and many of those logs most likely would be burned, creating serious health problems and spreading air pollution during the dry seasons, or simply would be left on the ground to eventually rot away. Purchase and use of these byproducts by craftsmen contributes to forest sustainability."

Today, of course, gatherings of turners regularly have for sale band-sawn disks of timbers from around the world, burls and root sections already encased in wood sealer, and exotic pods and nuts. But wood experts increasingly worry about what climate change and pests may be doing to domestic species. Allen Nemetz, a turner and IWCS board member in Connecticut, notes that ash is threatened by insect borers to the point that forestry officials believe the species could be close to extinction by 2020. Some varieties of oak and walnut also are succumbing to an invasive blight and could go the way of the elm and American chestnut.

For those who love to turn wood, it is worth paying attention to the need for stewardship of the trees that provide the raw material for our bowls, sculptures, and evolving art forms.

Stan Wellborn is a writer and woodturner based in Washington, DC, and southwest Colorado. He joined the AAW Board in 2011.

Creation's egg

2008: Hollow Form by Pascal Oudet, Goncelin, France, white oak, hollow-turned and sandblasted.

This amazing wooden egg, turned and sand-carved and shown here at 2x life size, could not have been created if the artist had not picked up new insights and techniques at symposiums and conferences where woodturners get together to share information. Two key ingredients shaped the American Association of Woodturners from the very start. They were the workshop format, which put turners of all skill levels together to share ideas and techniques, and the Instant Gallery, which gave every turner a level tabletop for displaying recent work, seeing the work of others, and discussing it all. Rotating workshops covering every conceivable woodturning topic remain a feature of the AAW's annual symposiums, as does the ever-popular Instant Gallery (page 170), which now attracts more than 1,000 pieces and fills a cavernous convention hall.

1985: Birth of the American Association of Woodturners

Between 1975 and 1985, numerous woodturning weekend symposiums had been organized, notably in Philadelphia and Provo, Utah, and there had been ground-breaking exhibitions of turned wood. Many late-night conversations had tossed around the idea of an organization for woodturners, one that could continue to produce symposiums, exhibitions, and events, and become a clearing house for information and ideas. But the concept did not gel until October 1985 during the *Woodturning Vision and Concept* conference held at the Arrowmont School of Arts and Crafts in Tennessee. On the second day of the weekend event, 13 interested people gathered on the porch of the student dormitory, discussed the idea, and agreed to form the American Association of Woodturners. Their diverse recollections follow.

Vision & Concept at Arrowmont

We needed to communicate

Dick Gerard

To tell the story of the founding of the American Association of Woodturners, it is necessary to begin in the late 1970s. That is when I became interested in turned wooden bowls. My first exposure to these bowls was from *Fine Woodworking* magazine. In the summer issue, 1976, I saw bowls by Al Stirt. Later, in other issues, I was exposed to turnings by David Ellsworth, Mark and Melvin Lindquist and other turners. This solidified my growing addiction to turning wooden bowls. Some of the techniques mentioned in those articles raised questions in my mind, and, being a library rat, I set off to discover if there were guilds, associations, or other groups of woodturners.

My search was entirely manual as this was pre-computer days. My search yielded a list of many kinds of groups for all manner of media, including weaving, quilting, glass, lace-making, all sorts of metalworking from iron to precious metals, jewelry, pottery, ceramics, basketry, and of course woodworking, but nothing specifically for woodturning. With a growing sense of frustration, I had to conclude that there were no groups to which I could turn to for answers.

About this same time, my wife spotted a small advertisement in *Fine Woodworking* for a woodturning-related gathering to take place at Arrowmont in October 1985. She suggested that I attend and perhaps take a survey to determine if there was sufficient interest in forming an association of woodturners. Ironically, the theme of the woodturner gathering was *Woodturning: Visions and Concept*.

My "vision and concept" for such a group only extended as far as maybe a periodic newsletter (mimeographed of course) sent to anyone who was a member. The contents would be mainly "how to" articles, some tool techniques, sources of supply, but most importantly, contact information so that those with questions and/or problems could contact one of the experts for additional information.

I registered and attended the October 1985 meeting at Arrowmont. While there, I badgered, bothered, and bugged the two persons who were the prime movers for this event, Sandra Blaine and David Ellsworth. At every opportunity I could find, I attempted to lay out my ideas for forming a group. Finally, they agreed that a meeting could be held on the back porch of the Red Barn dormitory.

Mark Lindquist was another of the driving forces that helped the 1985 *Vision and Concept* meeting

October 1985: Woodturning: Vision and Concept *brochure, Arrowmont School of Arts and Crafts. The simple brochure unfolded to list workshop topics, which ran the gamut from philosophical to highly technical.*

become the seminal movement for AAW and helped form its future. Mark was an early supporter of AAW and a generous contributor. His efforts are all the more noteworthy because few of the attendees were aware of his deep involvement and commitment.

At that first meeting, my main argument for forming a group was the need for communication among this bunch of work-alone artists and craftspersons from all over the world. Nearly 250 people from all over the world had given up time in their own endeavors, spent their own money to travel to Arrowmont, and paid for lodging, food and drink. It was obvious to me that if we could not form an organization from this die-hard group of woodturners, then it probably was not possible.

At an all-attendees meeting following the impromptu Red Barn session, the idea of forming a formal group was presented. Immediately, two patrons of woodturning, Ray Leier of del Mano gallery (Los Angeles) and Rick Snyderman of Snyderman Gallery (Philadelphia) each offered $500 seed money. David Ellsworth volunteered to act as a lightning rod to draw attention to our nascent group. Somewhere along the line an election was held to determine the first Board of Directors and officers were selected.

In February 1986, the AAW was incorporated as a non-profit organization in San Marcos, Texas, with Bob Rubel acting as our volunteer administrator.

The original vice-president, Albert LeCoff, decided to leave to devote more time and energy to the Amaranth Gallery and to his own vision and concept, which ultimately led to the creation of the Wood Turning Center in Philadelphia (incorporated November 16, 1986). I was offered the member-at-large position on the board after Leo Doyle assumed the role of vice-president.

From the earliest teleconference of the board members, Palmer Sharpless insisted that we should assist in the formation of local chapters. Thanks to his early efforts we now have over 300 local chapters in every state of the union plus Canada, Europe, Japan, and Australia. The first local chapter formed was the North Coast Woodturners of Ohio on December 30, 1986.

The first issue of *American Woodturner*, the journal of the American Association of Woodturners, was published

1985: They didn't have video projectors nor lathes up on a stage, but they did have plenty of enthusiasm, as demonstrated by this avid woodturner finding his own way to see over the crowd at Arrowmont. Photo by Nancy Gerard.

in 1986. This first issue was a newsletter and is now quite scarce. At one time, I had gathered together about a dozen of these newsletters, and over the years, I donated them to various symposiums to be auctioned off for fund-raising.

The Symposium

The first AAW symposium was held in Lexington, Kentucky, in October 1988. All of the work, from the original contact with the site managers to set up to the demonstrations, was performed by the Board of Directors. The Lexington symposium was a gamble that paid off. The success of this first symposium confirmed that additional symposiums were a good idea. Later, the board decided that the location for future events should be moved around the country so that the maximum number of people would be able to attend. Later still, the timing was changed from fall (October) to summer. This change was a response to members with families and children in schools who found it impossible to attend in the fall, but who could combine summer vacations with attending the annual AAW event. It should be noted that many other changes and additions to the AAW have been made throughout these 25 years, most in direct response to the wishes and desires of the membership at large. Even the Professional Outreach Program (POP) is a result of such requests from the professional woodturners in our group. Youth programs, Education Opportunity Grants, Disaster Relief Funds, and insurance policies also resulted from such requests.

Board Meetings and Finances

No one on the original Board of Directors had the slightest idea of what we were getting into. We were not corporate types. We were unpaid. We had no previous experience or training. We had only the $1000 start-up funding mentioned earlier, which, incidentally, was supplemented when Mark Lindquist purchased a full-page ad in the journal. Many times I have remarked that the success of the AAW was because we did not know that we could not create and sustain such an organization with all these elements missing.

What we did have was a non-voting president, a love of woodturning, and a desire to see woodturning not only continue, but to grow. Eventually, three notable women joined the leadership group: Mary Lacer became our administrator (1990), Betty Scarpino our editor, and Bonnie Klein joined the Board of Directors. Except for reimbursement of expenses, none of the board members, editors, or administrators were paid positions, at least not initially. Most agreed to a verbal contract that promised they would be paid at some future undetermined date when the AAW's finances might be healthy enough.

Early Board of Directors meetings were held by teleconferencing. On those occasions where board members, the editor, or the administrator needed to talk to one another, phone calls were made, notes were kept and when the originating caller's phone bill came in, it was submitted to the treasurer for reimbursement. During my time as treasurer, there were a constant series of calls between Mary Lacer and myself and sometimes to David Ellsworth regarding approval to make expenditures. Finances were so tight in those early years that often the administrator was required to seek approval from the treasurer to spend more than $25. Outlays of $50 or more required approval from both the treasurer and the president. If the proposed expenditure was $100 or more, the Board of Directors approval was required.

In our Board of Directors, as in any such group, it is inevitable that members will bring their own agendas, personal quirks, and biases to the meetings. And the decisions made in those meetings will be heavily influenced by those factors. I am proud to say that the board meetings I was privy to were notable in that the overriding factors influencing our decisions were, "what was best for the field of woodturning, what was best for our members, and how could we improve growth, fellowship, and communication amongst our members."

We tried to check our egos and personal agendas at the door and to focus on what was best for the organization and its members.

I believe that the end result, these 25 years later, points to our success in meeting these goals.

Dick Gerard served on the AAW board for six years, four as treasurer. When he retired in 1992, he devoted more time to exhibiting and developing his turned work.

As his artist's statement reads, "The majority of my designs are simple forms that seek to complement and accentuate nature's inherent beauty through objects that have a strong tactile and aesthetic appeal."

In 2004, Dick was made an honorary lifetime member.

The early board

The first board of directors of the American Association of Woodturners was:

> David Ellsworth, President
> Dale Nish, Vice President
> Ernie Conover, Treasurer
> Rus Hurt, Secretary
> Albert LeCoff
> Bill Hunter
> David Lipscomb
> Palmer Sharpless
> Alan Stirt

Between the date of incorporation and the first Journal (June 1986), Albert LeCoff replaced Dale Nish as vice president and Leo Doyle was added as a member at large.

Later, in December 1986, some changes to the board were made, resulting in this line up:

> David Ellsworth, President
> Leo Doyle, Vice President
> Ernie Conover, Treasurer
> Rus Hurt, Secretary
> Bill Hunter
> David Lipscomb (replaced June 1987 by Rude Osolnik)
> Palmer Sharpless
> Alan Stirt
> Dick Gerard (became Treasurer in late 1988)
> David Lipscomb, Editor

Board of Advisors
> Rude Osolnik
> Dale Nish
> Edward (Bud) Jacobson
> Albert LeCoff

For a complete listing of officers and directors, see page 248.

VOICES

Kip Powers: you had to join to vote

My name is Kip Powers and my membership number is 111. I had the good fortune to be in attendance at Arrowmont's *Woodturning: Vision and Concept* conference where the idea of forming an association was first suggested by, if I recall correctly, Dick Gerard. A beginning turner at the time, I was overwhelmed at the skills of the demonstrators: David Ellsworth, Del Stubbs, Al Stirt, and several others. Things I recall: Al's easy manner, Del's enthusiasm, David blowing up a hollow cylinder. "I forgot that it was poplar," he explained.

There must have been a list passed around to sign, as shortly thereafter I received a mailing from Bob Rubel, who had volunteered to be the administrator, mentioning what dues would be and listing nominees for office for whom to vote. Figuring that you needed to be a dues payer to vote, I sent back a check—$25 if memory serves—and a ballot. I received a note from Bob that he'd hold the check should the formation not go ahead—it was a few months before it was cashed.

Some time later, I became a member of the Gulf Coast Woodturners (GCWT), the Houston area chapter of AAW. I resided in Port Arthur, Texas, about 100 miles east of Houston

at the time and for several years there were a few members who carpooled over to Houston for the monthly chapter meetings. I learned much—probably most of what I know—from interactions with the GCWT members and from attendance at the annual symposiums and workshops at Arrowmont.

After I retired from a career as a research and development chemist in the oil industry, my wife and I relocated to Northwest Arkansas in 2002. There was, on our arrival, no organized turning activity in the area, and it didn't take long for me to realize that I missed having it. Starting by emailing members gleaned from the annual AAW directory, we had a couple of preliminary meetings at my home and organized to become the Stateline Woodturners, now the AAW Chapter serving northwest Arkansas, southwest Missouri, and northeastern Oklahoma. I was privileged to serve the chapter as president for its first two years. We have grown from the initial group of five sitting around our kitchen table to an active group with over sixty members. My membership in the AAW and local chapters has been a source of joy and inspiration, and I look forward to continuing to learn from and, I hope, contributing to the organization.

Judy Ditmer: I was enchanted, and case furniture was doomed

In 1985, I was new to woodworking and had virtually no knowledge of turning. I had seen an ad for the *Vision and Concept* conference at Arrowmont. I love the Smoky Mountains and was curious about turning, so I decided to go.

When I walked into the opening of the show at the conference that first night, I was stunned. I had no idea what kinds of things were being done with lathes. That exhibit was a revelation. I looked at the pieces over and over. During the weekend, I attended as many demonstrations and events as possible, and returned again and again to the gallery to look at the work and to listen to people discuss what they were seeing. I was enchanted, and although I didn't know it yet, my plans to continue building case pieces and other furniture were doomed from that day.

Most of the technical aspects of the demonstrations, of course, went right over my head, but I watched them closely anyway. (It later surprised me how many things from those sessions returned to me in the next few years as I became ready to make

use of them. This has informed my own teaching ever since.) I was fascinated by how straightforward this process was, by how little had to come between the turner and the work, and by the many ways people were using this simple machine to produce such a huge variety of objects. I drove back to my lodgings at night with visions of bowls, gouges, and shavings spinning in my head; I went to sleep with mental pictures I could not yet understand of round things exploding and becoming entirely different.

I clearly remember sitting by the creek at the picnic where I met Dick Gerard, who was talking to anyone who would listen about the idea of starting an organization of and for woodturners. How little I imagined what that idea would lead to and how so many of the people I had met that weekend would become a remarkable part of my life. After twenty-five years of turning and nearly that many of teaching, I continue to add to the treasures this field and this organization have helped to bring into my life.

Two Big Things: Workshop Format, Instant Gallery

David Ellsworth

To appreciate the significance of the formation of the AAW in 1986, let's look at what had occurred in the woodturning world just prior to that date. There was accelerating growth in the numbers of turners involved, the origins of workshop classes in multi-media craft schools, advancements in innovative tools and techniques, a renewed consciousness in design and standards of quality in making, a series of national and international woodturning conferences, plus a growing number of exhibition venues that included craft shows, galleries, and museums. The era was ripe for some form of service organization that could address the collective needs of a growing field that included novice-to-advanced levels of turners, gallery owners, collectors, and museum curators.

It was clear that in order to become effective, this new organization would need to be a not-for-profit (501-C-3), be membership-based, and have a basic philosophy that focused on education, plus a means of communication with its members. The final element was an annual conference that would become the gathering place for one-on-one communication and would provide the collective boost that all organizations need to keep the energy moving.

There were very few academic institutions that provided training in woodturning at the time, the most widely recognized being the woodworking programs led by Rude Osolnik at Berea College in Berea, Kentucky, and by Dale Nish at Brigham Young University in Provo, Utah. Both men were highly recognized turners, and Dale had recently completed the third of three books, which together became the most widely read books in the history of modern woodturning. But, for this new

organization to promote education to members that covered the entire country, the academic model was too restrictive and too slow. Instead, we used the model that had been most successful up to that point: the workshop format.

The workshop format began with the formation of the Philadelphia woodturning symposiums that were held twice each year between 1976 and 1981 at the George School in Newtown, Pennsylvania. These events were the brainchild of Albert LeCoff, while the nuts-and-bolts of these gatherings were managed by Albert's twin brother, Alan, and the late Palmer Sharpless, the legendary and long-term (38 years) woodshop teacher at the George School.

The core philosophy

Two primary elements evolved during these symposiums that would directly affect the core philosophy of the AAW. First was the opportunity for individuals at any and all skill levels to gather in a down-and-dirty, elbow-rubbing environment where the latest and greatest ideas in woodturning technology, methods, and design approaches could be shared. These were non-hierarchical learning events that focused on demonstrations of techniques targeted to the needs of the attendees rather than the teachers.

Second, these events were the first opportunity for attendees and instructors alike to show their work in an informal, non-juried setting: tables or benches with white paper covers and sometimes just tables and benches. Critiques were held in a discussion-like format where the instructors offered commentary on every conceivable

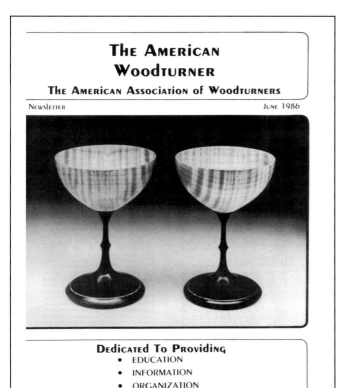

June 1986: The cover of the AAW's first and last newsletter announcing the ambitious formation of the new organization.

September 1986: The first issue of the AW Journal, *American Woodturner*. It had twenty-eight black-and-white pages and sported five photos.

subject from technique to selection and interpretation of material to design. These Instant Galleries have become a major feature of today's AAW annual symposiums. They provide a pulse of the growth of the field, as well as a chance to discover new talent.

The decade prior to the formation of the AAW saw enormous growth in the number of turners. This, plus the technical and aesthetic achievements that occurred during this decade, led directly into the need for some form of support system for what was beginning to look like a "field of woodturning" rather than simply a large group of talented individuals. To emphasize this idea, consider that by 1982, four years before the formation of the AAW, all the primary design styles in contemporary turning had been established and had reached a modicum of maturity. These included bowls, platters, spindles, architectural forms, sculpture, hollow forms, and segmented forms. Surface decoration involving both color and carving was also highly advanced.

Collectively, this extensive growth in such a short period provided the energy, content, and personnel that would help pull woodturning out of the confines of its industrial past and onto a stage in the decorative arts that was shared with the established fields of ceramics, glass, fiber, and metal. It is also important to recognize that unlike these other media fields, woodturning did not have an academic or art(full) base. In effect, woodturning had never graduated beyond high school woodshop class, while the other media fields had gone on to graduate school in university art departments.

Important exhibitions

Parallel with this vast growth of individuals and the objects being produced was a growing number of national and international exhibitions of turned objects. These visually exciting exhibitions helped define the upper limits of the field and led both seasoned vets and their young admirers to step forth with work that constantly challenged their own skills.

...by 1982, all the primary design styles had already been established: bowls, platters, spindles, architectural forms, sculpture, hollow forms, and segmented forms...with surface decoration via color and carving...

These most important exhibitions began with *The Art of the Turned Bowl*, 1978, mounted at the Renwick Gallery of the Smithsonian Institution in Washington, D.C. It featured works by Ed Moulthrop, Bob Stocksdale, and Mark and Melvin Lindquist. It was followed by the *Gallery of Turned Objects: The First North American Turned Object Show*, in 1981. Obviously a questionable title, this exhibition was put together by Albert LeCoff, then director of the Amaranth Gallery and Workshop in Philadelphia, and juried by Rude Osolnik and myself. A small black-and-white catalog was published with images photographed by Bobby Hansson. Having first been exhibited at Bucks County Community College in Newtown, Pennsylvania, and afterward having gone on to several regional museums, this exhibition could fairly claim to be the field's first traveling collection. The American Craft Museum in New York City had a show in 1983 titled *The Art of Turned Wood* that was curated by its director, Paul Smith. The *Edward (Bud) Jacobson Collection of Turned Wood Bowls* exhibition opened at the Renwick Gallery of the Smithsonian Institution in April, 1986. And finally, the International Turned Objects Show (ITOS), titled *Lathe-Turned Objects* was organized by Albert LeCoff of the Wood Turning Center and shown at the Port of History Museum in Philadelphia in 1988. This was the premier exhibition of the time, featuring a color catalog with images photographed by Eric Mitchell and juried by Rude Osolnik, Albert LeCoff, and myself.

As these exhibitions show, by the early 1980s the "art" aspect of woodturning had clearly made its presence known and helped create an interesting duality that would continue to challenge the basic philosophy of the AAW. That is, how to address the craft-to-art conundrum

1985: Arrowmont School of Arts and Crafts, Tennessee. Arrowmont's broad crafts curriculum made it the ideal incubator for the conference where the AAW was born. The school later installed the nation's first art-based teaching facility for woodturning.

1985: After a hard day demonstrating turning, the then-young Del Stubbs (left) and Al Stirt laugh it up on an Arrowmont evening. Stirt created a career of turning and teaching, and in 1997 became an honorary lifetime member of the AAW. Photo by Bill Ramsay.

when approximately 95% of your projected members are traditional craftspersons while the other 5% (at best) are the contemporary artists getting all the public attention. This dynamic was certainly nothing new to the other, more mature craft media groups, but it would definitely become a factor for our young organization.

The final link that connects all these various elements of growth in woodturning would be the multi-media

MEMBERSHIP

We now have slightly over 500 members! The states with the largest number of members are California (47), Ohio (36), Pennsylvania (33), Tennessee (30), Texas (23), and Colorado (21). We have members from almost all of the states, including Alaska (4) and Hawaii (5). The geographic spread is fairly even: 100 members in the Northeast, 96 in the North Central, 87 in the Southwest, 78 in the South Central and 77 in the Southeast. That leaves the Northwest, Alaska and Hawaii with 41. We have a few members that are out-of-country. Five or so from Australia/New Zealand and four from Canada. One member lives in Belgium!

1985: David Ellsworth (left) and Stoney Lamar (center) confront Mark Lindquist's marriage of chainsaw and lathe, *Vision and Concept* conference, Arrowmont.

1986: Membership report from the first issue of *American Woodturner.*

1985: Ed Moulthrop, left, already widely known for his huge turned orbs (page 37), shares the Arrowmont evening with woodturner Dana Curtis. In 1994 the AAW recognized Moulthrop as an lifetime honorary member. Photo by Bill Ramsay.

craft schools that sponsored woodturning workshops. The most significant of these would be the Anderson Ranch Arts Center, Appalachian Center for Craft, Brookfield Craft Center, Penland School for Craft, Haystack Mountain School, and, most important, the Arrowmont School of Arts and Craft in Gatlinburg, Tennessee.

Mark and Melvin Lindquist initiated Arrowmont's woodturning program in 1981 with the full support of then-director Sandy Blain. I began teaching there in 1983 and have taught one-week classes every year since. Mark was also a major player in organizing the October 1985 conference titled: *Woodturning: A Motion To The Future.* This conference featured a superb exhibition, *Vision & Concept.*

Equally important, Mark encouraged Bob Rubel, from San Marcos, Texas, a man I had only briefly spoken to prior to the event, to attend the Arrowmont conference. And when the rumblings of forming a national woodturning organization began to stir, Bob volunteered two free years of service to be the administrator. Dick Gerard was also part of that rumbling, as he brought with him a huge stack of papers outlining the details of forming a not-for-profit organization.

The net effect of all this energy was a meeting on the second day of the conference by thirteen interested people on the porch of the Red Barn student dormitory. It was here that we sat down to figure out what this all meant and what we were going to do to make it happen. Out of that meeting came the basic concepts of what the new organization might look like, its intent and purpose, and the role each of us might play in its formation. To say the least, it was a very challenging and exciting meeting. Turning fantasies into reality had suddenly taken on a whole new dimension.

...turners at all skill levels could rub elbows and learn from one another and show their work together in the Instant Gallery

VOICES

Stephen Hogbin: the times were highly charged

I was there when the AAW was forming. The picture in my mind is clear with a number of excellent turners milling around after a demonstration, hotly discussing the pros and cons of a new organization. How well I remember could be challenged but Mark Sfirri, David Ellsworth, Stoney Lamar, Mark Lindquist, and I think I was meeting John Jordan for the first time as well.

The first meeting was more of an impromptu gathering, and whose idea it was will be for others to remember. I think it may have been just after a demonstration by Mark Lindquist, who would look across his chainsaw mounted on a massive lathe, and it felt like he was looking us in the eye saying "Yaaaaaaaah!"

The times were highly charged. David Ellsworth produced the ultimate feminine forms that seemed to evolve from a primal source that takes viewers back to the origins of human experience. Interestingly, he had a way of presenting the forms in a masculine manner. Lindquist's masculine vertical and totemic forms equally touched the primal nerve endings. Unlike the simple object delights of Prestini and Stocksdale, the work was packed with emotional energy. For me, it was hardly the time to start another organization. There was too much action on the ground. The strong design sensibility was also at play through Mark Sfirri's investigation of multi-axis turning, Merryll Saylan's sublime and elegant forms, Steve Loar's evocative music-driven works, Robyn Horn and Stoney Lamar's sculptural investigations, and Michael Hosaluk's evocative approach that's still endlessly evolving. The possibilities seemed endless and remain endless today.

There may have been other moments in restaurants where I felt like the joker rather than conspirator for a new organization. As a Canadian, it felt like an American concept and organization, but more importantly I was stretched to my limit involved in volunteering with Canadian non-profit organizations. Single media organizations never interested me in the same way as multi-disciplinary ones, as I preferred the chance to meet people working in other fields. I remember turning away from the group of turners, shaking my head at the scale of the proposal, in part because Albert LeCoff was already organizing excellent professional and educational programs. How wrong could I be to have thought it might not work, since the AAW now has many thousands of members and a vital program? Meanwhile, the Wood Turning Center holds the enviable international reputation for the domain. They coexist as two vital organizations, often fulfilling different and complementary needs. The third organization in the triumvirate is the Collectors of Wood Art. The AAW would be a very different organization were it not for the collectors who have shaped the field through their purchases. At first, I decided not to join the AAW, but I later did join—I was an early naysayer but wished the infant organization well. Now I am bowled over by its size and the excellent quality of the members' work, even when it is a bit decorative for my tastes and interests.

When I started, there was no organization for any woodworker, turner, or furniture maker. I was hardly aware of Prestini, Stocksdale, or Osolnik. Perhaps I had seen their work but it did not impress on me the possibility of turning. Teaching a design course had led me to read about creativity. In the late 1960s, education in creativity was controversial, with some saying it's impossible to teach and others saying well, let's at least try. I learned how to start making and trying out ideas, and I found that the lathe was a great way to try out a lot of different ideas quickly. While potters, weavers, and glassblowers were making challenging objects, woodturning was moribund and stiff. Today the field is vital and challenging due in large part to pioneers such as Ellsworth and Lindquist who brought their humanity to the object, turning it into a subject. Since then the domain of turning has grown exponentially.

1974: Stephen Hogbin showed this astonishing group of turned pieces at a Toronto gallery during the 1974 World Craft Conference, to the amazement of woodturners and the larger craft world. As the woodturning writer and educator Mark Sfirri has said, "Hogbin was 20 years ahead of his time, and now, 30 years later, he's still 20 years ahead of his time."

Merryll Saylan: why I didn't go to Arrowmont

The 25th anniversary of the AAW made me remember those early days and the fact that I did not go to Arrowmont when the AAW got its start. I had gotten rejected from the exhibition that accompanied the symposium, which might have contributed to my decision not to attend. But it was also predicated on other symposiums I had attended.

The first one was at Dale Nish's where, for the show & tell, I brought my Jelly Doughnut and a bowl with no bottom, held together with an acrylic butterfly that stood on a stand constructed with wood and acrylic rods. It seemed a surprise to many when I said I made it. I found out I scraped! I had never seen or used gouges, but I had bought my steel from Jerry Glaser. Jerry had demonstrated his special steel at my school so how could that be bad? I attended the big anniversary symposium put on by The Wood Turning Center in the early 1990s and won a merit award for the Jelly Doughnut, but I was also asked why would anyone bother to make that piece. Both conferences had demonstrations on techniques, tool use, and tool angles. I always wondered how you could know a wall thickness in thousandths of an inch.

But I was impressed enough with what happened that I put on a small conference in Oakland, California, where David Ellsworth and Bob Stocksdale demonstrated. And yet I decided not to go to Arrowmont; just too much tool talk and angles, and on top of scraping, I was now dyeing wood black and using transparent dyes in pastel colors.

But I've changed since then, and I do use a gouge. And the field has changed. Now I hear turners say, "I don't care about technique." In 1990, I won a residency to work in England. The Association of Woodturners of Great Britain and the woodturning community were so welcoming that when I returned to the States I decided to get involved and be a part of our American organization. After a stint on the board, I found myself the president of the AAW in 1995. To be president and have the conference that year in my own backyard at UC Davis was great. I've made lifelong friends from that experience, but eventually I stepped down—as one of my sons said to me (he's been in nonprofits his whole career), "Mom, you're an artist for a reason." Right he was. To then win the POP Merit award in 2009 and stand up at that symposium with David Ellsworth to receive it, what a wonderful, yellow brick road this has been.

Artist and craftsman

1979: Jelly Doughnut by Merryll Saylan, poplar with cast polyester resin.

Saylan is a sculptor who uses the lathe in the service of her artistic vision. The American Association of Woodturners has always enjoyed creative tension between turners who describe themselves as artists, and those who prefer to be known as artisans or craftsmen. The organization is a big tent, with more than enough room for everyone.

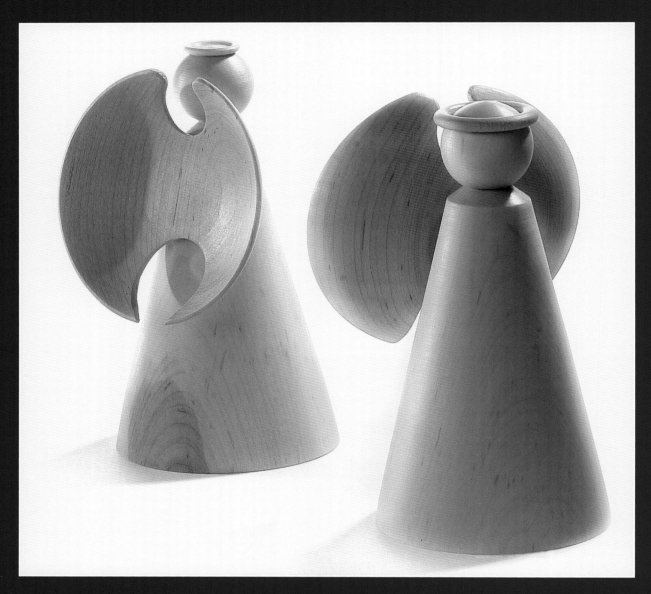

Professional turners

Nick Cook, Christmas angels, approx. 10" tall, hard maple.

Nick is a professional woodturner living in Marietta, Georgia, where he operates the only full-service turning studio in the Atlanta area. Nick is one of a number of expert woodturners who came out of the woodwork and joined the AAW during its formative years. Today, Nick is a popular teacher and demonstrator, and in 2002 was made an honorary lifetime member of the AAW.

Nick first designed the Christmas angel in 1992 for a community arts fundraiser, then presented the piece as a project in *American Woodturner* for Winter 2004. Many woodturners find that making holiday ornaments is not only a satisfying diversion, but also a bounteous source of special gifts for family and friends.

History of the American Association of Woodturners 1986–2011

What does it look like when a craft organization grows from zero to more than 13,000 members in just 25 years? What are the struggles and triumphs? In this section, five former presidents of the organization write about the time when they were most active. Alongside the budget struggles and the eternal problem of how to manage constituencies of members within a large and diverse organization, the AAW soon began to organize its own exhibitions of turned work. Some of these exhibitions were invitational, some were juried and open to all comers, and some were themed. The photographic record of these exhibitions tells a parallel story to the organizational one, a story about the rapid evolution of the woodturning craft itself.

1986–1990

Whatever You Do, Keep Politics Out of It

David Ellsworth

"Whatever you do, try to keep politics out of the organization."

These words, and the wisdom they convey, came to me from an old friend Al Gruntwagen, when we first conceived the AAW in 1985. Of course, any two people in any discussion is basically a political event in some form, so the idea of forming a national organization of woodturners absent of any political conflict would have been unrealistic. That said, we did try.

The first AAW Board of Directors was formed by write-in votes from approximately 100 of the 250 delegates who attended the 1985 Arrowmont conference. As established by our new administrator, Bob Rubel, individuals receiving the highest number of votes would be elected president, vice president, secretary, and treasurer. The remaining five would be known as board members at large. As a result, the originally elected board as of fall 1985 consisted of myself as president, and Dale Nish as vice-president, followed by Albert LeCoff, Ernie Conover (treasurer), Rus Hurt (secretary), Bill Hunter, David Lipscomb, Palmer Sharpless, and Al Stirt. Edward ("Bud") Jacobson and Rude Osolnik were selected as Advisors to the board.

The original financing for the organization came from that same group of delegates with annual dues set at $15 per year, $50 for businesses. Ray Leier from del Mano Gallery in Los Angeles and Rick Snyderman from the Snyderman Gallery in Philadelphia were generous enough to kick in $250 from the start, and Mark Lindquist of Lindquist Studios in Quincy, Florida, was our first Corporate member with a $1,000 donation.

It was expected that the beginning of any organization would be filled with a number of rocks and rolls and, as expected, the first year was an event-full experience. As president, I received the first rock when Bob Rubel informed me that the printer he was using in Texas had mixed up the pages in printing our first newsletter. Without time to consult the rest of the board, I suggested that we could take either the Chevy approach or the Cadillac approach and that we'd better take the Cadillac route even if we had to pay for the repairs out of pocket. Printing was expensive in those days, especially for such a small number of copies. Fortunately, the printer ponied up for their mistake—I think that's what they call it in Texas—and we were only a week late in getting the first issue into the post.

My second rock in the road came in March 1986, when Dale Nish resigned to devote more time to Craft Supplies, U.S.A., a supply house and catalog company with teaching facilities for woodturning classes that he had begun in 1982 and based in Provo, Utah. Leo Doyle was brought onto the board to replace Dale, and Albert LeCoff became vice-president.

The next event evolved through a proposal made by Albert at our first sit-down board meeting in April 1986 at the Renwick Gallery of the Smithsonian Institution in Washington, DC. Albert very much wanted to pursue his dream of creating a center for woodturning in Philadelphia. Thus his proposal—complete with working drawings—was to build a round building that would include spaces for an office, a lathe room for classes, a library where one could do research, plus a gallery for exhibition and retail sales. There was much discussion about the potential of developing this Center and what it might involve, especially as we already had an office in San Marcos, Texas, with Bob Rubel as administrator. The other obvious problem was financial—a membership-based, grass-roots organization with less than 500 members could never afford the scale of such a project. The board also felt that a center in Philadelphia would not be able to geographically serve the needs of a membership that was broadly spread throughout the country and the world. By consensus of the board, it was agreed that Albert would leave the AAW board and form his own organization called the Wood Turning Center (WTC) to satisfy his dream. This decision became effective in the summer of 1986, and the Wood Turning Center received its 501-C-3 status the following November. Albert was asked to be on our Board of Advisors, and he accepted.

Why split in two?

Understandably, Albert's shift to form the WTC was met with mixed reactions by many AAW members. After all, why would a fledgling organization suddenly split in two, and who needs a second organization anyway? It would just mean paying more for membership in two organizations.

The reality is that the WTC has evolved to become a perfect complement to the AAW. Both groups focus on education as their core mandate, and while there was understandably some overlap in method, the WTC was able to address this subject in a manner that the AAW could not. The WTC, located at 144 North 2nd Street in Philadelphia, has subsequently developed an extensive library for academic research, has promoted many exhibitions called Challenge shows, and has a gallery for exhibitions and retail sales. The Center has a vast permanent collection and sponsors the International Turning Exchange (ITE), which brings four to six artists together each year for a crash-and-burn two-month long work session culminating in an exhibition. So, while the AAW has always maintained a strong lean toward education beginning at the grass-roots level and working up, the focus of the WTC has always been more toward the interests of the professional. That includes writers, makers, curators and collectors.

Other differences are that the AAW began as a membership-based organization, so its financial base remains pretty secure. The WTC has a much smaller membership base and relies primarily on grants and donations, making it more vulnerable to fluctuations in the economy. The bottom line is that the "field" of woodturning is far stronger today with both organizations than it could ever have been with only one.

More events involved Dave Lipscomb resigning from the board in the summer of 1986 to pursue his career as a medical consultant and expert witness. His vacancy on the board was filled by Dick Gerard…lots of changes in a short period of time.

Enormous personal energy

Looking back, then, at the AAW's first board, what characterized this group was individuals with an enormous amount of personal energy, a high degree of professionalism, and an equal amount of dedication to the membership that we were elected to represent. They also had almost no amount of experience in forming and running a not-for-profit organization. The details of that foundational structure would come from Bob Rubel, who also happened to be the administrator for the National Alliance for Safe Schools.

There were, of course, numerous other talents among this group that gave us what we needed: Dave Lipscomb, our first editor, was a medical doctor; Dale Nish, Leo Doyle, Rus Hurt, and Palmer Sharpless were university and secondary school educators and provided the connection to academia and a greater understanding for the need of having woodturning in the classroom; Albert LeCoff was well known as a workshop organizer and promoter of woodturning; Dick Gerard, who worked on promotion and later became our treasurer, worked in finance and computer system design for the federal government; while Bill Hunter, Al Stirt, and myself represented the faction of professional (unemployed) studio woodturners with direct connections to both the grass roots woodturners and the public marketplace. Looking back, it was quite a well-rounded selection of individuals. What none of us could have known was that each of us would invest around 30 hours each week to get the job done.

Our board meeting at the Renwick was also significant as it was synchronized with the closing of Wendell Castle's stunning exhibition of *13 Clocks* and the opening of the equally dynamic *Edward (Bud) Jacobson Collection of Turned Wood Bowls*.

Historically, the Jacobson exhibition would inspire Jane and Arthur Mason to begin their own private collection of woodturnings, which, along with those of Edward (Bud) Jacobson and Dr. Irving Lipton, represented the beginning of many major private collections of contemporary turned objects in the United States. All of these collections, in part or whole, would eventually go to museums throughout the country, which greatly helped to raise the stature of woodturnings as a viable artform within the decorative arts.

With the help of a lawyer friend of Bob Rubel, the AAW had already secured its 501-C-3 status with the IRS in February of 1986, so this April meeting was a ground-breaking-event designed to nail down the structure, philosophy, and direction of the organization. The enormity of this task was made easier by the fact that we were all good friends who trusted one another and, what was vitally important, any personal agendas were left at the door. Our ideas of what we each thought was important were tossed around and bantered about in an atmosphere of free exchange until the core elements were agreed upon. Leo had brought nine of his hand-carved and painted folk art birds, and whenever we were ready to vote on a motion, "yes" votes were issued by allowing the birds to stand while "no" votes saw the birds topple. I also remember that in all our votes, nary a bird ever bit the dust.

Critical to this meeting was the need to follow the guidelines we had received at the Arrowmont conference the previous October when we were present to hear the voices of our constituents. Stephen Hogbin from Canada developed the fundamental idea for our mission statement, which became: "Provide information, education, and organization to those interested in woodturning." To us, this meant "…to all those" who were interested in woodturning, whether they be hobbyist or professional. So, we first agreed that whatever topics or ideas we presented would have to somehow positively impact the membership directly. Leo Doyle came up with the name of the newsletter, *American Woodturner*, which would, by the second

issue become a journal rather than just a newsletter. Rude and Palmer established the ideas for forming local chapters that we hoped would become the grass-roots foundation of our membership. Also, the need for an annual conference similar to the Arrowmont event was agreed upon by all members present.

What is a woodturner?

As this new AAW board would discover very quickly, before we could fine tune our ideas to better serve the membership, we had to learn more about the membership itself. In other words, what was a woodturner? What did people want and need? How could we convince them to actually do work in a volunteer organization? And once you found people, how could you get them to join something if they weren't joiners? The answer to that last question, of course, is to provide value in everything that you offer.

Probably the most difficult period in these early years came in January 1989 when Bob Rubel was let go as our administrator and replaced with Dennis Hormann. Hormann struggled with personal problems and only lasted about six months on the job. That's when our treasurer, Ernie Conover, discovered ASMI, a professional group specializing in running non-profit organizations. ASMI was given a one-year contract, but it was not renewed. We discovered they simply had no idea what a woodturner was, couldn't keep up with the volume of correspondence required, and provided no personal connection to our members. They were a paper-pushing business, and no two telephone calls were answered by the same person. Then we found Mary Redig, who later became Mrs. Mary Lacer, and who single-handedly rebuilt our computerized membership list and structurally saved the organization with good administrative skills, an excellent memory, and equally if not more important, she was a woodturner and spoke woodturning!

Another related obstacle focused on the articles that appeared in our journal. All these articles were written by our members. The problem was that there were many people out there doing important work both technically and aesthetically, but if you couldn't get them to write about it, or if they had no writing skills, our ability to get valuable information out there was severely reduced. People rightfully complained that there would be one primary article in each issue and the rest was fluff, which in many cases was true.

I am certainly guilty of providing some of that fluff. If an article wasn't directed to the weekend hobbyist turner and filled with technical information and pictures of flying shavings, it qualified as fluff. And not one of my twenty "President's Page" articles had anything to do with technique or ribbons of shavings. What I was trying to do was lay out numerous subjects that related to the world of the arts and crafts, of which woodturning was becoming a major part, even though most of our members knew nothing about it. After all, the majority of AAW members, then and now, are retired persons who have come to woodturning as a hobby. They were already successful in their respective professional fields, but more often than not, they had no direct experience in the arts. It was of little value to them if someone presented information on rainforest depletion or exhibitions in other countries or the hazards of copying other people's work or the limited history of contemporary woodturning compared to that of other media. What they signed up for was how to mount a piece of wood on the lathe and enjoy shaping it without getting bashed in the head.

In my defense, and as an educator, I felt a responsibility to help our members grow in ways that went beyond their present experience, beyond the lathe, beyond technique, even beyond wood, so that there was no glass ceiling to their own efforts as their personal skills increased. Obviously, many people did appreciate those efforts as it did help them understand that woodturning was a small room in a very large house known as the Modern Movement of Craft. Still, it was discouraging. I knew that one of the greatest values in turning wood was that the objects we make do share equal space with ceramics, glass, and baskets, many of which provided the inspiration for our turned wooden objects. But I did get enough complaints that in 1988, I finally backed off and stuck with local rather than global subjects. It bores me even today to read some of those later articles.

Balancing competing needs

This also relates to my greatest personal frustration and the most perplexing element of any grassroots craft media organization: How do you create and maintain a balance of the needs of hobbyist, semi-professional, and professional makers, knowing that if you're doing your job, those needs will grow, will evolve, like cell division over time? I feel that the AAW has done an excellent job of providing that balance simply by presenting images and articles in our journal showing objects and techniques that directly represent the ever-changing styles and types of work being produced. And it's great fun tracing the growth of those styles and types over the past twenty-five+ years. Just look at the work that appears on tables at local chapter gatherings or at the Instant Gallery in our annual conferences where people feel the freedom to experiment with things like piercing, painting, carving, inlays, and stitching, or the simple presence of pure form in a candle holder or a salad bowl. It's the ultimate in the beauty of people brave enough to play with their skills and to take a chance, not because it's right or wrong or good or bad, but just because it's a challenge to fully express what we feel when we're making something, and definitely because it just feels good!

And then you rail when someone cancels their membership simply because they don't like some object shown in the journal. Maybe it's been painted or carved or had more hand-work in it than lathe work. Or maybe it's because there are a few articles on fluff instead of all the articles being on technique. Times like these, one's objectivity begins to wane, and it seems impossible not to judge. So…did we manage to keep politics out of the organization? Yes…and no. We certainly created an arena where politics could grow, and we faced quite a number of difficult obstacles that we managed to steer our way around, over, or through—four administrators within a two-year period being the most extreme example of the problems involved.

Professional jealousy

One area of struggle that we never anticipated related directly to our stated mission of trying to satisfy all the needs of all types of woodturners from beginner-level to professional. That is, professional jealousy. Up until the mid-1980s, we never encountered this as a problem because there were so few of us in the country that we pretty much knew one another. Also, those of us who taught were working one on one with beginners in the classroom, so any hint of jealousy was neutralized by direct contact among us. But, after the organization was formed and began to grow, the distance between the known and the unknown also began to grow. This was further complicated by the division and confusion between the craft and art in woodturning, with most of the early group representing the art side. A lot of people thought that board members were just a bunch of hippies run amuck. Some joked half seriously (I think) that you had to have a beard to be a successful woodturner, and one fellow wanted to know how much board members got paid! Thank heaven there were no Internet chat rooms in those early days, or we'd never have survived the rumors and the blather.

One way that we did manage this growth was to offer members progressively higher quality in the journal and in conferences. The journal was obviously our primary tool of communication, and we have consistently drawn about 10% of our membership to conferences. It was here that people were able to rub elbows, make new friends, and dispel the hierarchies. Using these tools, I believe that board members during my tenure managed to turn adversity to our advantage and ultimately, if not immediately, to the advantage of our membership. That's an indication of how politics can work for you instead of against you.

Oddly, where we did see the downside of politics was within the local chapters. It was expected and encouraged that our chapters would work to satisfy the needs of their own members. This can only be done on the local level, not through any directives or mandates from the national organization. In fact, one didn't even have to be a member of the AAW to be a member of a local chapter. What we didn't expect were the number of glowing egos that emerged in quite a number of the chapter presidents, some of whom would later became members of the AAW board. There is just something about putting people in charge of other people that brings strange things out in them.

Fortunately, time does heal. And part of this healing process has been a greater awareness among chapters of the value in bringing well-known professional turners to demonstrate at chapter meetings. Not only does this give members direct exposure to new techniques and methods of work, it helps them gain valuable perspective on how people approach different topics differently. It also helps prevent the sense of isolationism that so often occurs within chapters when they have no input from the outside. In effect, it's like a huge

university with national and international teachers moving around the country in search of students.

In hindsight, I feel that our early desire of providing education, information, and organization has been realized through the strength of our journal, our conferences, our local chapters, our scholarship programs, our youth programs, and a solid administrative structure. That's great value for the dollar. I am thrilled to have been a part of this process and am very proud to thank my friends and fellow board members at the time for their insight and hard work in helping to make this organization a viable and working reality.

In addition to his role as the innovator who developed techniques for hollowing wood like an eggshell, David Ellsworth holds AAW membership card No. 1 and served as president of the young organization from its inception until 1990. In 1992 he was made an honorary lifetime member.

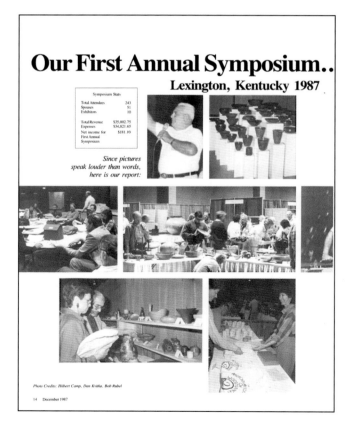

1987: The fledgling *AW Journal* begins to publish photographic coverage of AAW events, such as this page reporting 243 attendees at the first annual symposium held in Lexington, KY.

THE PRESIDENT'S MESSAGE

Greetings and welcome to the first newsletter of the American Association of Woodturners.

In October of 1985, about 250 woodturners from six countries gathered at the Arrowmont School of Arts and Crafts in Gatlinburg, Tennessee, for a national Woodturning Conference, "Woodturning: Vision and Concept." With all the meeting and greeting of old friends and new it soon became clear that what had brought us to Tennessee was more than just a lust for tools and techniques, it was also a thirst for the process of learning. Several hundred turned objects were on view in both formal and informal display -- as if the energies of the past decade were brought before us in one moment. It was more than an awesome display, it was a moment of pride. "Woodturning: A Motion to the Future" was the title of the gallery exhibition, and if there was a single thought on everyone's mind it must have been "where do we go from here?" It is that thought, from those 250 people, that ultimately gave birth to the American Association of Woodturners.

Before I describe the purposes of the AAW - the whos, whats, wheres and whys - let me say that this is not only the first newsletter of AAW, it is also the last. In fact, this is the introductory issue to what will soon appear as The American Woodturner: Journal of The American Association of Woodturners. The decision to publish a Journal instead of a Newsletter was really quite simple. First, we wanted to give our membership something of value; and second, we wanted a product with good graphic appeal -- a product that would look good in the workshop, in the home, and in the gallery where many of our objects are being displayed and sold. So, The American Woodturner: Journal of the American Association of Woodturners will be published quarterly beginning in September 1986. It will be the voice of our membership, the source of much needed information in the field, and the link to the international movement of woodturning .

Who are these "we's" I keep referring to? In this case, "we" began with over 100 woodturners from the Arrowmont conference who responded to an extensive questionnaire describing the type of organization that should be formed and the ways it could best serve the woodturning community. "We" are also the Officers of the Board of Directors who were elected by those same woodturners at Arrowmont. "We" are people like Dick Gerard, who presented us with the first survey of interest in forming an association; Bob Rubel, who offered his energy and administrative experience to take the concept of an organization and make it into a legal and working reality; Rude Osolnik, who has given freely of his wisdom as an advisor to our cause. "We" are the 500 plus members - woodturners, gallery owners, collectors, and so forth - who have contributed over $16,000.00 in membership fees and contributions to help get the AAW off the ground before there were any formal announcements that the AAW even existed. And of course, "we" are you, the current and future members of the American Association of Woodturners. In effect, this is OUR association and because we are dedicated to the principles of education, information, and organization the benefits we receive come directly from the contributions of our own members.

(Concluded on next page.)

As you read this newsletter and, later, our Journal, you will notice that the topics fit a few major categories including:

- Interview-of-the-Issue
- Collectors' Corner
- Technical Topics
- About Wood
- Calendar of Shows/Events
- Suppliers' Side (products)
- The Gallery View
- Classified Ads

As if that weren't enough, one page will be called THE TURNING POINT, where I will touch on subjects related to the field of woodturning from my own experience.

If we keep in mind that the AAW is a service organization devoted to the needs of its membership, one can see that the size of the Journal and the type of information will fluctuate in direct proportion to what has been received from you, the members. So, be thinking of things that you would like to know and things that you would like to contribute. We have a lot of room and a lot of time to help each other grow.

David Ellsworth, President

1986: President's message from the inaugural *American Woodturner,* issue #0.

THE AMERICAN WOODTURNER

THE AMERICAN ASSOCIATION OF WOODTURNERS

NEWSLETTER   JUNE 1986

DEDICATED TO PROVIDING
- EDUCATION
- INFORMATION
- ORGANIZATION

AMONG THOSE INTERESTED IN WOODTURNING.

	MEMBERS	CHAPTERS
1986	1,510	1
1987	1,863	10
1988	1,890	24
1989	1,221	27
1990	2,405	31

1986

Formation of the American Association of Woodturners, followed by the on-going publication of *American Woodturner* as its official journal. The expression of a huge number of hobbyists and amateurs and, to a much lesser degree, practicing professionals and academics. Wild enthusiasm with disposable income fuels technology and materials.

1986–1990

David Ellsworth is elected the first AAW president and leads the organization through its formative years.

1986

Formation of the Wood Turning Center followed by the ongoing publication of *Turning Points* as its official journal. The WTC grows out of the George School symposiums. The personal vision of Albert LeCoff leads the WTC to look worldwide for an ever-broadening interpretation of wood art, grounded by an intense interest in work from the lathe. The WTC champions the history of woodturning as well as working with youth.

1986

Collaboration is born. Inspired by a series of exhibitions at the The Gallery at Workbench in New York City, Mark Sfirri teams up with painter Robert Dodge. Mark develops furniture pieces by multi-axis turning. Robert then applies decorative finishes. This initiates a large body of work created through 1992.

1986

Sculpting Wood, by Mark Lindquist steps beyond Dale Nish's books with the introduction of the chainsaw, grinder, carving, and the controlled but rough surface. Radical hair-raising stuff. Lindquist also makes it clear that notable work would need to draw upon art, as well as craft.

1987

243 woodturners attend the AAW's first annual symposium, Lexington, Kentucky.

1987

The Turners Challenge exhibitions and catalogs begin. Curated by Albert LeCoff and sponsored by the Craft Alliance Gallery (St. Louis) from 1987–1989, they continue to the present under the banner of the Wood Turning Center. The *Challenge* exhibitions showcase the very finest innovative objects via juried selection, traveling venues, and high quality catalogs. These include thoughtful and challenging commentary from respected authorities from diverse fields. These influential and perfectly named events help establish woodturning as an art form with a record of invention.

1988

250 woodturners attend the AAW's second annual symposium, Philadelphia.

1988: panel discussion at the second AAW symposium, Philadelphia. Left to right, Melvin Lindquist, Rude Osolnik, James Prestini, Bob Stocksdale. Photo: Mark Lindquist/ Lindquist Studios

1988

The *Lathe-Turned Objects* exhibitions begin with the first *International Turned Object Show* (ITOS). Sponsored by Albert LeCoff and the Wood Turning Center, these world-wide explorations do much to establish woodturning as a world-wide phenomenon. Held at the Port of History Museum in Philadelphia, ITOS is a sumptuous celebration that substantially bolsters reputations.

1989

278 woodturners attend the AAW's third annual symposium, Seattle.

1990

292 woodturners attend the AAW's fourth annual symposium, at Arrowmont, in Gatlinburg, Tennessee.

Dale Larson: didn't want any social stuff

In early 1989, I saw an article I believe in *Fine Woodworking* that said a bunch of woodturners were getting together in Seattle. I'd been woodturning for 11 years and had never met another woodturner. I thought that a trip to the Seattle symposium would be fun. I sent in my application. They sent back a letter asking if I wanted to go to the barbecue one night and the banquet another night. I didn't want to do any of that "social" stuff, I just wanted to go see the woodturning. I didn't understand what I was missing. I went up to the symposium at Denver's school where I met Denver and Bonnie. The instant gallery was in the school library with the woodturnings just sitting on top of the book cases. I remember two things

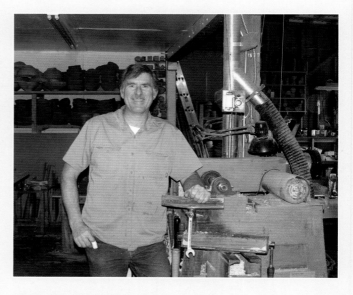

1989: Dale Larson in his workshop.

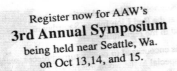

Register now for AAW's
3rd Annual Symposium
being held near Seattle, Wa.
on Oct 13,14, and 15.

The Symposium is being hosted by the Seattle Chapter - AAW at Overlake School and they extend to you a personal invitation for this very outstanding event.

This is the first time that a local chapter has been a symposium host and we are working hard to make it one that will be long and well remembered.

Overlake School is about 15 miles east of Seattle and is located on a 53 acre rural setting amidst many beautiful tall fir and cedar trees. The school gym, campus, library and school shop will house such activities as the demonstrations, general meetings, instant gallery, and trade show, and will provide a comfortable place to meet old friends and make new ones during lunch breaks. There are many lawns and paths to explore. There is space to park recreational vehicles for those of you who travel that way, with easy access to the showers and restrooms in the gym. Arrangements can even be made for those that would want to camp or tent, if we know in advance.

Overlake Library

from the instant gallery. I saw Ron Fleming's lily vase and just kept walking around it looking at it. Frank Cummings had three small goblets with the wavy carved rims. They were inlaid with gold, jewels, and ivory. The three were priced $1500, $2500 and $3500. Each was marked sold, sold, sold. I realized that there was something in woodturning besides flat-bottomed dry, bowls. I remember three booths in the tools show. One booth was selling Nova Chucks. The cost was $195. I'd paid $212 for my Craftsman's lathe. It took me three days to decide to buy the chuck. I now own six lathes, and the last two cost slightly more than the Craftsman lathe. I can honestly say that trip changed the path of my life. I have now travelled all around the United States and gone to four foreign countries to teach and turn wood. I have friends all over the world. This past January, Eli Avisera and I took a lathe down to the Dead Sea and turned two spheres on the shores. Not a bad life.

Dale Larson 20+ years later: symposium set-up day

The Portland AAW symposium was June 29–July 1, 2007. The critical day was Thursday, June 28, setup day. There were 22 local committees that had a hand in organizing the symposium. Local planning started nearly a year earlier. In late January 2007, the AAW board came to Portland to check out the symposium site and meet with the local committee chairmen. As the symposium dates approached, pieces of the puzzle started coming together. Everything needed to be organized locally so that on Thursday, setup day, everything could be moved into the convention center and end up in the right place.

The first major issue was local shipping addresses for stuff that was coming in from around the country and some foreign places. Local turner Fred Kline had a business about a mile from the convention center. He became the central shipping point. Starting about a month before the symposium, boxes started arriving. The AAW sent its entire office, including all the AAW products and equipment needed to run the symposium. The JET mini-lathes came to Fred's then went to Tom Reiman's place to be assembled. The tightest problem was the traditional Japanese full-sized lathe. It got hung up in the port of Long Beach, but finally made it to Fred's business in time. Dale Larson's place received two van loads of art work for the different art exhibitions.

The AAW board arrived on Monday. Mary Lacer and Eunice Wynn started working with Fred and pulling boxes as they were needed by the AAW. Dennis Thomas's committee started stuffing registration packets. Tom Reiman, Doug Brown and crew put all the Jet mini-lathes together in Tom's shop. John Wirth pulled together all the equipment requested by the demonstrators. The wood for the youth turning room was organized and cut by Glenn Burki and crew. All this equipment, wood, and supplies were pre-staged for Thursday.

When Thursday morning arrived, everything started moving into the

Portland convention center. Tom Reiman used his company's truck to move the JET mini-lathes into the youth turning room where Doug Brown organized them. John Wirth and Glenn Burki brought the tools and wood. Don Ditto was in charge of setting up the video equipment for the demonstration rooms. Cindy Ditto helped set up the AAW products sales table. Dale Larson hauled artwork to the exhibitions. Howard Borer and Randy Rhine unboxed and set up the grinders in the demonstration rooms. Kathleen Duncan organized the demonstrator lounge. Bob Tuck organized the registration committee. Craig Taylor set up and ran the Learn to Turn lathes where anyone could come and try turning. Paul Rasmussen organized the biggest committee, the demonstrator assistants. Mike Meredith organized volunteers for the Instant Gallery.

By 3pm, the registration desk was open, the Instant Gallery was open and Learn to Turn was up and going. By 7 pm, the art exhibitions were open. The symposium was on!

2007: The orderly appearance of the trade show floor at the Portland symposium belies the enormous amount of volunteer labor that went into organizing it. Many woodturners come to the AAW to see the shavings fly off the lathe, but they stay for the fellowship. After helping set up the 2007 symposium, Dale Larson went on to join the AAW's board of directors and in 2010 served as symposium liaison between the organization and the local Hartford, CT, organizing committee. Not bad for a guy who, as he recalls, "didn't want to do any of that social stuff."

1991–1995

The Young Organization Struggles for Stability

Alan Lacer

Excerpted from editorials Lacer wrote in the AW Journal in 1991, near the start of his term as AAW president, and 1994, as he left office.

1991: Filled with optimism

"The end of a year is always a good time to pause and look back as well as to glance forward to see what's on the horizon. When I do this with our organization, I am filled with optimism.

The AAW is very much in existence and has had the same address for our national offices for some time now! This may not sound like much for newer members, but those who have been aboard from the beginning know what a struggle it has been to launch and stabilize a national organization. For the first four years, the AAW moved its offices about once a year, tried different administrators, and grappled with its role and direction. The success of surviving those times causes us to give thanks to those who kept the association afloat. We recently set a record: The AAW offices have been in the same location and with the same administrator longer than at any time in our existence! What's more, our records and administrative functions are emphatically in the best condition ever. Renewal notices and election ballots go out on time, members receive information in a timely manner, and the journal makes it to your door when it should.

This last year has been a real turning point for the AAW. In 1990, we ended the year in the red (about $13,000). We were not sure who our members were, had just made a big decision to move our office to Minnesota, and we changed the date for the national symposium. Well, you stayed with us—we now have the largest membership we have ever had, we are the largest turning organization in the world, financially, we have paid off our debts, and we will end the year in the black. This turnaround was due to the hard work of the administrator, journal editors, board members, the many volunteers who pitched in when things were at their darkest, and of course those members who stayed with us.

That was my backwards glance—what about the future? At long last we may not have to be obsessed with mere survival and can ask the real question: What can such an organization do for the craft and for its members?

Let's start with four areas currently being addressed: the journal, national symposiums, scholarships, and directories. The journal continues to blossom as a resource document in the field of woodturning. Each journal has a general theme with the intent of reaching a broad spectrum of skill and interest levels.

The national conferences are as strong as ever. Symposium sites will move across the country on a regular and anticipated pattern—east, central, west. We are working to be at least three years ahead of the event in terms of location and intend to offer more variety at each conference with topics targeting the novice as well as advanced turners (focusing on design and surface treatment). The movement around the country is essential if we are truly to be a national organization. Advanced planning will allow adequate time to find a suitable site, obtain the desired demonstrators, and allow time for members to plan their vacations to coincide with the symposium.

On the issue of scholarships: We will continue to award scholarships to individuals and local chapters. What is exciting is that one of our scholarship funds (the Daphne Osolnik Memorial), is now over $30,000.

Changes are in the making for the directory. Last year we produced a membership/demonstrators directory. This year, you will receive a directory comprised of all current members, a listing of all official AAW chapters, and a list of demonstrators. This year's directory will be a dramatic improvement over your first one, and next year's will be even better. We are building toward adding a "turning resource" category of sources for materials, tools, lathes, publications, courses, and schools that are of interest to turners.

There are other ideas being considered. The notion of having small, specific conferences around the country has been met with serious interest. Two types are being mulled over: a beginner's conference (green woodturning?) and a design or marketing conference for those a bit further along. Neither of these would be for large numbers—maybe 40 to 60 individuals—and would have a high degree of direct involvement by all attending. Personally, I would like to see the fall of 1992 as the time to launch the first pilot.

I have also had some favorable responses concerning special video projects. I see these occurring in at least three areas: 1) Specific topics such as sharpening, design, friction drives/jigs, or finishing; 2) Documenting specific turners, especially some of those who have been involved in the craft for many years; and 3) The national symposiums where some classic interactions and demonstrations have occurred, but where little record survives. We are working on obtaining grants to fund this type of project.

What can a national organization do for the craft and for its members? The above are some answers—we are open to others. But please keep these points in mind: we are still here, we are solvent, we are stable, and we are alive and growing!

1994: The full compass of woodturning

"It's time to say good-bye. Six years on the board and four as president have surely been enough for anyone to serve in a voluntary position. I would like to share some thoughts, looking forward as well as back.

I came to the board during a time when few ran for positions and few voted in board elections. I chose to run because of two strongly held beliefs: that there weren't enough people participating in woodturning's organizational life and that the interior of the country was being grossly neglected. Also, due to several physical challenges, I was forced to dramatically reduce my time at the lathe. Involvement with the AAW gave my interest and passion for the field an outlet.

My first years on the board found me in the midst of a struggling organization. Oddly, there are times when I miss the crises days. The days of financial turmoil, survival loans, discussions of shutting down the AAW, relocating our office, multiple administrators, petitions and the like played an important role in the shaping of this organization. As painful as those times were, they helped formulate a mission and vision for survival and growth. In the struggle to exist, we probably had the closest working relationships within the board, with volunteers, and with the editor and administrator that we have ever seen.

Successes

"Like most things in life, there has been a mix of success and disappointment during the past six years. On the positive side, there is economic stability, strong growth in membership (from about 1700 members in 1989 to 5000 this year), record-setting national conferences the last three times out, increased scholarship awards, a proliferation of local chapters, liability insurance for our board, the capacity to provide inexpensive insurance to local chapters, involvement in several woodturning exhibitions and the impetus behind a significant number of others, the first steps in a burgeoning video program, the totem landmark at Arrowmont and the birdhouse project in New York, the publication of a project book and annual resource directory, an orderly movement of national conferences around the entire country, the advent of sharply focused mini-conferences (with the Arizona conference this month, we will have run three of these), a quarterly newsletter, a much improved board-selection process, and strong renewal rates (last year was at eighty-seven percent).

It is amazing to me that we have accomplished so much with only one increase in dues since 1987—none of my magazine subscriptions can match that! We have also left significant endowments at two universities, given a sizable donation to the speaker's fund at another, contributed in a meaningful way to the Arrowmont building fund to create a first-class woodworking educational facility, and cleaned up our own in-house scholarship fund that functions much like an endowment. It has certainly been rewarding to be one of many players in these events.

The future

"Where do I feel the AAW should be going? Foremost, I hope it continues to strive for balance and breadth in the field: amateur and professional, beginner and veteran, production turner and studio artist, local chapters, and non-chapter members across the whole country, indeed, throughout the world. Magazines and product-oriented businesses usually target a group of likely consumers. We need not be driven solely by economic concerns and can give play to all kinds of special interests. Our publications can (and do) include an attention to design, technique, art, production, ornamental turning, embellishment, projects, debates, profiles, news, and advertising, all to better reflect our whole field. Let's continue to represent the full compass of wood turning, focusing on no one interest to the exclusion of any other.

There are other ideas that need exploration. The size of our national conferences has reached the unwieldy 500-plus level, which makes it hard to deal with a new location and new volunteers every year. If we continue at the current level, we will need a conference coordinator to maintain continuity from year to year and provide necessary management. Offsetting the demands of a full-size annual symposium is the evolving idea of the mini-conference, where only 50 to 100 participants can focus on a specific topic in a more informal atmosphere.

Our publications ought to continue evolving too. Regarding the recurring question of color in the journal, I personally would like to see a color section, perhaps a membership gallery, with the balance of the journal kept black and white. There could also be value in a new biennial publication, a photo documentary of selected works of members—the AAW 500? Our video program should grow, and the idea of doing specialized documentaries of veteran turners has promise.

Exhibitions? Yes!

"And finally, on the question of whether the AAW should be more involved in woodturning exhibitions, I answer with a strong, "Yes." I am not alone in that sentiment—almost three-fourths of those responding to our survey felt the same. This must be done cautiously and fairly and on a limited basis, but I see real benefits to expanding the public's awareness of our field and giving exposure to the work of more turners, especially the unknowns.

I leave office with our organization financially healthy and on solid ground. I couldn't feel stronger about the quality of our current administrator and editor. This January, almost half of the board of directors will be new, and I anticipate a tremendous infusion of fresh energy and ideas. Although I will miss exploring many of the issues before the board, I applaud the new team.

My sincere thanks to so many of you for your support and encouragement over the years—for both the organization and for me personally. It has been a satisfying six years."

Alan Lacer was the AAW's second president, serving from 1991 to 1994, a time of rapid growth and organizational maturation. Lacer, who lives in Minnesota, is a highly regarded demonstrator and teacher, and for many years has been American Woodworker magazine's contributing editor for woodturning. In 1999 he was made an honorary lifetime member of the AAW.

1991–1994

Alan Lacer is the AAW President.

1991

256 woodturners attend the AAW's annual symposium, Denton, Texas.

1992

512 woodturners attend the AAW's annual symposium, Provo, Utah.

Honorary lifetime members: David Ellsworth, Ed Jacobson.

1992

Collaboration grows as a way of inciting invention and creating a sense of community beyond the individual. Mark Sfirri and Michael Hosaluk develop work via an active serial exchange that first makes itself known as the Mark & Mikey Show in 1994. Meanwhile, Steve Loar initiates an indirect form of collaboration, creating narrative scenes fueled with cast-off and unresolved components donated by other woodturners (page 132).

1993

520 woodturners attend AAW's annual symposium, Purchase, New York.

Honorary lifetime members: Dale Nish, Rude Osolnik.

1993

The first *World Turning Conference* is sponsored by the Wood Turning Center. Elevated thinking and community are the mission of these events. Interdisciplinary interaction is encouraged, if not provoked, with talk and emotions rising well above, "how'd you do that?" Subsequent venues occur in 1997 and 2005.

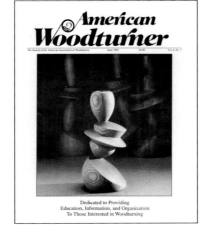

American Woodturner

Dedicated to Providing
Education, Information, and Organization
To Those Interested in Woodturning

1994

543 woodturners attend the AAW's annual symposium, Fort Collins, Colorado.

Honorary lifetime members: Melvin Lindquist, Ed Moulthrop.

	MEMBERS	CHAPTERS
1991	2,832	39
1992	3,626	49
1993	4,073	58
1994	5,003	63
1995	5,757	74

1990s

Noteworthy collections of wood art are begun by Edward Jacobsen, Irving Lipton, Jane and Arthur Mason, and Robyn and John Horn. These will, in part, become major public collections as gifts to Arizona State University, Los Angeles County Museum of Art, the Mint Museum of Craft+Design, and Yale University Art Gallery respectively.

1995

Bucks County Community College (Newtown, Pennsylvania) becomes the premier post-secondary institution for woodturning with the inclusion of a required class in its two-year fine woodworking program taught by Mark Sfirri.

1995

The International Turning Exchange Residency Program, sponsored by the Wood Turning Center, begins. The ITE encourages collaboration and the creation of challenging new work by bringing together four artists, a journalist, and a photographer for ten weeks in the workshop. Ten weeks often prove a long stretch given the intensity of working, and in the early days, living together. Still active, the ITE is a hothouse of invention.

1995

498 woodturners attend the AAW's annual symposium, Davis, California.

Honorary lifetime member: Bob Stocksdale.

1995

Merryll Saylan is the AAW President.

1996–2000

Adolescent Growing Pains

David Barriger

When I retired from teaching, I had it in mind to become a full-time turner, but just for enjoyment, with no intentions of living off my earnings. Having struggled to learn turning on my own before the AAW had come into existence, I felt a strong loyalty to the association. When President Charles Alvis called and asked if I would run for the board, I felt totally unqualified, but thought if I could help the AAW in any way I would certainly be willing.

My first board meeting was January 1996 in San Antonio, the location for the 1997 Symposium.

Although I had little idea of how these things were handled, I assumed we were just there to look at the facilities we would be using. I was surprised to learn we had to find a facility because it had just been decided to hold it in San Antonio after the original location fell through. The only place available turned out to be the city auditorium. This seemed doable since we had never had much more than 500 attendees. By the time we finished the meeting, I had been appointed chairman of the conference committee for 1997 and the San Antonio symposium turned out to be not only my initiation, but also one of the most interesting adventures during my time on the board.

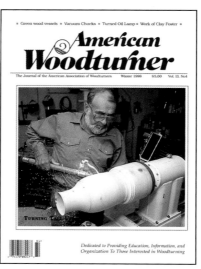

To add to my worries about being new at this, over 950 turners attended Greensboro that June. It was a real challenge to lay out the auditorium to handle 14 break-out rooms and the possibility of 800 or 900 attendees. The biggest problem was where to fit in the trade show. We decided the best place was on the main floor of the auditorium. Originally, they had told us there was plenty of lighting so we didn't worry about it. After a lot of measuring and calculating, we were able to come up with a floor plan that would work.

Feeling satisfied with our plan, we spent our time on demonstrators and scheduling, and all went well until two weeks before the symposium. That was when I received a phone call from the auditorium manager saying she had decided we could not place the trade show there because there was a weight limit of, I think, 250 pounds per square foot. She had found out we had lathes weighing much more than that. I had to convince her that a lathe covered enough square feet to average out.

The big crisis was when we met with the auditorium staff on Wednesday with the show starting Thursday afternoon. As soon as I walked into the room, I was confronted by the city fire chief who said we could not bring wood into the auditorium main floor because there were no sprinklers. The city was more than a little paranoid, we learned, because this building had burned a few years earlier. By convincing them that most of the wood was green and agreeing to walk the building with a fire marshal at opening and closing, we were able to go ahead. There were many other problems, not the least of those being damage to the stage floor where we brought lathes and pallets of wood across it and for which we had to pay to repair. Another thing we found out as the vendors finished setting up was that there wasn't nearly enough light, so the vendors had to buy lights to properly show their products.

In spite of our skepticism, the symposium did come about, and most people were satisfied with it. That was because a lot of AAW people pitched in and did what had to be done. I knew then that this was a great organization because of a lot of great people. Since then we have come a long way, constantly improving our symposiums. We first hired coordinators for the 1998 symposium, and the presentations have become more professional each year. The real winners have been those who have benefited from the thousands of dollars raised for Educational Opportunity Grants. The *AW Journal* went from black-and-white, first to color cover, then to color center pages, and now to full color as well as improved quality.

By 2000, we had added the chapter collaborative program and expanded the Instant Gallery and trade show considerably. We had improved the video coverage of the symposiums, added some informative tapes, and had started the popular Masters series of videos.

I think of the period from 1996 to 2000 as the adolescence of the AAW. We had many problems to overcome, like growing pains, and we always worked through them and kept our eyes on the goal. As you would expect, over the years the AAW has had to deal with a few individuals with selfish, personal agendas, but the majority were there to serve for the good of the AAW, and this is expressed in our success. It has been amazing to see the progress in woodturning both in quantity and quality, much to the credit of the AAW education programs. There is no telling how many lives have been enriched through turning, collecting, purchasing, or just observing.

In my opinion the most (or possibly the only) consistent factor from 1996 to the present has been Mary Lacer. Her offices have gone from a small storage building in her back yard to a crowded two-room office to a somewhat larger space in another building in Shoreview. Now, it has moved to what I consider a great area in the Landmark building in Saint Paul, which even has a nice space for our gallery. Mary has had a few title changes but she has consistently represented and guided the AAW. We have seen continued progress since 2000. I think we all eagerly await the future and are proud to be a part of it.

Dave Barriger of Apopka, FL, served as the AAW president in 2000 and 2001.

1996

940 woodturners attend the AAW's annual symposium, Greensboro, NC.

Honorary lifetime member: Palmer Sharpless.

Turning Ten exhibition features 15 leading AAW members known for their willingness to share their expertise with others. The AAW's first published exhibition catalog.

1996

The Design Challenges begins as a regular part of AAW annual conferences under the initial tutelage of Steve Loar (Greensboro, NC).

1996

The first biennial international collaborative takes place at Emma Lake, Saskatchewan, Canada. Organized by Michael Hosaluk and the Saskatchewan Craft Council, Emma Lake is the outgrowth of a series of successful woodturning and furniture symposiums, begun in 1982, that were held at the Kelsey SIAAST trade school in Saskatoon. Emma is a few heady days in the woods by a lake with an amazing buffet of all the tools and materials that were possible to bring together. While encouraging collaboration, it allows for the free flow of ideas in a free-for-all of "making" followed by an auction that draws in the community as well as some far flung collectors.

1996–1997

Charles Alvis is the AAW President.

1997

Out of Focus, the turning field's first Internet exhibition and first "*salon de refuse.*" A good many big names get shunted out of the juried Curator's Focus exhibition and catalog, and they don't like it. Have the rules changed for these mid-career artists?

1997

The first Collectors' Weekend is held in Little Rock, Arkansas, resulting in the formation of the Collectors of Wood Art in the fall of 1998. A bold fusion of collectors, artists, and galleries, CWA becomes an important force via annual forums, exhibitions staged at SOFA-Chicago, and through visiting artist grants to university programs.

	MEMBERS	CHAPTERS
1996	6,634	86
1997	7,124	105
1998	7,609	119
1999	8,278	138
2000	8,794	153

1997

705 woodturners attend the AAW's annual symposium, San Antonio.

Honorary lifetime member: Alan Stirt.

Turned For Use is the first themed exhibition at the AAW annual conference. It seeks to tap the undercurrent of production talent that can blend utility with fine design (San Antonio Museum of Art).

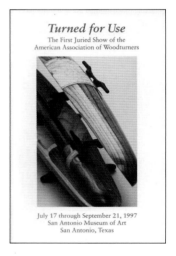

Turned for Use
The First Juried Show of the American Association of Woodturners

July 17 through September 21, 1997
San Antonio Museum of Art
San Antonio, Texas

1997

Dedication of the new wood studio at Arrowmont school, with the largest educational woodturning facility in the United States, and possibly the world: a 13-lathe bay adjoining a complete furniture studio. Lathe artists are encouraged to collaborate with furniture makers, thus bridging the artificial abyss between contemporary wood art and studio furniture.

1998–1999

David Wahl is the AAW President.

1998

The annual Echo Lake conferences begins. A joint venture of the Bucks County Woodturners and Bucks County Community College, this first progeny of Emma Lake is followed by events in Australia, New Zealand, and Pennsylvania: collaboration, community, and free-flowing ideas.

2001

Wood Turning In North America Since 1930, by Yale University and Wood Turning Center. Whilst only the catalog to an exhibition, this book defines the age. The intellects of Edward S. Cooke, Jr., Glenn Adamson, and Albert LeCoff are brought to bear on the creation of this sumptuous exposition. Some felt that it assayed a field still in its adolescence, full of vigor and bound for a bright future.

2001

831 woodturners attend the AAW's symposium, Saint Paul.

Honorary lifetime member: Ray Key.

Nature Takes a Turn: Woodturnings Inspired by the Natural World. The exhibition features 22 juried artists and 16 invited ones recorded in the AAW's first full-color printed catalog.

2000–2001

David Barriger is the AAW President.

2002–2003

Bobby Clemons is the AAW President.

2002

916 woodturners attend the AAW's symposium, Providence.

Honorary lifetime member: Nick Cook.

Put a Lid On It: Containing Human Experience. Exhibition jury selects turnings with lids by 34 AAW members. Plus 11 invited master craftsmen.

2003

823 woodturners attend the AAW's annual symposium, Pasadena, California.

Honorary lifetime member: Bonnie Klein.

2004–2005

Phil Brennion is the AAW President.

	MEMBERS	CHAPTERS
2001	8,829	170
2002	9,800	189
2003	10,804	204
2004	11,407	226
2005	11,926	252

2004

American Woodturner moves to full color print.

2004

895 woodturners attend the AAW's annual symposium, Orlando.

Honorary lifetime member: Dick Gerard.

From *Sea to Odyssey* exhibition features a wide array of contemporary turned art with a nautical theme.

2005

The Center for Turning and Furniture Design at Indiana University of Pennsylvania becomes the first university program in the nation to offer a studio emphasis in both turning and furniture design leading to undergraduate and graduate degrees in fine arts. Instruction in newly renovated and significantly enlarged facilities begins in January 2006, with a dedicated turning facility, a state-of-the-art furniture studio, and CNC tooling for both.

2005

1,150 woodturners attend the AAW's annual symposium, Overland Park, Kansas.

Honorary lifetime members: Arthur and Jane Mason

With a Kansas venue, the AAW's annual exhibition takes the theme *reTurn to the Land of Oz*, inviting imagery drawn from *The Wizard of Oz*. Forty-four artists, juried and invited, participate.

Hands-On Youth Instruction is formally initiated at the AAW annual conference. Just the tip of the iceberg of years of work with youth by many chapters nation-wide. It is a forceful response to the graying of the organization and the demise of Industrial Arts in public schools. A very important endeavor.

Nature Takes a Turn

Juried exhibition, Saint Paul, Minnesota

This ambitious exhibition featured work by 22 juried artists, plus 15 invited ones, who all take their primary inspiration from the natural world.

Cosponsored by the Minnesota Museum of American Art, *Nature Takes a Turn* traveled to three high-profile venues and generated the AAW's first full-color exhibition catalog (page 256).

Themed exhibitions such as this have become a specialty of the AAW, allowing the organization to highlight and advance artistic trends in ways that broad curatorial surveys cannot.

Vase by Matthew Hill, silver maple, 8" dia. "...an attempt to suggest the sensuality of the human body."

Shell Series No. 7 by Gary Stevens, walnut burl, 18" wide.

turnings inspired by the natural world

Unicellular Vessels of Love by Neil Stoutenburg, various species, largest is 8.5" high x 3" dia. "...the individual personality is not necessarily that of the group and the group personality changes as the group dynamics change."

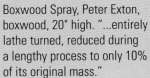

Boxwood Spray, Peter Exton, boxwood, 20" high. "...entirely lathe turned, reduced during a lengthy process to only 10% of its original mass."

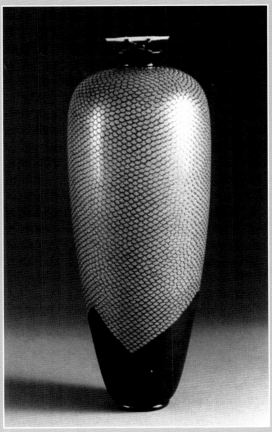

Trinity, Mike Lee, Gabon ebony, silver, African blackwood, largest is 3.5" long. "These pod forms...are symbolic of the birth of new life."

Piscatorial Vessel No. 5 by Dick Codding, cherry with aniline dye, 20" high.

Put a Lid on It containing human experience

Juried exhibition, Pasadena, California

If it weren't for the container, we would all be without a home. Yet, the challenge of this show is much more than to make a lidded turned-wood container. It is to create work that functions, reflects our times, or offers an exploration of an artist's vision.

—*Kevin Wallace, juror's statement*

Pearl Jar, Michael Mode, holly, wenge, ebony, walrus ivory, 9" tall. "The inspiration comes directly from the Pearl Mosque in Agra, India."

Fluted bowl with cover, Harvey Fein, afzelia burl, maple, purpleheart, 6" dia.

Maple jars, Bob Hinshaw, Norway maple with inlays, largest is 7.5" dia.

From Sea to Sea

Juried exhibition, Orlando

The Orlando symposium venue generated the nautical theme. Jurors Jacques Vesery and Mark Sfirri chose work by 45 artists. The exhibition was documented on a CD, not with a printed catalog—an unsatisfactory alternative the organization has not pursued. Instead, in recent years the AAW has encouraged broad participation on-line, with extensive galleries of event photographs as well as member portfolios (www.woodturner.org, www.galleryofwoodart.org).

Nautilus by David Nittman of Boulder, CO, maple with dye, 22" dia.

Keel's End, by Jack Shelton of Fort Pierce, FL, Honduras mahogany, 11" dia.

Ring of Fire by Linda Fifield of McKee, KY, maple with glass beads, 3.75" dia.

Lumba Lumba by Douglas Weidman of Green Lane, PA, box elder, acrylic paint, 10" tall.

reTurn to the Land of Oz

Juried exhibition, Overland Park, Kansas

As befits the location of the 2005 symposium, entrants were asked to create work based on L. Frank Baum's *The Wonderful Wizard of Oz.* This theme lends plenty of easily recognizable objects and characters. In Oz, we find images that have become modern-day icons of our culture; as a challenge, we wanted to see how artists could incorporate these icons into their woodturning.

—Linda Van Gehuchten, exhibit co-chair

Over the Rainbow, John Noffsinger, Annandale, VA, 13" dia., maple platter turned, pyrographed and dyed; walnut stand.

Surrender Dorothy, Dixie Biggs, Gainesville, FL, 4.75" dia., jacaranda with African blackwood rim, turned, carved and painted.

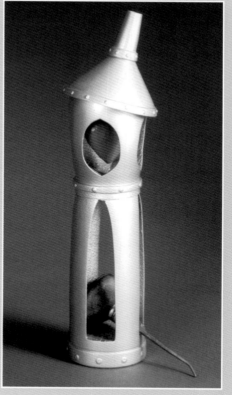

The Tin Man, John Lucas, Baxter, TN, 25" tall, turned, carved and painted wood.

Dorothy's Wild Ride, Jim Keller, Richmond, TX, spalted pecan, 13" dia.

All photos in this spread by Bob Hawks.

New York City, What Else?, Harvey Fein, maple and gold leaf, 14.375" dia.

Good Witch of the North and Wicked Witch of the West, Fred Klap, Toronto, Ontario, pear and walnut, 12.5" high.

2006–2011

Building Bridges

Angelo Iafrate

A flurry of controversy ended as I became a board member. I remember that first board meeting well. It was held in Atlanta. By 4:00 p.m. of the first day, most, if not all, of the board members arrived at the hotel. President Phil Brennion called the meeting to order after dinner. We worked until about 11:00 p.m. The meeting was adjourned until after breakfast the next morning. The next day was a repeat of the previous evening and running until the midnight hour. A "bored" meeting, in those days, took a substantial amount of time because it consisted mostly of committee work. Feeling that we had not accomplished all that we could, the president expressed his displeasure that many board members were leaving mid-afternoon on Sunday. The hours were grueling. I thought to myself, "if this is the way the board works, I will never make it!"

I persevered and tried to encourage and help others, as well as manage my own committees to have work done before we went into session.

Here is an example of the amount of work done by the Board of Directors. The biggest meeting, by far, was the meeting held at the symposium. We would arrive at the symposium site the weekend before the event began and attend meetings pretty much nonstop. I needed a week to recover! Later, when I became president, I encouraged board members do their committee work off site, and bring only their presentations to make at the face-to-face meeting. By doing this we were able to arrive at the symposium site the Tuesday before, saving board members valued time.

As conference committee chair, I depended heavily on my team of coordinators, Butch and Pat Titus, who were responsible for the day-to-day operations of the symposium for the entire week. Butch and Pat, I believe, were grossly underappreciated, and I would like to take this opportunity to extend a sincere thank-you to them for all of the work they put in, for the benefit of our membership, to make each symposium better than the last. Later, Carol Kuc and her team would take over the task.

If there was a positive direction of the board, it was the mantra that we improve service to the members and become more professional in our presentation to the public. As board members, we would occasionally hear from members who felt they were unfairly treated by the AAW. We tried to rectify all of these complaints as completely and quickly as possible. I cannot remember more than a handful of these instances.

As conference committee chair, I also heard complaints from our demonstrators. It was with this sector of our membership that I focused some effort on building bridges to bring these demonstrators "back into the fold" (as the board termed it). I began building bridges. Some of the people that were brought to the consciousness of the general membership include Mike Darlow, Richard Raffan, Melvyn Firmager, Giles Gilson, and Mark Lindquist. To my great pleasure, the AAW bestowed the gift of honorary lifetime membership on both Giles Gilson and Mark Lindquist—long overdue.

Because the AAW was growing so fast, it was important to me that the work of these turners was brought to the forefront so that newer members would have a sense of our history and where we came from as well as how the work evolved through those years.

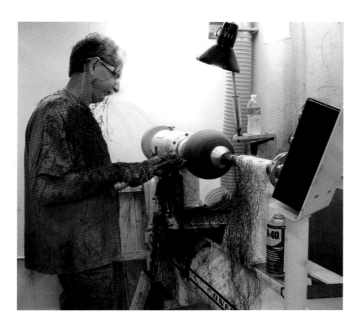

2007: Robert Lyon turns a bowling ball at the Echo Lake symposium organized by Bucks County (PA) woodturners.

This book is the highlight of that effort, celebrating 25 years. It was decided by the board that the book should be apolitical. In an effort to avoid the book having a single author and a single viewpoint, we decided that the more stories we told, the better we could paint the picture of AAW. Accordingly, we hired a professional editor who was knowledgeable about turning but who had not been associated with the AAW.

I think my single most important achievement was the Japanese Bowls show at the 2007 Portland symposium. In the winter of 2006, I was invited through the AAW office to attend a urushi exhibition to be held in New York City. It was called *Genuine Japan* and was to highlight the best work of the big name urushi (lacquerware) artists along with fine samples of saki. The lacquer artists began with simple wooden bowls, partially turned, and there was a large supply on hand. At the end of the weekend event, I was told that "we are going to throw these bowls away, do you want them?" "Yes," I said in gross disbelief. I took the wooden bowls home like a big game hunter takes home a trophy. I was elated. Now, what to do with them?

A story came to mind where, in a similar situation, a number of big name turners were given a piece of wood and asked to turn something from it and return it to the AAW for a show. My fear was that we would throw a party and no one would attend. The best story was the block that was sent to Giles Gilson was burned, and the ashes were sent back to the AAW. Gotta love that guy!

As time went on, the board created a list of about 50 turners, each of whom was to receive a partially turned bowl and finish it in their own style and liking. The resultant body of work was to have its own show at our 2007 Portland, Oregon, symposium. The pieces would be displayed alongside the work of the Japanese urushi artists and woodturners (who I invited to be featured demonstrators). I was nervous. As word got out about the show, we received requests for bowls when we had none. I turned about a dozen more blanks from local cherry and sent them out. I was encouraged.

The show opened to critical acclaim. With this, the Professional Outreach Program now had a venue to call its own. The group followed up with their *Spheres* exhibition at the 2008 Richmond, Virginia, symposium, in which I was myself able to partake with X-Box (a turned prop for magicians).

At the end of the Bowls show, the Japanese contingent awarded the AAW an extraordinary piece for our permanent collection. In return, they were allowed to choose three of the bowls to take back to Japan for their museum. Building bridges.

As time went on, I worked through three years as president of the Board of Directors. At the end, I was spent. The politics of the organization wore me out. I was ready. It was my hope that the work we did during that time was good. It was also my hope that, in the words of David Ellsworth, we were able to keep politics out of it. I know we tried. Sometimes we succeeded and sometimes we did not. I hope that it all averaged out so that we added a few more ticks in the "good" column.

Angelo Iafrate of Providence, RI, was president of the AAW during 2007 and 2008.

2006–2008

Angelo Iafrate is the AAW President.

2006

1,932 woodturners attend the AAW's annual symposium, Louisville.

Honorary lifetime member: Mary Lacer.

Turning 20— Still Evolving, an international invitational exhibit of 23 artists who were active from 1986 to 2006. In celebration of the 20th anniversary of the founding of the American Association of Woodturners, Kentucky Museum of Art, Louisville.

1987: Mary Lacer organizes the initial meeting of what would become the Minnesota Woodturners Association, then serves four years as its president. She is elected an AAW board member in 1989, and a year later becomes the organization's full-time office manager. In 2008, Lacer becomes executive director and serves until her retirement in 2010.

To mark the Louisville venue, AAW also organizes *Step Up to the Plate*, a baseball-themed juried exhibition of turned wood art.

2007

1,585 woodturners attend the AAW's annual symposium, Portland, Oregon.

Honorary lifetime member: Jerry Glaser.

Turning Green is the theme of the annual AAW exhibition, featuring work by 51 artists and a full-color catalog.

The AAW's Professional Outreach Program (POP) honors three of its leading

Giles Gilson, winner of the 2007 Professional Outreach Program merit award for lifetime achievement, congratulates Mark Lindquist, the AAW's honorary lifetime member for 2010.

members, Giles Gilson, Mark Lindquist, and Stephen Hogbin with a special exhibition of their work. POP also organizes an exhibition titled *Japanese Bowls: A Western Perspective*, in which Western artists take as raw material rough-turned Japanese bowls otherwise destined to become lacquered dinnerware and make something else of it.

	MEMBERS	CHAPTERS
2006	13,008	259
2007	13,096	285
2008	13,137	302
2009	13,500	320
2010		
2011		

2008

1,591 woodturners attend the AAW's annual symposium, Richmond, Virginia.

Honorary lifetime member: Albert LeCoff.

The AAW mounts two concurrent exhibitions, both with full-color catalogs. *Turned for Use II* features 44 artists making utilitarian work. *The Sphere* invites 48 artists to meditate upon the perfect sphere.

the Sphere

2009

Bill Haskell is the AAW President.

2009

1,291 woodturners attend the AAW's annual symposium, Albuquerque.

Honorary lifetime member: Giles Gilson.

The official AAW exhibitions feature desert imagery as befits the symposium venue and wood art derived from spindle turning. The POP committee honors Berkeley artist Merryll Saylan with an exhibition of her work alongside a startling exhibition of "twirlings" by the Oakland furniture artist Garry Knox Bennett.

2010

American Woodturner moved to bi-monthly publication.

2010

Emma Lake: Unplugged boldly investigated a major craft collaboration without electricity.

2010

Tom Wirsing is the AAW President.

2010

1,200 woodturners attend the AAW's symposium in Hartford.

Honorary lifetime member: Mark Lindquist.

2011

The American Association of Woodturners celebrates its 25th anniversary by holding the annual symposium in its headquarters city, Saint Paul. John Hill, a longtime stalwart of the organization, is named an honorary lifetime member.

2008: Notables sign books displaying their work, Richmond, VA symposium. From left, Dewey Garrett, Harvey Fein, Binh Pho, and Gorst Duplessis.

2008: Albert LeCoff, left, receives the AAW lifetime achievement award from his twin brother Alan. The two men organized the 1975–1985 woodturning symposiums that preceded formation of the AAW.

2009: Mysterious turned cylinders by Dick Veitch get a close inspection during the amazing Instant Gallery. Photo by Andi Wolfe.

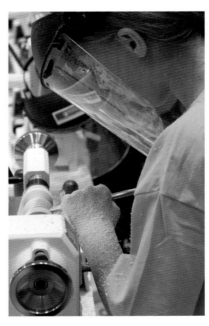

2010: This girl gets a great start learning to turn wood at the AAW 2010 Hartford symposium. Photo by Andi Wolfe.

Turning 20, Still Evolving

Invitational exhibition, Louisville, Kentucky

This major exhibition highlighted the evolutionary work of 22 studio turners over a 20-year period. The collection showcased significant turned pieces from each maker from 1986, 1996, and 2006. The exhibition catalog included photographs of all three pieces by each participant, along with essays by David Ellsworth and Alan Lacer, both past presidents of the AAW, and by wood artist J. Paul Fennell.

At age 20, the organization had grown up and had become capable of organizing and curating a complex exhibition such as this. These pages feature the most recent work by makers whose early work can be seen elsewhere in this book.

Bruce Mitchell
LEFT TO RIGHT:
1986: Teardrop Urn, spalted teardrop oak, 14" tall.
1996: Fin Spin, osage orange, 10.5" tall.
2006: Double Image, redwood burl, 28.5" tall.

2006: Connection, Stephen Hogbin, ash, glass, paint, 27" high.

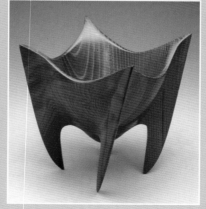

Two Grinds Please, salt or pepper mills, Don Leman, Columbus, OH, various hardwoods, 9" tall. Photo by Sharon Bierman.

Not Your Grandfather's Old Bagpipes, Ray Hughes, Shallowater, TX, tulipwood, buffalo horn, Delrin, leather, cloth, 30" long.

Ball Vase magic prop, Angelo Iafrate, Johnston, RI, black and white ebony, 6" tall.

LEFT: Kitchen set by Mike Mahoney, Orem, UT, quilted poplar with African blackwood, 10" tall.

The Sphere

Invitational exhibition, Richmond, Virginia

The Sphere is the second in a series of Professional Outreach Program exhibitions. The challenge presented to over 50 artists from around the globe was to finish an object no larger than 6 inches cubed. The invited artists were encouraged to expand on the concept of "sphere" rather than feel restricted by it, and it is obvious they did just that.

—*Jacques Vesery*

Corrugated Sphere, Jason Schneider, Colorado.

ABOVE: Stars Sphere, Eli Avisera, Jerusalem, Israel.

RIGHT: You Can't Be Spherious, Julie Heryet, Bristol, England.

Spiked Star in Sphere, David Springett, Warwickshire, England.

The Spindle

Invitational exhibition, Albuquerque

For woodturners, the spindle is not only a shape, but also a technical term for wood held on the lathe at both ends or "between centers." Traditional spindle forms include stair balusters and newels, chair legs, and pepper mills. *The Spindle* was the third in an ongoing series curated by the Professional Outreach Program of the American Association of Woodturners. Forty studio turners were invited to participate.

The Guardians, Douglas J. Fisher, Parksville, British Columbia, Canada.

Return to Earth, Satoshi Fujinuma, Tokyo, Japan.

Sleeping Beauty, Louise Hibbert, Gloucester, VA.

Popular Mechanics by Douglas W. Jones, Las Lunas, NM.

The Teapot

Invitational exhibition, Hartford

Try to see the forest through the trees and the teapot through the tea.

The Teapot is the fourth in the Professional Outreach Program's ongoing exhibit series. Invited artists from around the globe percolated the challenge. The boiled-down idea was to create some of the most extraordinary and unordinary forms blending utility and inspiration. Wood may not seem the appropriate medium for a teapot, yet it serves as a wonderful canvas to explore revelation from tradition.

Steeped in the aroma of history, these contemporary containers are a collective thread of thinking outside the box or tea chest. Conservative, witty, or thought provoking, all are as diverse as tea itself.

—*Jacques Vesery*

Helga, by Arthur Liestman, big-leaf maple burl, ebony, 5" tall.

Lip Service, Dixie Biggs, Gainesville, FL. Cherry, acrylic paint, 7" wide.

Having Tea with My Good Friend Wiley-O, by Cindy Drozda, Boulder, CO. Sea urchin shell, metal leaf, African blackwood, garnet in 14K gold inlay, 5.3" high.

"Outside of the chair, the teapot is the most ubiquitous and important design element in the domestic environment, and almost everyone who has tackled the world of design has ended up designing one."

—David McFadden

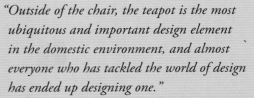

Bitter and Twisted, by Julie Heryet, Bristol, England. Boxwood, sycamore, acrylic, 8" high.

ABOVE: Cha Hu, by Curt Theobald, Pine Bluffs, WY. Cherry, 6" high.

Earth Tone Tea Stains, by Ray Feltz, Celina, OH. Walnut, maple, cherry, holly, 6.5" high.

Self-Portrait as a Teapot, by Michael Hosaluk, Saskatoon, SK, Canada. Maple, acrylic, copper, 6.5" high.

Maple Medley *an Acer Showcase*

Juried exhibition, Hartford

Maple trees, noted for their fall colors, are prevalent in the Northeastern United States, site of our 2010 Hartford, CT, symposium. *Acer* is the genus of trees and shrubs commonly known as maple. There are approximately 125 species worldwide. The word "*acer*" is derived from a Latin word meaning "sharp," referring to the characteristic points on maple leaves.

Maple wood is cherished and used to great advantage by both woodworkers and woodturners. While wood from the *Acer* family can sometimes be very bland and uninteresting, it also can have a regal appearance. It sometimes has wonderful figure and coloration patterns that are a special treat to wood lovers: tiger-striping or fiddleback patterns; ambrosia beetle streaks; fine black spalted zone markings that seem like India ink lines; marvelous and sought after birdseye, blister quilting and curl patterns that display rich and deep chatoyance; lovely and intriguing burl; and the brilliant red streaks of boxelder (*Acer negundo*). The maple family indeed produces an opulent palette of figure and color, which can be seen in the work selected for this juried exhibition.

—*Bill Haskell*

Natural-edge Maple Burl Hollow Vessel, Mike Jackofsky, Escondido, CA, bigleaf maple burl, 15" dia.

ABOVE: Marbleized Maple Vessel, by Andy DiPietro, Burlington, VT, bleached spalted ambrosia silver maple, 6.75" high.

LEFT: From the Artifactory, Beth Ireland, Roslindale, MA, maple turned and carved, 20" long.

Dancing in the Moonlight II, Neil Kagan, Falls Church, VA, bigleaf maple burl turned and carved, 7" high.

Alchemist Vessel, David Marks, Santa Rosa, CA, bigleaf maple, Gabon ebony, snakewood, walrus ivory, silver and gold leaf, 20" high.

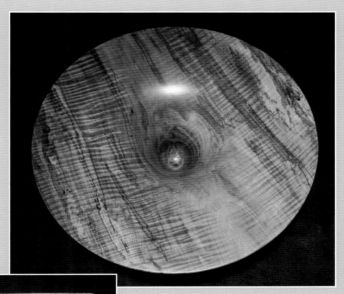

Flared Maple, by Phil Brown, Bethesda, MD. Curly red maple kept wet for a year to spalt, air dried, epoxy hardened, and turned. 18" dia.

Telling a story

2007: Knight Fall by Derek Weidman, Green Lane, PA, mahogany and boxwood scraps, turned, carved, painted. 12" high.

Turning wood brings us into intimate contact with a natural material. We hold it, we examine it, we analyze it. We cut, scrape and bore into it. We are often covered in it, shavings fresh, wet, and aromatic. To acquire wood, we are made to consider its origin. Did it come from a healthy, sustainable forest or did it come from a dwindling supply in a badly managed area of the world? If we are open and receptive, woodturning can teach us a deep appreciation for the gifts of the earth.

Because it is the substance of plants that are vulnerable to changing conditions, wood is an apt material for making statements about the health of the planet. For the 2007 AAW exhibition *Turning Green*, Derek Weidman created Knight Fall. Says Weidman, "This figure is the Green Knight, and instead of standing for chivalry and righteousness like the more common White Knight, he is fighting for the environment and conservation. He is showing wear in the 11th hour..."

Woodturning in the Era of the American Association of Woodturners: 1986–2010

The American Association of Woodturners has played a crucial role in the development of contemporary woodturning and wood art. Its chapters have created a venue for woodturners all over North America to get together, share information, swap tools and materials, and show their current work. Its annual symposiums have brought together turners from all over the world in an open sharing of ideas as well as techniques. Without the organized sharing this organization has made possible, it is not likely that the field as a whole could have advanced so rapidly in so few years. This section also presents a taxonomy of the field—a careful attempt to group and order the main trends in contemporary lathe-turned art.

So Far, So Fast

A *new tradition of woodturning emerges*

Steve Loar

Being part of the contemporary woodturning field as it developed from a handful of isolated makers to the immense field it is today has had a very special feeling to it. Well into the early 1990s, the field seemed to embody classic, stereotypical American attributes. We were seen as inventors and innovators, rather brash, anxious to be striding ahead, and not very tolerant of, or even interested in, traditions. For many of us, woodturning felt like Manifest Destiny. We believed that the United States was the center of the universe and saw more and more of the world's turners wanting to be part of our action.

Contemporary crafts were born out of the post-WWII search for new forms, new processes, and new meanings. For some, it was an attitude of challenging the gods of tradition. There have been repeated attempts to set the canon of who was the "first generation" of practitioners and teachers, who was second, and who has been left to follow, but the genesis of contemporary woodturning is widely acknowledged to be in the work of James Prestini, Bob Stocksdale, and Rude Osolnik. These individuals worked in near obscurity as the crafts related to furniture, ceramics, metals, and fibers gained momentum and broad recognition.

The half-century that encompasses contemporary woodturning seems to have washed together into a scene reminiscent of Han Solo throwing his space ship into star-drive in the first *Star Wars* movie. Whoosh! ...and away it went in a blur of individual points smeared into a veil. Within that blur, woodturning's particular moment was the decade spanning 1976 to 1986 with its public acknowledgment of the field as something of a phenomenon. Especially significant moments were the 1986 *Vision and Concept* turning conference

Traditional woodturning

1980s: Gail Redman, Railing with Newel Post, redwood, 44" high, Wood Turning Center Museum Collection.
Redman's artful renovations of Victorian homes in San Francisco gave tradition and utility a solid grounding toward a contemporary synthesis of use and art. Redman's passing in 2000 robbed the field of a superb talent.

at Arrowmont, the 1981 *Gallery of Turned Objects* exhibition and catalog, followed by the 1986 formation of the American Association of Woodturners. The 1980s clearly marked the blooming of a new and vital field.

The contemporary woodturning field has grown rapidly and has covered a great deal of investigatory ground since a critical mass of practitioners began to develop in the mid-1970s and early 1980s. There has been an unrelenting investigation of what the lathe can do, especially as it relates to wood and to work from the faceplate. The field's most obvious obsessions have been with a basic process, a basic form, and as many big tools as a person could afford. The interests and investigations of the field-at-large have fueled remarkable innovations and refinements to the machinery and tooling that have become commercially available. The thin-walled vessel has been intensively explored. The most remarkable indicator of the enormous and sustained interest in turning can be seen in the membership of the American Association of Woodturners, long ago topping 10,000. As a result, these last 25 years have brought us a new tradition of woodturning.

Sculptural expression

1993: Crow Pond, Neil Donovan and John Vahanian, basswood, cherry, ebony, colored pencil, paint, 30" dia.
Crow Pond is a pastoral scene that remains one of the most satisfying pieces of the movement. With suggestions of Boullee's 1784 Monument to Isaac Newton, scale and perspective are played with at every turn. A beguiling early use of mixed media.

Tradition

Tradition may be defined as the handing down of statements, attitudes, beliefs, legends, and customs from generation to generation by word of mouth or by practice. Traditions are valued ways of doing things and are a function of time and repetition. What is important is sorted out, patterns are established, and these are passed along to others. If a new tradition in woodturning is to be understood, it will be helpful to understand what came before it.

Prior to World War II, turning could be defined as a process of rotational carving to rapidly produce elements out of an inexpensive and widely available material—wood. The primary use of the lathe as a mass-production

tool placed a premium on minimizing cost, so that where hand operations were still used, skill was equated with accuracy in speed of production. For the first 75 years of the 20th century, the long historical tradition of woodturning embodied several distinctive attributes:

- Turning was taught in most secondary schools, along with introductions to general woodworking, metalworking, and drafting. It also was taught by master to apprentice, by father to son, and by self-education.
- Turnings were commercially produced in volume, primarily for utility as housewares and structural/decorative elements in furniture and architecture, and in industrial patternmaking en route to cast iron objects.
- Pattern books were often used as the style source, thus continuing aesthetic traditions even where details were modified or when the worker reinterpreted the specified form.
- Turnings were generally monochromatic, whether of a single wood or as the result of paint.
- Turnings did not tend to result from personal artistic expression.

Contemporary woodturning

2000: Cycles, Virginia Dotson and Edward Wood, Italian poplar plywood, paint, music CD. The artists have turned a vessel then cut it apart, arranging the recombined pieces. These finely articulated fragments suggest the whole vessel, while their composition evokes landscape, dance, and unheard music.

New traditions

Since the formation of the American Association of Woodturners in 1986, a new tradition of woodturning has developed with a lengthy list of its own attributes:

- It is process-oriented and, by definition, reveres the single media of wood.
- It is enamored by faceplate work, rather than spindles and has set the thin-walled vessel as the standard reference for skill.
- It accepts speed-of-production as the common denominator of skill rather than quality, sophistication, or repeatability.
- It has little concern for utility/function.
- Although many turners first saw a lathe in industrial arts class or were self-taught, today turning is most often taught in intimate small-group situations.

- It can claim only a few formal college or university programs in higher education and has steadfastly eschewed formal education in art or design.
- In the rush to be "modern," turners have exhibited little knowledge of, or interest in, historical precedents.
- It was, until the early 1990s, composed almost entirely of middle-aged to elderly Caucasian American right-handed males.
- It is seen by many practitioners as a hobby or entertainment, often centered upon the size and number of machines, tools, and gadgets.
- It is involved with one-of-a-kind production, even when made for retail sale.
- In wanting to be all-inclusive, it has failed to define a boundary, edge, or limit to what constitutes "turned."
- It sees itself as apart from, and not a subset of, the field of furniture.
- It has bestowed the title of "artist" on all turners, without assessment of the actual merit of the work.
- It has an extraordinary sense of community and a unique level of sharing and has led the other crafts in its exploration of artistic collaboration.

The big plateau

The arc of contemporary woodturning has metaphorically brought it well out onto a large plateau. It ascended so quickly that it was all a blur, with no need to look anywhere except straight ahead. Following this rapid rise to visibility, recognition, and acceptance, several worrisome factors have been converging to slow this progress. The field has begun to slow in its levels of ingenuity and discovery. Innovation and invention are by no means dead, but for several years there have been fewer and fewer truly original forms or ideas offered up and even fewer noteworthy technical achievements. The list of new traditions (above) suggests that what made contemporary woodturning burst forth and achieve so much in so short a time were unbridled enthusiasm, brawn, native wit, a sense of community, and the time and disposable income

Turned, and mostly carved

1981: Suspended Flora, Ron Fleming, redwood burl.
The artist considers this a breakthrough piece, because he has pressed both turning and carving into service of the story he wants to tell. Fleming has always been a master of the 360-degree experience, not constricted by the spinning symmetry of the lathe. He offers drama and mystery within an easily readable fusion of flora and vessel. Like the best sculpture, you are drawn to wonder what the other side looks like.

to acquire the tools, materials, and training to establish a fulfilling hobby. The list also suggests a narrow focus that could hinder and slow the field as it moves into the future.

Many of the early "young guns," the ones who set the pace in the late 20th century, have aged and entered mature phases of their work. Their progress is now measured in sophistication of form and process, rather than outright discovery. Their original insights and levels of execution have been assimilated by legions of apprentice-like devotees and former students.

"The field has come through the easy part with brilliance. Now it gets harder."

Unfortunately, the nature of apprentices is to work mechanically without a deep understanding of the artistic or conceptual processes necessary to continue development. The result has been a diminishing of the overall level of originality and a proliferation of ephemeral turned wood knick-knacks and trinkets. Ironically, the wide-spread acquisition of sophisticated tools and techniques, including digital photography, can make the early and important work appear pale by uninformed comparison.

While the field appears to be robust, many works have been lauded as innovative when the lathe was not a central driving force in either conception or resolution. It is puzzling why numerous works that only use the lathe for excavation have been given heightened visibility while beautifully imagined and executed inquiries that happen to be with furniture have been ignored. Additionally, post-lathe processes and surface manipulations often render forms so altered that they lose their references to a birth in turning. It is fitting that one definition of "render" is, "to portray in another language." This is not to deny that there is engaging and magnificent work being made, but there is an interplay of arcs and swells that identifies an object's origins on the lathe. The very essence of woodturning is this interplay of arcs and swells.

Several years ago in an exhibition review in the journal *Turning Points*, Robin Wood lamented, "One of the drawbacks of this movement toward complexity is that each year, in order to make a mark, we have to make something a little more complex." That is true because every culture, including woodturning, goes through definite stages of development, generally moving from simple to complex. In the first stage, the basic strategies

of survival are solved. Generations of survivors slowly build more comfortable lifestyles. Things gradually improve, and more people live longer. More and more of the basic stuff of living becomes commonplace, and more about that culture's universe is discovered, tested, and accepted as the current truth. For every culture, there comes a time when most of the basics have been figured out. For our culture, we have heavier-than-air craft, the World Wide Web, the means to obliterate our entire species, and we have set our sights on figuring out gravity, black holes, cloning, and computers that use other dimensions. There is a point in every culture or field's development where native genius and enthusiasm simply are not enough. The new discoveries tend to be made in esoteric and expensive endeavors. Woodturning is in such a time. The cycle of history might continue to ascend, but it can also flatten into an ongoing plateau, or even diminish. Woodturning is in such a time.

As our field came into being, something of a tragedy took place as woodturners allowed themselves to be dressed in the clothes of "The Artist." True, what might be called a "studio woodturning movement" was developing, but most turners are and were interested more in the tools and the techniques than in the concepts, ideas, or statements that come out of a "studio." The historic struggle within the American Association of Woodturners to balance the content of its journal, *American Woodturner*, reflects this clearly. Being artful is quite a different kind of work from gaining technical prowess or feeding a fascination with tools and hardware. So while it may be glamorous that some have allowed themselves to be called artists, the field's obvious fascination with faceplate work and especially the thin-walled vessel disguises a narrow exploration of possibilities (albeit, a very intense one!). Even the seeming breadth that is now applied to describe what is "turned" masks this narrow inquiry. In addition to all but ignoring its own rich roots in architectural and production/multiples work, turning has failed to brave the adjacent field of contemporary "studio" furniture or the world of contemporary sculpture. There have been a few notable attempts to at least acknowledge furniture and historical references, though. Notably, the AAW and the Wood

Complexity

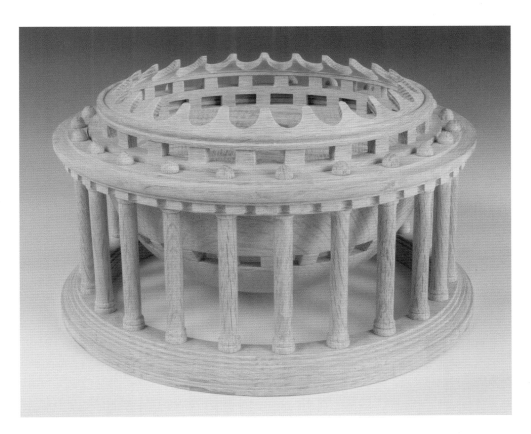

1999: Et Tu, Colosseo series, Dewey Garrett, bleached white oak.
Garrett, an engineer in Livermore, CA, uses ingeniously jigged routers in combination with precision lathes to create complex pieces with historical and architectural themes. Earlier work explored the bowl's skeleton, supported by mysterious and faultless craftsmanship; truly architecture of the vessel. A prolific and incessantly curious talent, Garrett has created numerous lines of innovative and finely wrought work.

Turning Center have repeatedly created educational introductions to major exhibits with displays that offered historical information about furniture and turning, and included both spindle work and furniture. A workshop student of mine once summed it up quite succinctly: "Most of us don't have studios. We have shops."

The woodturning field could coast ahead on inertia for quite a while before an adoring public, relatives, or even the dedicated collectors realized that they were getting warmed-over goods, yesterday's bread without the zing, or variations on the same-old same-old. Significant heights have been attained and new lands have been discovered and conquered, but our Age of Discovery is over. Productivity and invention have already leveled off, and I see a future that might diminish quite rapidly as aging practitioners become unable to participate in their beloved hobby. This thinning of the ranks has massive implications. Without a large base of purchasers, woodturning's commercial network may dramatically shrink. Without a large base of practitioners, innovation may dramatically decline. Without the large base of novices that is the mainstay of the AAW, the array of workshops and schools for them will wither.

The proliferation of turning workshops and conferences, like the number of tools available, indicates a large and active field. Turning is wildly popular. Enormous. But unabated growth of any kind cannot continue forever, as we can see in the larger U.S. economy. While there is no data on the average age of woodturners, a visit to any conference will suggest that it is, quite simply, elderly. Discretionary time and money, and for many, postponement of a fulfilling avocation are the primary drivers. In the last few years, the field has lost many of its ground-breaking pioneers: James Prestini, Rude Osolnik, David Pye, Melvin Lindquist, Ed Moulthrop, Bob Stocksdale, Skip Johnson, and Palmer Sharpless. Studio Furniture has experienced similar passings with Art Carpenter, Sam Maloof, James Krenov, and Alan Peters. Their ages were not much more advanced than many current woodturning practitioners. All of this leaves us with two wildly different theories about the near-future of the woodturning field: my fretful vision is that advancing age will soon significantly diminish the number of turners, becoming a profound negative force, as opposed to the brighter view, held by several of my very informed colleagues, that sees a large part of the baby-boomer generation just moving into

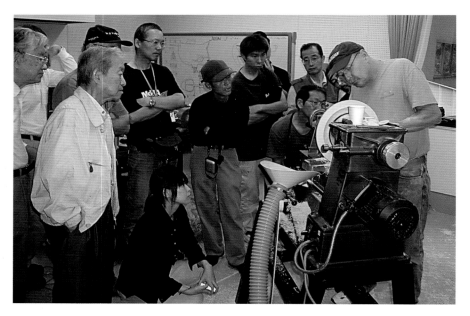

Teaching by demonstrating

In a scene repeated many times each month at AAW chapter meetings, John Jordan of Cane Ridge, TN, teaches a group of woodturners about his tools and techniques. Fueled by the American Association of Woodturners demonstrator scheduling service, education at this level is ongoing nationwide, but it is not so easy to fill a weeklong workshop on advanced techniques or design ideas. Photo courtesy John Jordan.

Neither a diminished level of originality or the potential for diminished numbers of turners need cripple the field. There are vast regions of unexplored terrain—we just need to take our interplay of arcs and swells on that journey rather than abandoning them. We need to "change, renew, rejuvenate ourselves." The need for education in the arts and the crafts, at all levels and by all means, will have never been greater.

Education

The vast number of workshops and conferences have created a huge base of technically capable hobbyists and amateurs. Rarely, however, have these workshops been the crucibles necessary to create individuals who will truly advance the field. Due to a significant portion of the field being self-taught, especially in the early years, there is a widespread lack of formal art/design education. Other crafts have matured because they developed foundations in post-secondary academia, usually in the early years of their post-war incarnation. These programs established rigorous environments of invention, inquiry, scholarship, and critique. They acted as birthing grounds for both practitioners and teachers. This has not yet been the case for woodturning. The handful of workshop-type schools of significance still demand "product" as content. Course titles and descriptions that dare to suggest an academic or design emphasis still tempt cancellation for lack of interest. Art and design topics certainly fill rooms for the hour-long conference rotation, but interest is slim-to-none for the commitment of time and money for a one- or two-week workshop. The level of serious craft instruction in many workshops has been dampened by the shortness of the sessions and corrupted by the vacation mentality of many enrollees. But maybe I'm just carping and asking the old dog to learn new tricks.

Where the old dogs have been committed to their own brand of inspiring education, though, is through

retirement, placing any downturn in the number of practitioners at least 40 years away.

"We're approaching the mountains now, and from these new heights there will be many stunning and inspiring views, but the terrain will be rugged and life there will be more demanding than it has been on the plain. The field of turning is at a threshold. Not a threshold as in a doorway, where one has the choice to go back or to proceed ahead, but a point similar to puberty, where one moves onward from one existence to another, never really able to turn back or regain the innocence of previous years." That was my voice way back in 1995 in my commentary, "We're Not in Kansas Anymore," for *American Woodturner*, the AW Journal. I was uneasy then, and I am far more anxious now. The field has come through the easy part with brilliance. Now it gets difficult.

Native genius and enthusiasm have carried the field along at a break-neck speed, but the absence of an interest in art and design has begun to exact a serious toll. Finding our way off the big plateau will require more from us than those paths that brought us here. It could also be made more difficult by having far fewer of us on the journey.

the AAW itself, its chapters, its long-lived journal, and its commitment to the young potential turner. The now-celebrated fathers of contemporary turning—Prestini, Stocksdale, Osolnik, and Moulthrop—gathered their creative energies from a wide cultural influence and some inner need to make and investigate. As people, they lived and marked a changing of the cultural guard. This changed in 1976, with the gathering at the Arrowmont School of Arts and Crafts. Much like the droplets in a cloud finally gathering enough mass to fall, a group of makers came together and saw themselves as turners. Both the American Association of Woodturners and the Wood Turning Center coalesced from that moment. They have both cultured a vital camaraderie that has nurtured more and more work, more and more processes, and more and more ideas. Prestini and the others were isolated hit-spots in the young and unformed sensibility that would become contemporary crafts. With the formation of AAW, the WTC, and the events they created and enabled, there came to be a true movement. Whether you were conservative or liberal, traditional

or artsy, whether you cut or scraped—you were part of something big and vital. Rude Osolnik laughed at my scrapers when I took a class with him. But I was there as one of the first "professionals" to receive an AAW scholarship, and he was there because there was a group of enthusiasts big enough to support a class.

Through the AAW conferences and through the work of many of the chapters, the importance of youth to the vitality of the field has been clearly expressed. This could be casually seen as a concern with the "graying" that has every craft organization scrambling to identify and nurture a next generation. For turners, though, a less cerebral answer comes to mind: It is the nature of maturity to want to pass along its skills and wisdom, to invest years of insight in the young. The program I have helped initiate at the Center for Turning and Furniture Design and our two-year counterpart at Bucks County Community College represent a great portion of academia's very limited interest in turning. And what of the youth that is excited by the AAW interest? With school workshops limited to "18 and older" and

It's not about the wood

1995: Where I Live, Al Stirt, ceanothus burl, barbed wire, turned and sandblasted, 8" dia. Photo by Alan Stirt. Collection of Mint Museum of Craft+Design.

The vessel-as-canvas in an unexpected way, both loud and quiet at the same time. So very evocative, it doesn't matter whether or not it's wood. Stirt said, "I started the piece before the Oklahoma City bombing and finished it just after. The Holocaust is echoed in the imagery."

It tells a story

2006: Spirit Whites on Sky Blue Pale, Ron Layport; maple, 9" dia.
Layport pushes the limits of the thin wall in the service of creating a powerful narrative screen. This dimensionally graphic surface fully engages light to magnify its exquisite imagery. While fully modern, it also suggests many cultures and many times.

math and science, industrial arts lost its way. It was never able to articulate the many profound aspects of its mission. The damage incurred to our nation with the loss of industrial arts and its sister home economics, and now with the growing threats to fine arts in American K-12 education, cannot be underestimated. For turning it could be a mortal wound. At the very least, we may be about to experience a long and slow decline for the lack of on-going opportunities.

Tomorrow's pioneers

Tomorrow's pioneers, like the individuals who have helped make the way for us, will be at the forefront of exploring what is acceptable in contemporary woodturning. They will continue to develop new processes and apply old ones in new ways, to create new forms and compositions that will express contemporary concepts and concerns. These future pioneers, like those of our shared history, will not be so concerned with what can be done as with what might be done. Figure, gesture, architecture, landscape, and pattern will likely be increasingly common interests

the larger part of the nation's industrial arts programs eliminated, there are few places to discover a youthful interest in turning. For the youth that are excited by the work of the AAW, there are few avenues for them to continue to grow. The very experiences of adolescence and the continuum of experiences that gave this mature generation its grounding no longer exist. There is a fusion of hand, mind, problem-solving, and disciplined work that turning and furniture-making embody, and they have been largely removed from our experience. Long before the fine arts became expendable in the face of diminishing budgets and mandated success in

as inspiration is drawn from literature, music, narrative, ritual, philosophy, and as always, other artwork. The true leaders will seek to clarify their personal voices as they boldly investigate the expressive potential of the lathe. They will also more aggressively question the semantics of "wood"-turning. It is exactly through these pursuits that innovators will expand the field's technical repertoire as well as its visual vocabulary and language. These individuals will hone their intuition and design sensibilities and be comfortable with serendipity and ambiguity. These are particularly difficult tasks to discover and master in a field such as ours that is so predominantly left-brained and grounded in objectivity. It is a positive sign that the number of women in the field is growing, albeit slowly, and it would be very beneficial if youth and individuals of ethnic variety also were to become notable participants.

Within the many goals that contemporary woodturning has sought, one very important but overlooked attribute is the straightforward pursuit of beauty. Al Stirt's emotional reaction to the Gulf War as expressed through his War Bowl series is one notable exception. There was a statement to be made, and beauty was not the way to say it. Otherwise, most of the thousands of things that woodturners have been made have had a common motivation—the pursuit of beauty. It may not have always been pursued with rigor, but the desire to make beautiful things has always been there. Turned wood objects can be an antidote to the mass-produced degradation of the visual, emotional, and psychological environment that we are experiencing— but only if executed at exceptional levels of creativity and craftsmanship.

The cult of originality, initially given power in the myth of Michelangelo, became solidified through the myth of Pablo Picasso and what we still refer to as "Modernism." The ease with which woodturners took to calling themselves artists belies the work that is necessary to become one. Just as surely as the physical aspects of turning are a body of skills, imagining and designing are another body of skills. The business of finding and then making one's own mark is a body of skills like any other. It need not be a Totally New mark or the Never Before Seen mark. What it needs to be is your mark and your Voice. And that's where we come back to the work of education. In order to grow into the next phase of maturation, our field will need a deep commitment to nurturing many individual creative voices, whether your own or others. In a world that doesn't need any more objects, what will we make of our future?

New traditions have to start somewhere.

Let's begin the climb off this big plateau.

Steve Loar is director of the Center for Turning and Furniture Design at Indiana University of Pennsylvania. Steve is a noted innovator in the field with artwork in major public and private collections throughout the U.S. and featured in over 30 books and texts. Steve's studio experience informs his teaching, his scholarship, and his critical writing. He has curated many exhibitions and is a long-time and frequent contributor to *American Woodturner*. This text builds upon previously published essays:

1) Catalog introduction: Moving Beyond Tradition—A Turned-Wood Invitational, Decorative Arts Museum/Arkansas Arts Center, Little Rock, AR, October 19-November 19, 1997, pp. 6-11.
2) Commentary: Education…What Is It Good For?, *Woodwork*, December 2003, pp. 56-59
3) Commentary: We're Not in Kansas Anymore, *American Woodturner*, December 1995, pp. 44, 46.

1985: Bowl For the Coastal Tribes, Steve Loar, 13" high, spalted maple, dyed veneered plywood, paint. Photo by Jamey Stillings. Collection of David Ellsworth. In this wry piece, Loar lifts the humble vessel off the table, theatrically presenting its polished spalted-wood interior.

Steve Loar: play nice together

Collaboration is the hard work of cooperating, communicating, and working with others, be it with one person or a group. It is also the hard work of compromise, knowing as you enter into the relationship that the end-product will not be yours alone. This commitment is fueled by a belief that a better, more interesting, and yes, unpredictable piece of work will result. It is at least as much about process as finished product.

The annual conferences and the proliferation of chapters and their own events created a tornado-like effect by mixing large numbers of woodturning enthusiasts. If you bump into enough people, you find compatible friends and associates. You have experiences that would never happen if you worked alone.

Collaboration grew out of, and was nourished by, these interactions. The physical in-person type of collaboration can be seen as having grown out of the woodturning and furniture symposiums begun by Michael Hosaluk in 1982, later coming to full bloom in the biennial Emma Lake collaboratives. Personal collaboration was initiated by Mark Sfirri in his work with painter Robert Dodge and then in serial collaborations with Michael Hosaluk. Another type of

Collaboration

1996: Helplessly Hoping/Expecting to Fly, Steve Loar with Mark Sfirri, Clay Foster, and Chesley Kingsley; curly maple, birch, oak, redwood burl, cow bone; 25" high. Collection of André Martel, Quebec, Canada. Typical of the Emma Lake experience, Loar was drawn out of studio solitude to engage in a highly active exchange with other artists, with pop music providing the narrative inspiration.

Mixed media

1988: Secretaire, early collaborative furniture by Mark Sfirri and Robert Dodge, lacewood and paint, 48" high. Collection of Wood Turning Center, photo by John Carlano. This collaboration between turner and furniture maker Sfirri and painter Dodge crosses traditional media boundaries.

found-object collaboration was begun by Steve Loar, working with an experimental off-set leg by Mark Sfirri. The current interest in group effort grew out of all this early work.

Collaboration has been a growing cultural interest over the span of the American Association of Woodturners' existence. It was probably most visible in popular music and seems to be part of the widespread interest in events beyond one's self: the search for "authenticity." The AAW and the Wood Turning Center enabled an ever-expanding network of opportunities for makers to mix with their peers. The hobbyist, the amateur, the professional—all were welcomed within the embrace of woodturning. Through teaching, individuals were forced to

articulate their methods, ideas, and discoveries. In so doing, they became better at what they did, passed along their ideas, and also observed an array of translations of their work that in turn could excite new ideas. Two significant contributions that woodturning has given to the collaborative spirit have been both the openness of sharing ideas and the speed at which they were offered to the field at large. The habitual secrecy that still marks many other crafts is essentially absent in woodturning.

For another way that woodturners collaborate, see page 173 and page 184.

Themes: Decoding Contemporary Woodturning

Steve Loar

Prior to the Italian Renaissance, people who made things, whether fancy or humble, creative or strictly utilitarian, were known as artisans and craftsmen. There were other words that described whether they executed their work badly, or well, or with brilliance—but they were nonetheless artisans and craftsmen. With the virtuosity of Michelangelo and in the myth that began to build about him, even in his lifetime, the Western world began a love affair with the artist as a lone genius, one who exhibits a unique or divine originality. From this change in language and the supporting belief system that grew up around it, we have come to see art as a gift as opposed to the result of hard work by an artisan or craftsman. This paradigm reduces the craftsman to a mere mechanic. The work created outside the mythos of gift or genius is today relegated to mere craft.

With the Impressionists in the late 1800s, we see further refinements in the modern artistic sensibility. This work resulted from the artist's personal vision rather than from a vision that was translated, restrained, or structured by the salon, the church, or the school

within which he worked. A significant 20th century contribution to this line of thinking was the further narrowing of art into "big A" Art. Much of the purpose of this type of art was to actually disengage from the viewer as the content of the work became an esoteric conversation among critics, academics, and collectors. The lay viewer was seen as being below or outside of

Is this woodturning?

1996: Untitled So Far, Gord Peteran, 20" long, leather, wood, linen thread.
An iconoclast and provocateur, Peteran brings intellect and wide-ranging interests to bear upon his exploration of the boundaries of woodturning. This piece—quickly made during a conference by sewing an anonymously scrapped spindle into a leather case—was highly controversial among woodturners when it appeared on the cover of the *Curator's Focus: Turning in Context* exhibition catalog. Critics say Peteran didn't turn anything, and they are correct. What Peteran did is what all good artists do: he saw something and brought it to our attention.

this conversation. Why try to communicate with the rabble when they clearly lacked the language and the temperament to understand what they were seeing?

20th century art has sought to engage the viewer through provocation, assault, or offense rather than be compromised by considerations of beauty, communication, or viewer enjoyment. Fortunately, woodturning has been largely involved with these latter qualities, which characterize the decorative arts. Yet despite vastly increased opportunities for camaraderie, networking, workshops, sales, exhibition, and notoriety, the field continues to crave official sanctification as a legitimate art form. Repeated comments have been made about the long-standing lack of critical commentary and assessment from outside of the field. A generous answer to this quandary is that craft stands apart from art, while a more cynical answer is that we woodturners may not yet have made enough work worthy of serious discussion.

In their quest to gain the status and—let's admit it—the sales prices of Art, contemporary crafts have largely adopted the theories of originality and individual genius. The best of contemporary crafts, however, embody creativity in combination with a variety of intimate and enriching sensual properties that fine arts typically do not possess. This fusion of creativity and intimacy

(or accessibility), the idea joined with the materials itself, is clearly more important to the world of contemporary craft objects than any historic grounding in utility. Contemporary woodturning, in its rush to carve out a place of its own on the beachhead of modernity, quickly shed its roots in utility.

Is this woodturning?

2010: #213 Cypress Vessel, Howard Werner, Mt. Tremper, NY, 50" dia.
Sculptor Howard Werner carves whole logs of wood into furniture and simple forms. This huge piece, though entirely chainsawn, is highly regular and the offset hemispheres are truly round. Werner agrees that the piece might have been easier to turn than to carve, except he had no lathe that was large enough. What Werner did is what all good artists do: he had an idea, and he did not limit his expression to what the available tools could facilitate.

Finding your way in the world of woodturning and wood art

The pages that follow sort out the various themes and styles prevalent in contemporary wood art. In broad terms, the map looks like this:

The Elegant Vessel
The Thin Walled Vessel
Color/Pattern/Texture
Telling a Story: Narrative,
Humor, Politics

The Essential Vessel

Technical Variations
Multi-Axis Turning
Ornamental Turning
Segmented Turning
Metal and Other Materials

Sculpture/Wood Art
Architecture
Landscape
Human Figure
Furniture

Despite the fact that the woodturning field is notable for its level of sharing, community, and teaching, because of the cult of originality there has been a general unwillingness to concede personal influence or reference. To date, there has been no acknowledgement of genres or schools of thought within the field. The time lines throughout this book provide insights into the complex interplay of friendships, teaching, opportunities, timing, and influences that have been the genesis of contemporary turning. The images in this section present critical moments in the development of the field by considering the dominant attributes of important work.

The expansion of the ideas, the processes, the uses of materials, and even our perceptions of what is dangerous within contemporary turning are somewhat like the Big Bang Theory: everything we see around us expanded from a single point of super-heated, super-dense matter. Each noteworthy development took place in a moment of time and context. When we look back on any significant moment, given our current understanding and levels of accomplishment or expectation, these events and objects often seem simple or passé.

I have identified important works as if they were new and unexpected rays of light that pierced the fabric of what was known or expected. These works changed our perceptions of what was possible. From them often emerged whole genres of creations by others.

The makers of these works were pioneers, not only in that they got there first with a concept, a process, or a material, but that they articulated a coherent voice of originality. They were the primal thought of successfully synthesized concept, process, and material. For many on my list, this voice has been heard over a sustained period of time: perseverance is one essential component of talent. But the paradox of the singer/songwriter had to be considered as well—the inventor who is not always the most effective communicator of the fully rendered concept. And while my focus was on the emergence of new ideas, it was also necessary to acknowledge several pivotal innovations in process and material.

Perhaps this attempt to place a taxonomy on the field will elicit your own assessments of what should be considered significant moments or events. There are many more!

Portions of this text are from the first presentation of Some Significant Moments in Contemporary Turning, *Artistic Woodturning Worldwide 2000 conference, Puy-St-Martin, France; June 3, 2000.*

The Elegant Vessel

The naked wooden bowl. Cupped hands colored by the wildness of wood. The essence of what people love, but, ironically, what artistic woodturners have pushed aside in the rush to claim an individual artistic niche. And stranger still, whether controlled or organic, the requisite skill is no longer held as the necessary rite-of-passage before one attempts creative work.

Richard Raffan
1970s: Bowls, various woods, smallest are 6" dia.
This work embodies the tradition of high technical skill in the service of use. In combination with an ever-critical eye, Raffan has produced elegance, balance, the fair curve, and universal appeal. Utility remains a largely unexplored aspect of contemporary turning.

Ray Key
1986: Untitled, box elder, 6" dia.
This beautiful vessel by the popular teacher Ray Key features the wood figure and the outer surface of the log itself.

Helga Winter
2005: Bowl, bleached madrone root burl, 7" high, photo by Frank Ross.
This artist investigates the contorted shapes that occur when green wood dries. Then she pushes the wood-ness out of the piece by bleaching.

The Thin-Walled Vessel

This term generally refers to a vessel that at least turns in upon itself and, in most cases, to one with a small opening. The smaller the hole, the more adroit the turner is considered to be. Thin-walled vessels are almost entirely non-utilitarian. Their quality is measured by their thinness and uniformity—assessed by sight, by balance/sound/light, or your belief.

Once woodturners had learned how to make thin-walled vessels, some artists quickly moved beyond the sheer beauty of the wood itself. They pierced and carved these thin shells of wood, burned them and painted them, bent them, and put them to service as components in some larger system.

David Ellsworth

Ellsworth captivated viewers with the seemingly impossible small aperture through which he hollows the interior, then threw down the gauntlet of holes in the sides, which took the non-utilitarian ceremonial vessel and made it, somehow, "not usable." A long term range of investigations that allowed the use, control, and prediction of material unthinkable to others.

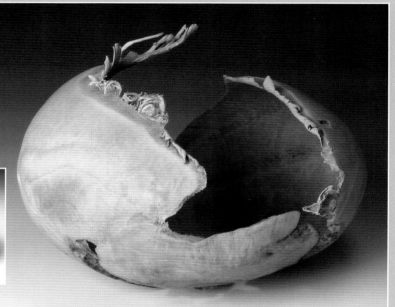

ABOVE: **1981: Vessel, walnut sapwood burl, 6.5" dia.**
ABOVE LEFT: **1979: Bowl, Brazilian rosewood, 8.5" dia.**

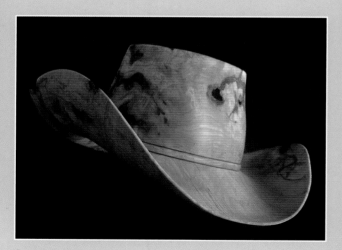

Christian Burchard
2000: Baskets, madrone burl, linen thread. The thin-walled vessel as an expression of fluidity. Compositional relationships would remain an important, vital ingredient to Burchard's many investigations.

JoHannes Michelson
2007: Range Rider, turned green and bent to shape.
The vessel made ever thinner, ever more useful, made possible through focused skills and the dramatic manipulation of material through invented "bake & bend" processes.

Frank Sudol
1995: Chalices
When tiny rotary carving tools became available, the Canadian craftsman Frank Sudol began to pierce the walls of vessels, creating lacy forms that intrigued many younger artists.

Frank E. Cummings III
1989: Nature in Transition, cork oak, 18K gold, 6.25" high. Photo courtesy Wood Turning Center.
A Victorian fussiness of decorative detail is countered by a broad simple plane, as if a doily had become a vessel, but one with modern sensibilities. A beguiling level of detail in both the grain and the invented portions.

LEFT: **Binh Pho**
2009: Eternal Return, box elder, acrylic paint, stones, 18" high.
The thin wall as a veil. Piercing is just one part of a broad palette of color and symbolism that is beautiful, autobiographical, compositionally refined.

Color/Pattern/Texture

These qualities differentiate how we perceive surfaces and affect our perceptions of shape and volume. The reverence for wood that fueled the field has given way to widespread experiments with surface effects that range from the sublime to the tawdry.

Al Stirt
1985: Fluted Bowl, butternut, 19.5" dia.
With pattern inseparable from the form, Stirt blends a sense of tradition with modernity. Physically bold and simple at first, his work increasingly involved complexity, scale, and subtlety.

Mark Lindquist
1982: Nehushtan, cherry burl, 14" high. Photo by Paul Avis, collection of Robert A. Roth.
A huge force of invention on many fronts, his investigations of aggressive texture and collaboration with the material were threatening to many and remain artistically powerful. Lindquist was the first of his generation of wood artists to break out of craft and into the art marketplace.

Siegfried Schreiber
2005: The Lovers, maple and pear, 23" wide. Photo courtesy Wood Turning Center. A sumptuous minimalism combined with literal movement, suggesting intuitive engineering. An unreal softness pervades the work and, even when at rest, evokes gesture and dance.

John Jordan
1995: Cherry Vessel, cherry.
Jordan's subtly textured surfaces reflect the light in new ways, lending a softness that invites one to touch the striking wood figure.

Giles Gilson
1982: Pearl Vase with Necklace and Drain, exotic woods with lacquer, 12" high.
With work refined to a nearly unimaginable level, Giles is a master of color and exquisite detail in a variety of media. Much of his work has the sense of a secret ritual or a fetish object.

Lincoln Seitzman
1987: Petrified Basket, walnut, zebrawood, purpleheart, satinwood, 14" high.
The faux dimension of the early objects, using marker pens, was sacrilegious to many and humorous to others. Far more than Ray Allen, Lincoln's work lit the fire of conversation regarding appropriation vs. "honoring the source."

Ray Allen
1990s: various hardwoods, 48" dia.
Early and consummate exploration of extreme size range, pattern scaled to the size of the form, and segmented construction. The question of appropriation vs. invention of pattern also entered the field.

Telling a Story: Narrative, Humor, Politics

Storytelling, plain and simple. Is there more to get out of viewing the piece than it simply being a turning? Does it evoke response beyond "wood" or reference to utility? Many artists use the vessel form as both palette and canvas to evoke our perceptions, memories, and references.

Ron Fleming
1991: Datura, basswood with acrylic paint, lacquer; 21" dia.
Powerful translations of flora from a painter and a carver. The thin-walled vessel becomes a true canvas or a sturdy pierced screen. Fleming's carvings have a muscularity and physical boldness that stand in contrast to his painted scenes.

Glenn Elvig
1991: It Certainly Was a Strange Night in Georgia, 40" tall.
Was Elvig just having fun with us? Fine craftsmanship served to exasperate the question of whether his pieces qualified as turned objects. His work still has the power to make you scratch your head—and smile.

LEFT: **Hap Sakwa**
1985: Against That Which All Else is Measured, poplar, maple, violin neck, 17.5" high.
One of our first storytellers. This work broke the rules before there were any. A new tradition, anyone? Artistically, something like an olive and pimento in the martini of woodturning.

Merryll Saylan
2005: Bessomimbusche, Spice Box, 47" high.
Widely known for her color, pattern, and composition, Saylan also did many fine explorations of the elevated form.

Michelle Holzapfel
1988: Cushioned Bowl, maple, 15" x 18" tall.
A consummate storyteller. Finely detailed compositions that call to us to spend time considering their plot and storyline. Visual treats are provided at every layer of investigation. The "one piece of wood" always adds to their seductive power and mystery.

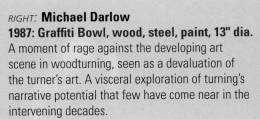

LEFT: **David Sengel**
1990: Caiphus, cherry, locust thorns, lacquer. Photo by Michael Siede.
Black thorns! Their captivating suggestions of Christianity and autobiography were later investigated as surface texture. Idiosyncratic investigations of story and meaning followed, some featuring spiny black birds.

RIGHT: **Michael Darlow**
1987: Graffiti Bowl, wood, steel, paint, 13" dia.
A moment of rage against the developing art scene in woodturning, seen as a devaluation of the turner's art. A visceral exploration of turning's narrative potential that few have come near in the intervening decades.

Jacques Vesery
2008: Diversity in the Round series, each 3" ball and its base is made from a single block of cherry wood: (left) **Junkyard Dog Ball,** (middle) **Roll Away the Dew,** (right) **That's a Wrap.**
Masterfully sumptuous color and fineness of detail support imagery that makes these forms irresistible. Gems.

Multi-axis Turning

The workpiece is painstakingly remounted and reworked for each round form. The turner usually must hand-carve the transitions between what can be turned and what's inaccessible on the lathe.

In no real way an extension of the ornamental complexity of the 17th and 18th centuries, multi-axis work shows the vitality of contemporary possibilities.

Hugh McKay
1996: Pentapot #2, madrone burl, 16" tall.
A masculine and polished dance of seemingly inflated forms impossibly joined—yet excavated. An engineer's sensibility at work in solving artistic puzzles.

Alain Mailland
2006: Seven Wise Men Dancing, hackberry, 21" tall. Collection of the Musees de Lochieu.
Mailland expertly anticipates how the wood will move as it dries, giving his work amazing animation and life.

**Peter Hromek
2006: Venus #1,
box elder, 16" tall.**
How can something feel weighty
and muscular yet, at the same
time, seem light and demure?
These perplexing and engaging
qualities are exceptionally
pronounced for work that is so
heavily involved in technical
problem-solving.

**Jean-François Escoulen
1995: Box, Brazilian
amarellio wood, 10" tall.
Collection of Albert and
Tina LeCoff, photo by
John Carlano.**
First and foremost of the
wave of French turners who
would follow. Typically French
madcap compositions display
stellar control.

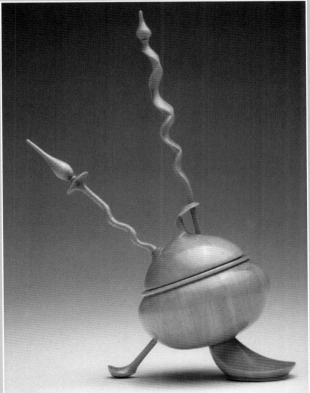

Ornamental Turning

Long before we had digital readouts, there were ornamental lathes such as the rose engine and the Holtzapffel. Much of the resulting 18th and 19th century aesthetic has been embraced and reinterpreted using these processes that allow precise, controlled, and repeatable effects simply not possible with free turning or hand carving.

Dale Chase
2005: Blackwood Box, 3" dia.
Chase's combination of modern masculine simplicity with the complex fussiness inherent in ornamental work makes for a mysterious and engaging object.

Bonnie Klein
2004: Red Boxes, cast acrylic, 2.25" dia.
Much like Saylan's Jelly Donut (page 65), Klein's acrylic boxes are engaging due to the surprising mix of material, process, and polished execution.

Jon Sauer
1993: Zig-Zag Bottle, blackwood and boxwood, 6" dia. The flavor of Sauer's work exists somewhere between the present and the late 1800s. It challenges modern sensibilities with its busy-ness yet does not quite taste antique.

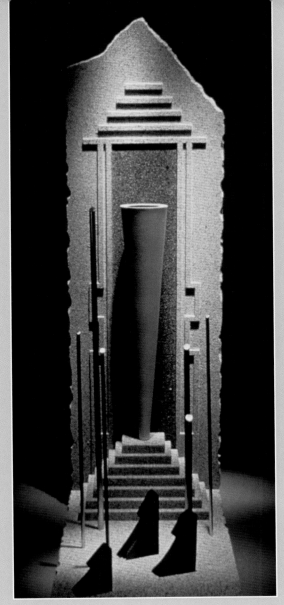

Richard Hooper
1995: Vector Warp, birch ply, 12" high.
While it was the primary intellectual/aesthetic design force of the 20th century, Minimalism didn't resonate with the turning field. Here we get it full force, but with just a hint of narrative. Pristine and monolithic, yet with a sense of gesture or impulse.

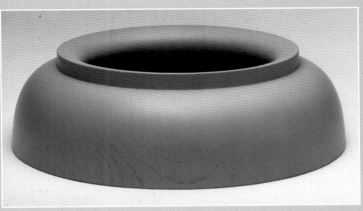

Maria van Kesteren
Volume, elm with gray paint, 10" dia.
Exquisite, minimal forms that isolate grain from "wood." As with all greatly refined forms, they look obvious. Powerfully quiet. Under-appreciated.

ABOVE: **Addie Draper**
1990: T Inscenario #6, ebony, pine, paint, 20" tall.
Draper's later investigations involved an expansive theatrical sensibility, within which turning was but one character, anticipating the world of installation, video, and time-based art.

Christian Burchard
1989: Dancers, madrone burl, mahogany.
The thin-walled vessel as an expression of fluidity and grace. While the technical threshhold that they crossed can only be dimly appreciated now, these dancers remain one of the most satisfying compositions of contemporary turning.

Architecture of the Vessel

If vessels had skeletons, they might look like this. A sense of structure that is quite different from the popular pierced screen of wood.

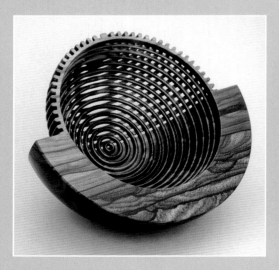

Hans Weissflog
LEFT: **1993: Broken Through, African blackwood, 2" dia.**
RIGHT: **2007: Half-Circle Bowl, African blackwood burl, 12" dia.**
A painstaking, machine-like aesthetic transforms the thin-walled vessel into an ordered veil which, nonetheless, gives evidence of fine handwork. Multi-axis designs complicate and heighten the intensity of these little universes.

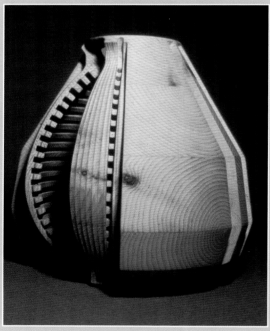

Gianfranco Angelino
1992: Ribbed Stone Pine Vase, pincus cembra wood, 10.5" dia.
If a turned container were a plant, it might look like this when cut open: compact from the outside while encapsulating a sense of expansive architectural space and scale within.

Dewey Garrett
1992: Lim #3, bleached maple, 12" dia.
Early work explored variations-on-a-theme of a bowl's skeleton supported by mysterious and faultless craftsmanship.

Landscape

A sense of our being in land and place is an essential aspect of the human condition. As with pieces that tell a story, we perceive landscape themes in many places, in various ways, and at different scales.

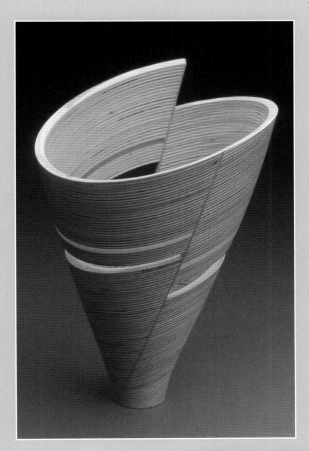

Virginia Dotson
1989: Cross Winds, wenge, maple, 13" dia.
Landscape as an easily accessible abstraction. Ever more sublime compositions.

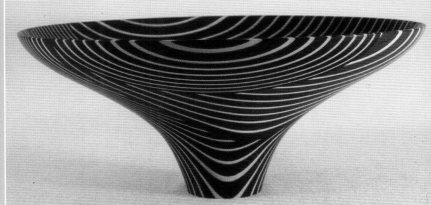

Michael Peterson
1989: Two Canyon Mesa, box elder burl bleached and sandblasted, 14" dia.
A direct fusion of vessel and landscape, this work offers a verisimilitude of the effects of weathering and aging. Always beautiful, quiet, and engaging, Peterson's later work became more visually complex while shedding most uses of turning.

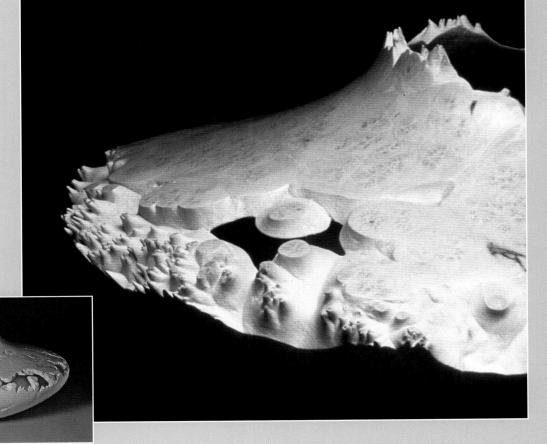

Human Figure

Even more than the landscape, the human experience is about the human figure. It is said that we walk and talk like our parents because they were our most intimate formative experiences. The figure can be inferred and evoked in an endless variety of ways.

LEFT: **Terry Martin 2009: Mr. Spindle and Son, limb wood, 12" high.** These pieces seem so incredibly simple, but they bring an adult's sophistication to the childlike vertical stroke that we identify as "human." They could also be the prototypes for a wonky chess set.

FAR LEFT: **Mark Sfirri 1997: Glancing Figures; cherry, ash, walnut with contrasting bases, tallest (on left) is 72".** A great wit at work. Ongoing important investigations of multi-axis turning, active collaboration, and popular culture as well as important investigations of turning and furniture make Sfirri's work difficult to categorize. Particularly notable are his investigations into altering the turned work to create new and unexpected forms.

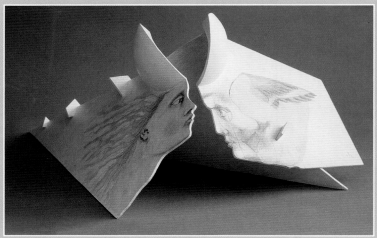

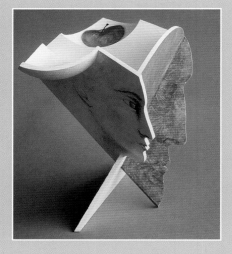

Stephen Hogbin
This high-risk little-seen series took the concept of "bowl" into the realms of painting and drawing. Not one to make work simply for adulation or sales, Hogbin's bowls are small expressions of a restless and brave artistic spirit.

LEFT: **1990: Psyche and Mercury, wood with paint and graphite, 23" wide, the Lipton Collection.**
RIGHT: **1990: Maturus, wood with paint and graphite, 10" high, the Lipton Collection.**

Furniture

The scarcity of examples underscores the field's love affair with faceplate work and the thin-walled vessel. Utility has been primarily explored via the table and bench.

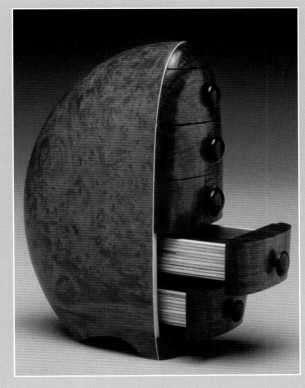

Ray Jones
1996: Halfmoon Box #1, madrone burl, claro walnut, ebony, birch ply, 10" tall. Photo by Tim Barnwell.
Wonderful small chests that speak of turning in a most unusual and intriguing way. As beautifully detailed as they appear.

Michael Hosaluk
1987: Zap!, Colorcore, maple, aluminum, glass, plexiglas, 37" dia.
One of the pre-eminent explorers of turning, Hosaluk's early furniture translated directly to small legged-vessel forms before going organic.

Michael Graham
1987: The Great American Bench, bleached and painted basswood, 72" long,
Also known for his curved drawer forms, Graham's bench remains one of the few large forms to come from the field. How odd to have a history so rich in spindle work inspire so little modern interest.

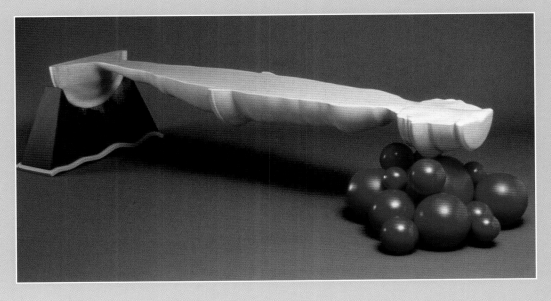

The Essential Vessel
Your Robust, Everyday Salad Bowl

This circular survey began with the elegant vessel (page 137) and ends with the every-day wooden salad bowl. Every American household has one, and every household has had one, as far back in time as we can reckon. Craftsman with simple tools plus chunk of tree equals essential vessel. This is why woodturning is a fundamental human craft and why it has such broad appeal.

1986: Jack Straka

1996: Liz & Michael O'Donnell

2006: Allen Jensen

2006: George Peterson

2008: Rudolph Schapron

2001: Unusual Fruit from the Shaker Period, Michael Hosaluk. Photo by Grant Kernan.

After the Revolution

Peter Exton

Twenty years ago I might've stockpiled wood like this—chunks of spalted maple, their inky zone lines scribbling unpredictably across the surface. With a little care, they could become beautiful turnings. Now, one by one, I toss them on the fire, hoping they're not too punky to burn.

Times change. We do something for a while and then we move on to something else. Woodturners who used to compare notes on smoothing the soft and hard areas of spalted wood are now as likely to discuss covering the wood with a film of paint and applying their own designs. We are still evolving.

Woodturning is very accessible. It welcomes the hobbyist and the fine artist alike. Without spending too much money or time, something can be made that provides immense satisfaction. It quickly opens material for aesthetic investigation, becoming an entry to creativity for many who might never have felt they belonged in a formal art class. Woodturning invites participation. It doesn't scare people away.

In the seventies and eighties, most turners concentrated on the lathe alone. Yet they have always been accompanied by at least a few who did a bit more. Adding other materials, painting, and carving have been with us all along, even as the great majority turned and turned and turned.

More recently, it appears that working only on the lathe doesn't attract the widespread devotion it once did. The great many who now work wood off the lathe are accompanied by a declining proportion who focus purely on woodturning.

This is probably a normal development as contemporary woodturning matures. After spending enough time on the lathe, many turners develop a very understandable itch to do more. The symmetry of a bowl or spindle doesn't satisfy as it once did. The relentless perfection might seem cold, canceling the warm vibe of the material. So the turner tries working funky pieces of wood to introduce some variety, or paints or carves or adds legs, or puts a box around the thing—just about anything that might make the result more interesting. Those off-lathe approaches have expanded the idea of what a piece of wood art might be, drawing more attention from makers. Consequently, the pendulum of interest has swung away from the lathe. For some, it's just one of many tools and may not even be very important.

Although many people have become deeply engaged in other ways of working wood, turning may have got them started and energized about making things. It's been a vital trigger, a catalyst for doing anything at all. Like the shortcuts to using new technological devices, woodturning is a "quick-start" method of engaging in creative activity. That's a good thing.

In a way, woodturning is also a jilted lover. Initially the object of some very intense infatuation, it's now too old-fashioned, too common, taken for granted. The fickle boys have turned their eyes elsewhere, chasing younger objects with their pretty colors and baubles. That's where the action is.

One day the pendulum will swing again and the charms of woodturning will find renewed appreciation. If you love turning and can't understand all the fuss about current fashion, take heart—you're the next avant-garde.

Although the new techniques have made things more interesting, they sometimes venture into unknown terrain technically. Wood hasn't changed. It still resists our efforts to control it, it still moves, and it may be another twenty-five years before we know for sure if it will retain the color of a dye or shed an acrylic paint.

There is another question surrounding all the new methods. At what point does the new technique define the work? That is, when does a carved turning become woodcarving, and when does painted wood become

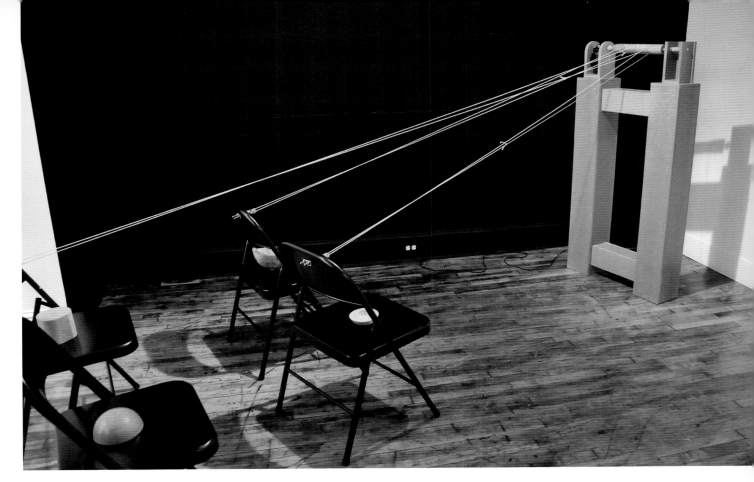

2006: Michael Stadler, Rhetoric, metal chairs, wood, string, motor, MDF, 50" tall. Unlike most contemporary woodturning, this composition won't display on a table or hang over the mantel. The object here is commentary and reflection. The lathe functions, but only to play a symbolic role, and interpretation depends heavily on how one reads the moving string device.

2009: David Belser, Stick Ball, 300 ash sticks assembled in a 3D grid. Belser says he "hit on the idea of supporting structures with wax while turning them; it turned out that making this 3D grid was harder than turning it."

painting? When should such work be evaluated in the context of those long traditions? Woodcarving is a very healthy activity in this country, producing work of terrific sculptural skill. How does the work of carving turners compare?

Looking ahead, woodturning will probably reflect more involvement by artists not necessarily bent on creating the beautiful object. Some of this has begun. During the 2002 International Turning Exchange in Philadelphia, Gord Peteran brought the pencil drawing to the lathe in Five Sounds, a series of drawings made by applying a pencil to spinning flats of paper, the method altered a little each time. The resulting circles are visual mantras, something to encourage meditation. The final drawing in the series reverses the application with a paper sheet mounted on a hand-held board trying to catch the mark of a circling pencil. The pencil is coy in its glancing touches, occasionally allowing controlled travel, but ultimately refusing to behave nicely. Such work takes turning out of the decorative arts. The approach and the response it generates are very different than we are used to seeing.

Another example is Michael Stadler's Rhetoric (2008), from the Wood Turning Center's *Challenge VII: DysFUNctional* exhibition. It consists of folding metal chairs holding crudely turned objects set before a towering lathe. They are connected by loops of string going round and round between the lathe and chairs, like woodturning demonstrators and the audience they serve, circulating the same information over and over.

The kinetics of the lathe could be used in many ways. There is music to be made with spinning wood. Different species and thicknesses can produce different pitches when contacted by a stylus as it rotates. Out-of-round spinning stock always creates a rhythm when it meets a tool. And the dreaded catch of the tool, which may signal the explosion of a bowl, could be designed to produce drama in performance. For some messy fun, a paintball gun could be fired at a spinning platter. Catch it on canvas and sign it.

There's another area that is both obvious and unmentioned: the sexual content of this activity called woodturning. The basic forms of spindle and vessel duplicate the phallus and womb. We enhance the look of a shaft with a series of circumcisions, even in purely functional work. Men lovingly reproduce plump feminine curves on vessels and derive real pleasure from plunging a hard rod deep into a hole to create the hollowed womb. There's plenty of material here for a psychological study; an artist could mine it, too.

Meanwhile, the question lingers: Is there more new ground to be broken in turning wood?

In the survey exhibition and book *Woodturning in North America Since 1930*, which toured in 2001-2002, we had a pretty good look at what had been happening in woodturning through the end of the 20th century. We may also have seen a clue to what might lie ahead. The exhibition included a small section called Engineering— so small it didn't warrant a mention in the catalog. There were only a few pieces in it, and just two artists, Stephen Hogbin and Mark Sfirri.

The small amount of work represented in that Engineering area probably indicates open territory for innovation. Two artists can't be the whole of creative ingenuity in this area. The lack of work shown just

2007: Jordan Gehman, Rollin' on 20, maple, 30" tall. Born in 1983, Jordan Gehman is too young to have been swept up in the hollowing frenzy of the eighties and nineties. In this piece from the Wood Turning Center's DysFUNctional exhibition, he uses the lathe to serve a very different purpose, installing an impractical chariot wheel prosthesis to mess with our assumptions of what a chair should be.

means it hasn't been created yet. But getting there may need a different sort of turner, with specific natural gifts. Hogbin and Sfirri share more than formal design education backgrounds. Almost certainly they have spatial visualization talents common to furniture makers, architects, and engineers. These talents help them imagine and then create complex structural work.

Woodturning doesn't seem to attract a lot of this type, but they're around. Every year at the annual symposium, the chapter collaborative competition features incredible, inventive constructions. These creations encourage expanding uses of turned work, combinations of form, problem-solving. Somewhere along the line, an artist with these talents will emerge and we'll see some great new stuff.

At the Museum of Science in Boston, there is a popular exhibit called Mathematica, where the amazing world of mathematics is illustrated and brought to life through displays and working models. Some of the exhibits demonstrate how much wonder a circle contains. For turners, these exhibits emphasize how little we have probed the circle for uses on the lathe and how much potential for new form it contains.

What's also interesting about Mathematica is who designed the exhibit. It wasn't a bunch of math wizards from MIT down the street. It was the husband and wife design team of Charles and Ray Eames. The Eameses are probably best remembered for their revolutionary, ingeniously simple molded plywood chairs. You might be sitting in one of many variations. They were a design giant of the 20th century, but we could also think of them as furniture makers with an enthusiastic appreciation of mathematics. Mathematics and woodturning can be a fruitful combination, too. Thankfully, the Eameses left those discoveries to us.

2007: Peter Exton, Rabble 407, bleached maple, 17" high.
Although this piece is turned, a lengthy process obscures its origins on the lathe. There seems to be some order in the arrangement of unfamiliar forms, but the result doesn't reference anything recognizable. Such work can absorb interpretations projected onto it, even while challenging the viewer to simply allow it to be what it is.

VOICES

Betty Scarpino: finding our voices

A number of the early woodturning innovators arrived at their expressions in wood at about the same time in a way that seemingly "just happened." This joint arrival nudged woodturning from its traditional roots into the outlying tendrils of contemporary art and craft. How that phenomenon came about is open to interpretation.

Interpretation of the woodturning field's rich history is complicated by the fact that vehicles for informing the world of what is taking place are in short supply. The Wood Turning Center's journal, *Turning Points*, has folded. Editorial viewpoints that shaped the AW Journal, *American Woodturner*, stemmed from traditional mindsets and backgrounds at commercial woodworking magazines. Innovative work is always being created, notably by the artists in the International Turning Exchange programs. Much of this innovation is simply not well recorded.

Our field suffers not so much from not having followed an academic path similar to that of our sister crafts (ceramics, baskets, glass), but more from an inability or perhaps unwillingness to recognize what is happening right before our eyes. There are innovators within our ranks today. Many of those innovators, however, have no idea of their own significance.

Our field is richly diverse because few of us have a traditional academic background. Our amazing mix of amateur and professional makers is unique to the craft world. Woodturning amateurs are creating incredible objects. We professionals are influenced. Woodturners are just beginning to find expressive written voices that can match the visual strength of our work. Let's see what happens in the next 25 years.

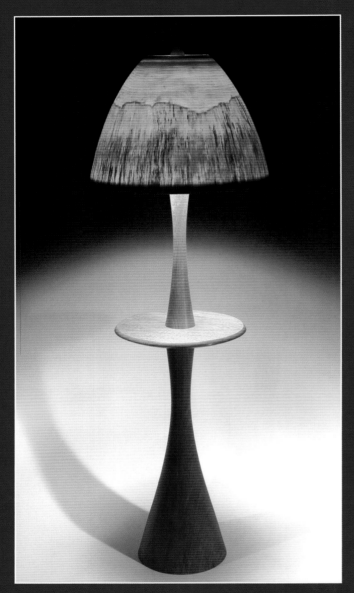

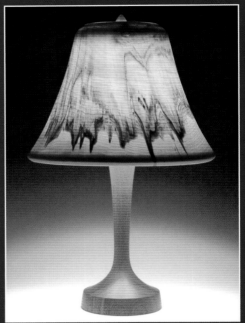

Shine a little light

There may be no better illustration of understanding the wood you are working than the lampshades of Peter Bloch. Aspen is the only wood he has found that can produce a warm firelight translucence, grows large enough, and is available in sufficient quantity. The growth rings must be uniformly concentric to minimize distortion and properly centering the blank is critical to producing a balanced form. Trusting his eye, Bloch achieves a constant translucence, and uniform thickness, by shining a light through the wood. In the end, he creates a triumphant blend of material, form and function.

Bloch is a professional turner from New London, NH. You might rub elbows with him, or see him demonstrate his art, if you were to attend an AAW symposium. This kind of opportunity—for turners of all skill levels to mingle in a friendly, egalitarian atmosphere—is a key ingredient of the association, as well as the turning field itself.

SECTION V

The American Association of Woodturners Today

Today the American Association of Woodturners is a club with more than 13,000 members organized into more than 300 local chapters. The association maintains an office with full-time staff in Saint Paul, Minnesota, along with gallery space to display temporary exhibitions and the permanent collection. Along with its annual symposium, the organization has expanded its activities to include publication of a bimonthly magazine *American Woodturner*, aka the *AW Journal*, a large website (www.woodturner.org), a Professional Outreach Program, a gallery of turned wood art (www.galleryofwoodart.org), and myriad other activities, as you will learn in this section.

A Shared Love of Wood is Our Central Experience

Kevin Wallace

Keynote address at the AAW annual symposium, June 2010, Hartford, CT

I have been to all manner of symposiums having to do with the arts, and I have to say that the annual AAW symposium is quite unlike any other. It has many of the same elements—educational outreach, demonstrations, lectures, exhibitions—but there are two things that really set the AAW symposiums apart. The first is that they resemble family reunions in so many ways—more so than any other event I've ever attended.

The second thing is that in the field of contemporary woodturning, it's not entirely clear who we are, where we are, or where we're going. A number of people have lectured and written articles and essays on the subject, and they are all very much like the story of the blind people touching different parts of an elephant and offering different descriptions of what it is. I wish I could say that I have the definitive answer about the who, where, what and how, but the best I can do is to try to find that place where we are in agreement and, perhaps, challenge some notions.

First of all, it's important to note that contemporary woodturning is not just one thing. There is an aspect of it that has to do with artists creating work that is exhibited at galleries and collected by museums, and there is the aspect that concerns people who love creating objects which are for the most part utilitarian, that end up being used in the home or given as gifts.

Then there is that blurry area in between, where the artists who are creating cutting-edge museum-quality works inspire those who enjoy creating objects in their garages for their friends and family. This can of course lead to family members eating salad out of bright red bowls with dressing dripping out of tiny holes while hearing stories about how much the maker enjoyed attending Donald Derry and Binh Pho demonstrations

at the last AAW symposium. But that's what keeps it interesting.

Getting back to what binds us together...although there are going to be some people who show up spinning metal or working in some other media, we know that a shared love of wood is central to our experience. Wood is, without a doubt, the most important material that we humans have ever had a relationship with. Millions of humans agree that if the Buddha was going to be enlightened, it had to happen under a tree, and if God was going to take one opportunity to walk the earth, he would choose to do so as a carpenter. It was wood that allowed us to move out of caves and build the shelters, boats and wagons that led us out into the world. Even with all of the technological progress and our ability to manipulate metals and plastics, how many of us here today live in a wood-framed house, sit and dine at a wood table while seated on a wood chair? The relationship between humans and wood is enduring, and that's not even touching upon what it has to offer us as a craft and as an art.

And I'm ready to take those words on—craft and art. I only wish that I could put an end to all of the "is it art or craft" dialogues for all time. Because woodworking is a craft. And you can create art in wood. And you can use craft processes to create a work of art. And craft has a rich history and art has a rich history and they occasionally converge. However, everything that is crafted out of wood is not necessarily art, and all art that is made from wood is not necessarily well-crafted and is therefore not necessarily craft at all. Craft and art can be the same thing, but they can be completely different things and ultimately one is not a higher calling than the other.

Speaking on behalf of Kevin Wallace, Terry Martin delivers the 2010 keynote address at the AAW 2010 symposium in Hartford, CT. With Wallace unavoidably detained by family business, Martin explained, "as family we help each other and in that spirit I will read Kevin's text." Wallace is a critic and curator specializing in contemporary wood art. Terry Martin, of Brisbane, Australia, is a turner and writer, and frequent commentator on contemporary woodturning.

I was very fortunate to become involved with this field at a time when I had the opportunity to meet James Prestini and Ed Moulthrop and get to know Rude Osolnik and Bob Stocksdale. One of the things that I thought was really wonderful is that Rude and Bob scoffed at the whole idea of "art" in woodturning. They were devoted craftsmen who didn't see their work as something that needed the mantle of art. Last year at the AAW symposium, I judged the instant gallery along with Merryll Saylan and Garry Knox Bennett, and we did the critique together. Although we disagreed quite a bit on the various works and artistic approaches, we all agreed when it came to good old-fashioned utilitarian salad bowls—that they were wonderful and an important part of contemporary woodturning. That utilitarian work that shows the natural beauty of the wood and shows attention to form and function, no matter how the field progresses, should always be an important part of it.

When I came to know the sort of forefathers of the contemporary woodturning movement, I also came to know the individuals who showed the potential this craft had to be art—and who actually gave birth to a bold new art form. Two of them will be honored this weekend: Giles Gilson, who received the lifetime achievement award last year but wasn't able to attend the symposium, and Mark Lindquist, who is being given the lifetime achievement award this year. Though there are a number of artists, from David Ellsworth to Stephen Hogbin, who helped to define this new approach to woodturning as an art, the impact that Giles Gilson had on the field through his exploration of paint—covering the natural beauty of the wood—was tremendous. At the time this shocked everyone. And Mark Lindquist, with his sculptural explorations from the use of mass to textures, changed the field forever. When you walk through the instant gallery this weekend, every time you see a work that utilizes painted surfaces or has sculptural intent, you are viewing work that builds upon the foundations established by these individuals. And quite often the woodturner might not really know the work of Giles or Mark and might not feel they have been influenced by them—because they were influenced by people who were influenced by people who were influenced by them. And this is why the AAW lifetime achievement awards are so important. Because if you want to know where you're going, you have to know where you're coming from. Our shared history is important.

I started off saying that the best I can do is to discuss the disparate parts of the woodturning field in order to find that place where we are in agreement—and these are the things that make us a family. These are the elements:

- A love of wood—the most remarkable and endlessly fascinating material in the human experience.
- A love of process—from the lathe to carving tools, from chainsaws to airbrushes.
- A love of craft—the rich traditions that we have inherited and share with the next generation.
- A love of self-expression—whether or not that means art with a big "A" to you—that is the driving force that causes us to see potential in our material and processes and drives us to create something that shows what we see.
- And a love of sharing—people coming together to show off their work, to share techniques, to share dinner or a drink, to swap stories, It's what makes us family and makes these get-togethers such a joy to attend.

Symposium

The AAW's annual symposium is a truly remarkable event that's easy to describe but hard to understand, until you attend one for the first time. Here's the list of ingredients:

- A big crowd of aficionados: 1,200 or more, many of whom make it their annual vacation with spouses in tow.

- An interesting venue: the event rotates around the United States. 2009, Albuquerque; 2010 Hartford; 2011, Saint Paul; 2012, San Jose, California; 2013, Atlanta.

- A huge roster of demonstrators and lecturers, 50 or more, showing-and-telling in 90-minute sessions. Each demonstrator performs several times, in rotations, so attendees can juggle their own schedules.

- The Instant Gallery: the world's largest collection of contemporary turned objects assembled for three days only. Any attendee may bring examples of his/her current work and lay it out for all to see, and most do.

- A chance to own wood art, maybe inexpensive, maybe not: Two auctions, one silent and one live, exchange 100+ pieces for $150,000 in scholarship funds.

- Excellent exhibitions: Themed, juried and invitational exhibitions attract world-class wood art along with amazing new talent.

Really big show

The Albuquerque convention center is big enough to wine and dine 1,500 woodturners, with excellent large-screen video capability—a real help for the fundraising auction of wood art.

Latest and greatest

The trade show gives vendors a chance to show the latest and greatest—and it's set up so they can run their machines and make shavings. This dude, making a very large bowl on a big, new lathe, works behind a plastic wall so spectators can't get hurt.

- Toys and wood: A trade show brings 50 or more vendors specializing in all things wood-turning.

- Youth turning: Kids learn to turn, and 25 of them take home the complete setups used at the symposium.

Many demonstrations

Symposium attendees choose the demonstrations they wish to attend. Here, Nick Cook shows how to turn a peppermill. Most demo rooms have complete lathe set-ups that local club members move in for the event. Many sessions are recorded and made available on DVD.

Video close-ups

Video operators show the action on large screens, so everyone in the room can see exactly what the demonstrator, Steve Sinner, is doing as he makes a small, thin-walled goblet on a narrow stem. Steve is miked, so everyone can hear what he is saying too.

Club meetings and regional events

Along with the annual symposium, AAW clubs around the country sponsor local and regional woodturning events. There's always information about upcoming events on www.woodturner.org. Here's a short list of regional events to attend:

January
Florida Woodturning Symposium
Tennessee Woodturners Symposium
Alaska Woodturners Symposium

March
Big Island (Hawaii) Woodturners
Turnfest 2010, Queensland, Australia
Totally Turning Symposium & Northeast Woodworkers, Saratoga Springs, NY

April
Dakota Woodturners Symposium
Southern States Symposium, Atlanta, GA

May
New England Woodturning Symposium, New Hampshire
Utah Woodturning Symposium, Orem, UT

July
Australian Woodturning Symposium, Queensland
California Mini Symposium, San Diego
Saskatoon Woodturning Symposium, Saskatchewan
Woodturners of Olympia, WA

August
Chicago Woodturners—Turn On Chicago
SWAT, Texas

September
Westcoast Roundup Woodturning Symposium, Vancouver, British Columbia
Rocky Mountain Woodturning Symposium, Loveland, CO
Ornamental TI, Wyndham near San Jose, CA
Association of Woodturners—Turning Southern Style, GA

October
Virginia Woodturning Symposium, Fishersville, VA
October 2nd Annual Honolulu Symposium, HI

November
Turners Anonymous Pittsburgh, PA
Chippewa Valley Woodturners, Wisconsin Guild Woodturning Expo
Segmented Woodturners, Tennessee

December
Maine Woodturning School & Maine LC

1987: First annual symposium

Lexington, KY
Total attendees: 243
Spouses: 51
Exhibitors: 10

"Carl Rich actually went around to each turning at our Instant Gallery. He counted 213 pieces made from 57 species of wood."

—AW Journal, *December 1987*

1996: Turning Ten

Turning Ten, the 1996 AAW symposium held in Greensboro, North Carolina, brought together almost 1,000 woodturners from all over the world, young and old. Rude Osolnik, 82 years old, demonstrated how he turns his signature candlesticks.

AW Journal editor Rick Mastelli wrote: "The high point of the 1996 symposium for me was the graciousness that pervaded most interactions, whether between demonstrators and audience, turners making or renewing friends, or the general public who came in to see the two symposium exhibitions and the turners who were delighted to satisfy their open curiosities."

The AAW's first nine symposiums were held on leafy college campuses. This was the first held in a downtown convention center—a move made necessary by explosive growth in membership and symposium attendance.

2000: 1,130 attendees, 58 demonstrators...

"...and more than 1,100 pieces in the Instant Gallery, which gets better and better every year. Most shows have been pre-selected for your viewing—not this one. The work of beginner and pro may sit side by side and you determine what you find interesting or pleasing. One participant said the Instant Gallery reminded him of the diving board experience: To spring high above the water, the board first takes you down a ways. The Instant Gallery at first made him feel like selling his lathe and tools, then inspired him to go back to improve his work.

"What really struck me about the sessions—and mentioned often by others—was watching someone so freely give information that maybe took months, years, or a lifetime of turning to develop or understand. Alan Batty

Instant Gallery

of England has been in the trade for 45 years and was a wellspring of information in his six sessions—most of his information is not in any books or videos, plus you had a chance to ask him questions."

—*Alan Lacer*, AW Journal, *Fall 2000*

2008: magical moment

"One Educational Opportunity Grant (EOG) auction item at the 2008 symposium in Richmond, Virginia, was a bright orange fiddle turned by Bernie Hrytzak, titled The Orange Slice Special. I decided to bid on it and make it a gift to the turner Andi Wolfe, a good friend and a fiddle player.

"Auctioneer John Hill moved the bidding up to $500 where it stalled. Rather than close the bidding, John said that he had intended to have someone come on stage and play it, but the volunteer couldn't be found. So he asked if anyone in the audience could play, and suddenly Andi appeared on stage, fiddle in hand. After a bit of tuning she played a jig to the delight of the audience.

"John reopened the bidding, the price went to $800, and I won. I then told Andi I had bought the fiddle for her, the sort of thing she could take to gigs for fun. Andi took the fiddle out of its case, and, as she rosined the bow, a young boy approached to ask if he could play it. As it turned out, Knick McKay was 12 years old and had been taking violin lessons for two years. He was in Richmond for the youth turning program, and his mother later told me that Knick had made numerous visits to the Instant Gallery to see the fiddle. Of course he hadn't dared to touch it. Without skipping a beat, Andi handed the instrument to Knick. He tucked it under his chin and began to play.

LEFT TO RIGHT: Andi Wolfe played the fiddle that Bernie Hrytzak made, but Knick McKay ended up owning it, thanks to Harvey Fein.

"I was standing about two feet away, and the energy coming off him literally stopped my world. When I regained my senses I looked over at Andi and I knew in that moment what I was to do. I leaned over and said to Knick that it was now his fiddle. "No, it's yours," he protested, and I responded, "Yes, it was mine, but I am giving it to you." He looked at me with total disbelief, then gave me the most ecstatic hug I have had in a long time. People were crying, people were applauding, and Knick was beside himself with joy."

—*Harvey Fein*, AW Journal, *Fall 2008*

Amazing Instant Gallery

A highlight of the annual symposium, the AAW's Instant Gallery is a truly mind-boggling display. Symposium attendees are invited to display one or several pieces of current work on long tables inside a vast convention space, and hundreds of them do. It's hundreds of woodturnings by amateurs and professionals, beginners and experts side by side on long tables.

The scale of the exhibition is both compelling and exhausting. You need to come back several times and spend a little time absorbing the work. And symposium attendees do—to marvel at the latest displays of utter mastery alongside astonishing innovations making their debut here, to take photographs, and especially to discuss with one another.

The Instant Gallery includes cash awards for merit, plus a silent auction followed by a live auction to raise funds for the organization's Educational Opportunity Grants program. Attendees convene late in the weekend symposium for a brisk critique led by the jurors who award cash prizes.

1001 woodturnings

The Instant Gallery is a highlight of any AAW symposium. Members display their work, explain it, discuss it, and enjoy being astonished by the skill and ingenuity of others.

Prizes awarded

Instant Gallery jurors select the best pieces from the 1,000 or more on display, then award recognition along with cash prizes totaling $10,000. For 2010 (above), the jurors were Marilyn Campbell, a professional turner from Ontario, Canada, Richard Hogue, a collector from Connecticut, and Terry Martin, a journalist specializing in woodturning.

Critical discussion

ABOVE: Garry Bennett dissects a woodturning at the Sunday morning Instant Gallery critique during the 2009 Albuquerque symposium. In this wide-open session, makers explain their work, the three critics analyze and assess it, and the audience chimes in. Merryll Saylan and Kevin Wallace, along with a large audience, are looking at an overhead projection of the piece under discussion.

LEFT: Betty Scarpino, editor of the *AW Journal*, conducts individual critiques of members' own work during the popular Instant Gallery at the 2010 Hartford symposium.

Artwork Auction Funds Grants for Education

Kurt Hertzog

When you think about the American Association of Woodturners, the first thing that comes to mind is woodturning education, whether it is the local chapter with their show-and-tell and meeting demo or the annual symposium. It is indeed all about education. Started back in the 1980s, the Educational Opportunity Grant program is the vehicle that can help a person, group, or organization with their educational needs.

Open to members, chapters, students, and organizations, the EOG program awards monies to assist in the woodturning journey. All that is asked of the recipients is that they share what they have learned with others. This woodturning education sharing is the cornerstone of the AAW.

The Educational Opportunity Grant fund raises funds via the proceeds of the auction held during the banquet at the annual AAW Symposium. The generous donation of woodturnings, tools, wood, and equipment made by our individual and business members creates a lively auction. These auction proceeds, along with fund interest and donations, create the ability to grant the large number of awards made each year.

Since the EOG first grants in 1988, the program has awarded over $1 million to many hundreds of applicants. We've helped schools and churches implement training programs for youngsters needing guidance. We've helped members enhance their turning abilities and branch out into new arenas. We've helped chapters modernize their

Two-stage rocket

At the AAW's annual fund-raising event, donated artwork is first accepted into a silent auction alongside the Instant Gallery. The pieces receiving the highest bids move along to the live auction, following the Saturday evening banquet. In 2009 at Albuquerque, auctioneer John Hill gaveled in more than $100,000. Auction proceeds support Educational Opportunity Grants and other educational events. In 2011, Hill, a long-time activist within the organization, was made an honorary lifetime member of the AAW.

equipment and capabilities to deliver demonstration programs to their members. Everything from library additions to special training programs in far-flung corners of the world have been aided by the EOG program.

Where will the EOG program go in the next 25 years? The needs continue to grow but so does the generosity of our supporters. From the humble beginnings, the program has grown and prospered and will continue to foster the legacy of sharing woodturning knowledge. Woodturning education is what we are all about.

Kurt Hertzog is chair of the Educational Opportunity Grant committee.

EOG Auction Proceeds	
1988	$7,600
1989	$9,700
1990	$7,200
1991	$13,200
1992	$10,545
1993	$15,500
1994	$13,300
1995	$13,000
1996	$17,000
1997	$16,000
1998	$24,000
1999	$43,200
2000	$41,750
2001	$32,361
2002	$34,258
2003	$32,900
2004	$46,555
2005	$67,710
2006	$151,675
2007	$99,440
2008	$69,555
2009	$102,700
2010	$167,900

National treasures

This artistic collaboration between Jacques Vesery and Bonnie Klein brought top auction dollar at the 2008 AAW symposium in Richmond, Virginia: $11,800. The upper portion is a spinning top. The piece includes historically interesting woods donated by Bill Jewell, notably, cherry from Mount Vernon and red oak from the grave site of Stonewall Jackson. The piece opens to reveal a representation of early Virginia history (inset).

—*from* American Woodturner, *Fall 2008*

My Personal AAW Journey

Mary Lacer

People often ask me how I got started in woodturning.

My personal journey from self-taught woodturner to helping the American Association of Woodturners evolve into a successful, thriving membership-based organization has been a colorful story. I was initially interested in working with wood and took a refinishing course—it was soon clear that wasn't what I wanted to do. I then took a woodworking course at a local vo-tech school. We were shown a video each week that highlighted a different piece of equipment in the shop. My goal was to learn to use every machine. The video on the lathe was the last one to be shown, and a lathe was tucked away in the back corner of the shop. The instructor didn't know how to turn, so I was on my own. The woodturning tools were so dull, they were blunt on the edges. Undaunted, I took an oak log from my neighbor's firewood pile, put it on the lathe, and somehow finished a lamp base, which I still have today. That was my introduction to woodturning. I finished the series of three woodworking courses and decided I wanted to concentrate on learning to turn. I was pleased to be able to turn my hobby into a woodturning business (Red Elm Workshop) for nine years prior to becoming administrator for the AAW. Little did I know that attending my first symposium in 1987 would lead to Bonnie Klein asking me to run for the board of directors in 1989.

Quite an adventure

I knew right from the start that I was going to be in for quite an adventure as I answered the phone to hear Bonnie Klein say, "I just shipped 60 boxes to your home. They will be there in three days." My response was, "What am I going to do with 60 boxes?" On July 1, 1990, I began my tenure with the AAW. It was a challenging time financially for the organization. My office was a 10-foot square space in my living room.

The garage was filled with all the boxes. As if things weren't complicated enough, the AAW was in the middle of a membership drive. The first prize was a full-sized lathe. One morning as I was sitting in my home office, I heard a large truck delivering the lathe. So, of course, into the already crowded garage it went. I worked out of my house for the first four and a-half years. The board originally determined that it would be a half-time position, but it became full time almost immediately.

As well as financial challenges, it was clear that we also faced some procedural and organizational ones. I immediately had to sort through all the boxes and determine what the most critical information was, in an effort to improve membership records and create an efficient system for tracking membership dues. The first step toward improving our financial situation was discovering that journals were being sent to 3,700 addresses—everyone in the database—when only 1,700 of them were current paid-up members. Looking back, there has been quite an evolution of the process for organizing, managing, and exchanging information. I began by going through papers in boxes, to using ledger books, upgraded to a modern computer system, and now an extensive website.

The *AW Journal*, over the years, has undergone quite a transformation from its beginning in 1986 as a stapled newsletter. It then progressed to a color cover and then evolved to become a full-color, professionally produced, top quality quarterly magazine that went bimonthly in 2010.

So that is how it all started for me, and it hasn't slowed down in the last 22 years. A second employee was eventually hired, and currently there are four full-time and four part-time employees to administer the tremendous growth of the organization.

AAW's Bright Future

I value every positive experience and personal connection I've made as an ambassador of the AAW. Over the years, I have seen encouraging signs that the art of woodturning will continue to grow and thrive. I look forward to seeing the AAW's future filled with an ever-expanding base of members, continued organizational development, and friendly fellowship. I can't help but imagine how much we'll accomplish together for the AAW in the next 25 years—and how much fun we'll have doing it.

On a personal note, I was greatly honored to be selected as an AAW Honorary Lifetime Member in 2006. It was gratifying to be honored by the AAW board of directors. The board is a dedicated and talented group that I have been proud to work with over the years.

Mary Lacer joined the board of directors of the American Association of Woodturners in February, 1990, was appointed administrator in July, 1990, and held further positions of managing director, assistant director and executive director over the next 22 years. She retired in 2010.

VOICES

Linda Ferber: fortunate to work for AAW

The opportunity to try woodturning presented itself back in 1999 when my dad had an auction, including his shop tools. He had been living in rural Foley, MN, but age and health required a move to a town home. He had an extensive wood shop and had made many nice furniture pieces for his children and grandchildren. I often helped with these projects. At his auction I chose the lathe, thinking that with this one piece of equipment I could continue working with wood.

I had no previous experience with a lathe, so I took a bowl-turning class and I joined the Minnesota Woodturners Association. I volunteered as a docent at the AAW Gallery of Wood Art. It is fun to assist the AAW at the Landmark Center Gallery and to see the response of visitors to the shows on display. When the AAW had a job opening due to Eunice Wynn's retirement, I applied and was hired full-time in 2007. I enjoy my job and feel fortunate to be able to work in an area I have such a passion for.

VOICES

Carolyn Lindval: children are the future

I would like to share a sweet and poignant moment with the AAW membership in honor of their 25th Anniversary: On my very first day working for this amazing organization, I was lucky enough to spend a Sunday afternoon in the gallery. It happened to be on a day when there was a very large family-oriented outdoor event downtown Saint Paul, and as a result, many families stopped by to visit the AAW gallery and gift shop. The gallery was filled with people of all ages and abilities, and sounds of "ooohs! and aaahs!" from the excited children filled the area. I realized right away that this was definitely not a stuffy museum, but was a place filled with fun, vitality and education…as well as beautiful works of art on display.

I was quite moved by a little girl, perhaps 6 or 7 years old. I heard her ask her older sister as she gazed at the professionally turned bowls and sculptures on display, "I have one dollar to spend. Can I buy any of these things? Her sister told her,

"Probably not…these are fancy." I chuckled quietly to myself and then noticed that as the little girl and her sister (and their family) were leaving the gallery, she saw our donations box.

She asked her sister what it was for. The older sister replied, "That's where if you liked this place, you stick money in there to tell them it was good." The little girl reached in her pocket, took out her dollar bill and popped it in the box saying, "This place was super fun! …now they'll know I liked it."

At that moment, I saw the future of woodturning. It is in the children. The family of woodturners will grow each time a child is made aware of the creativity, fun and beauty of the art. I knew then and there, that this is a truly special place.

American Woodturner
Jewel of the AAW

It's quite remarkable that the American Association of Woodturners has been able to continuously publish its magazine, *American Woodturner* or, as it is fondly known, the *AW Journal*, over a 25-year span. This has been due not only to clear focus by the Board of Directors, but also, and perhaps more importantly, to an unbroken string of excellent editors. Two of them, Rick Mastelli and Dick Burrows, had previously been senior members of the editorial staff at *Fine Woodworking* magazine, and one, Carl Voss, came over from *Wood* magazine. Under the leadership of the current editor, Betty Scarpino, the quarterly journal became bimonthly in 2010.

AW Journal editors

David Lipscomb, Summer 1986–Spring 1987
Dan Kvitka, Summer 1987–Fall 1988
Peter J. Hutchinson, Winter 1988–Winter 1990
Betty Scarpino, Spring 1991–Fall 1993
Rick Mastelli, Winter 1993–Spring 1998
Dick Burrows, Summer 1998–Winter 2002
Carl Voss, Spring 2003–Winter 2008
Betty Scarpino, Spring 2009–

ABOVE: Carl Voss

LEFT: The *AW Journal* took on a new look in 2009.

BELOW: Dick Burrows in 2002 at the end of his five-year term as editor of the *AW Journal*. Photo by Phil Pratt.

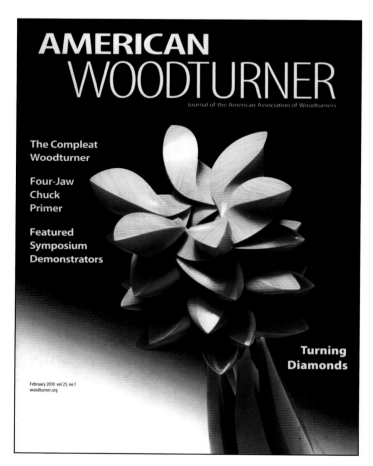

VOICES

J. C. Newcombe: mesmerized by AW Journal

I had only been turning for a short while when I received my first issue of *American Woodturner* magazine. I nearly gave up and threw all my equipment and lathe away!

It's not that I was disappointed in the magazine, quite the contrary. I was mesmerized by the photos and articles of these beautiful turnings submitted by other members. I thought I was getting good at turning, but when I saw these entries, I realized I was out of my head to think I was "good." Like I said, I almost gave up turning when I realized—and this is what I would like to share with others that may feel like I did—it's not about being competitive. It's fun and a relaxing form of art that can be appreciated in many different ways.

I compare it to race car driving. Some drivers have the very best in equipment and training, and others get by with what they have and what they learn, but they all do one thing: Race! I enjoy turning and like what I produce from it. My work is simple in comparison to some. Most of my pieces are usable and are appreciated by those to whom I give them. I have a lot of fun turning, and it relaxes me. I enjoy picking out the wood to see what kind of art I can release from it. To me, that's what it is all about.

J. C. Newcombe turns wood in his home workshop.

Betty Scarpino hoists the pigtail gouge presented to her at the end of her first term as editor of the *AW Journal*, 1993. Scarpino returned to the editorship in 2009. Photo by Robert Bahr.

Rick Mastelli (right) hams it up at the lathe with Del Stubbs, about 1990. Photo by Sue Roman.

A Vigorous On-Line Presence

Steve Worcester

In the beginning the computer-savvy woodturners hung out on rec.woodturning, one of the thousands of newsgroups in the public domain usenets. It was quite lawless in an Internet context—no moderators, no one approving users—but it was a lot of fun and a free worldwide exchange of ideas.

Then in 2003 there was an offer put out by AAW President Phil Brennion for moderators to help manage an AAW-sponsored and funded on-line forum. While this wasn't a new idea, there already were a few forums out there—Woodcentral.com for example—but for our organization it was an evolutionary big step. It would allow more people to use an online area with some civility and order, to discuss woodturning with their peers. You didn't even have to be an AAW member to participate, and this is still true today—anyone may join the forum whether or not they belong to the AAW itself. On May 4, 2003, moderated by Terry Delahay, the forum went on line.

Jeff Jilg soon took over and we added features like the Photo Gallery space that now shows high resolution pictures of more than 8,000 woodturnings from our forum members. To encourage participation, we started up quarterly contests based on articles in the *AW Journal*. Users would post photos and we would have well-known turners kindly critique and judge the entries, and the winner would get the picture of their piece featured in the print magazine.

Under Ken Grunke and now with Kurt Bird's devotion and diligence, the contest has become a very popular part of the forum culture, and recently was expanded to a picture of the week. The moderators choose a piece and it is featured on the AAW website,

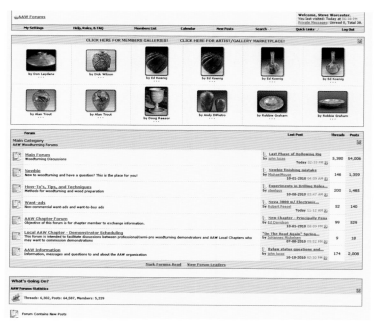

with the assistance of the AAW webmaster Ed Davidson. Ed forms the all-important link between the forums and the main AAW information site.

Today the forum has its own website with more than 5,000 users from all over the world. It gets millions of views each year. It shows hundreds of posts on how to do specific techniques, want ads for people to sell and buy woodturning garage sale items from tools and lathes to exchanging blocks of wood, a calendar of symposiums and demonstrators, talks of AAW business, and a great place to just find out about anything from chain saw sharpening to how to set up a vacuum chuck system. Our forum has evolved into a gathering place for thousands of like-minded individuals to share their knowledge of and passion for woodturning. We hope that users see it as a valuable benefit created by the AAW, and that they continue to support the AAW.

Steve Worcester recently retired as moderator of the AAW forums.

Return to the Community

In the AAW's Return to the Community program, the local chapter hosting each year's national symposium selects a local charity. AAW members and chapters are then invited to donate turned wooden items for the benefit of that charity. In the past, Return to the Community projects often focused on turned wooden toys that could be given to impoverished and hospitalized children. In recent years, due to changes in toy safety laws, the program has focused on turned items that may be sold to raise money for the target organization.

In 2010, sales of turned toys to people attending the AAW's Hartford symposium raised more than $1,200 that was donated to the Connecticut Children's Medical Center Foundation. In 2011, the target charity is Empty Bowls.

The goal of Empty Bowls is to raise money to help organizations fight hunger and raise awareness about the issues of hunger and food security. Many AAW local chapters have participated in the Empty Bowls project. At the Empty Bowl display during the 2011 AAW symposium in Saint Paul, bowls will be sold with the proceeds going to Second Harvest to fund food for the

Toys made by Oregon woodturners on display at the 2007 Portland symposium.

hungry. Purchasers will take home a bowl to keep as a reminder of all the empty bowls in the world.

The Return to the Community began in 1996 in Greensboro, at the AAW 10th annual symposium. The charity was Brenner's Children's Hospital. At the event Tops for Tots, a drawing was held and $331 was raised.

—*Linda Ferber*

Toys and tops made by local chapters of the AAW, for donation to local charities following the 2008 symposium. Photo by Ed Davidson.

Ray Simmons: starting a club in Lancaster, Pennsylvania

There are many reasons to join a group of woodturners in a club. I've learned that the best reason is to share the camaraderie of some of the most interesting craft persons you can find. I originally thought that the sharing of ideas would be top of the list, but in a conversation over what to do with a donated piece of wood, a turning club member told me he didn't know what he could use the wood for because he didn't turn. We were at a woodturners meeting, and I was at a loss for a reply. Gifted or cursed as I am with an active talking ability, I was experiencing a rare moment. This was a reminder that a club cannot lose sight of the member's reason for attending.

As individuals, we pick and choose our recreations to give us something. Rare is it that any club member hangs around if there is not some benefit. Whether it is something learned, something shared, or the affiliation with the organization, a connection has to be made to attract and keep an active membership.

Years ago, I had been living in northeast New York close to Canada and had no exposure to woodturning or turners. I was not aware of any local clubs. I had seen multi-colored rolling pins and a lamp of glued-up different colored woods. I made some pens and pencils after reading an article in a woodworking magazine, but woodturning was not yet something that called me. Then I turned some bud vases and I got a great reaction: a nondescript piece of throw-away wood became a sit-on-the-shelf treasure. I was hit by the woodturning lightning bolt.

My wife and I moved from New York to Lancaster County, Pennsylvania, to follow her job opportunity. Retired from the Air Force, I followed her and soon found new work in a technical field. With everything looking new and different, I was ripe for a new hobby. I had admired some small turned objects at a craft show and decided to try to turn small ornaments. So it began. A mini-lathe grew to a bigger lathe and the projects grew from miniature turned birdhouses to bigger and more challenging items. By 2008, I felt it was time to join others.

I found many references to woodturning on the Internet and ended up at the doorstep of the American Association of Woodturners. Membership for me seemed to force a commitment to understand this woodturning thing. Understanding requires input, and I wanted to maximize the quality of exposure. I have the pleasure not to be challenged in technical or mechanical ability and woodturning was an exercise in mechanics and the technical skill to create something new from a block of wood. Woodturning could be, in my mind, performing magic.

An AAW club met about an hour away at the Woodcraft store in Harrisburg, so I joined, I drove, I attended, I met some great turners, I drove, I attended, and I drove. Two hours on the road to attend a two-hour meeting. My job got me up really early, and the drive home was brutal. I needed a shorter drive.

The club was donated a downed tree that happened to be in Lancaster, and a number of members said they would help transport the pieces to a central location to distribute. I waited along the street while the tree service dropped the tree, with a number of club members who all lived near Lancaster. I asked why there wasn't a local club. The Lancaster area is rich in woodworking history with early years of European settlers and the many Amish woodshops today. This was a prime area for a wood craft club. I was told the club idea had been brought up a number of times, but didn't take off. I felt it was time to make things happen.

I had already talked to a few possible future members one-on-one and was assured that if a local club formed they could be relied upon. But if a club was going to happen, someone needed to make it so. I popped the question: If I got things rolling would you guys get on board? I had five assurances that there would be five members. We would meet in a garage if needed. The challenge was now mine. How do I start a woodturning club that would survive?

I researched the AAW information about finding a space, contacting possible members, how to do this, and how to do that. I had no seed money, no meeting place, no help, and what I felt I needed was a miracle. When you get the advice, "All you gotta do is…" it is usually a bit more involved.

It was personal reflection time. Could I make this happen? What did I want from the club? I decided if I could get enough interested people in one place at one time, I could sell the idea. I needed to put on my positive thinking hat and start the ball rolling. One thing I've lived by is that no one knows what you know. If you are positive, you can sell ice cubes to those living in cold places.

2009: Ray Simmons, third from right, and members of Lancaster Area Woodturners examine a turned spindle during a club demo evening.

The AAW resource directory was my starting point. I emailed everyone who had an address in Lancaster County, taking care not to get too close to the area covered by the other club. My intent was to attract local turners. I needed enough dedicated interest to get a start and was convinced once this ball started to roll it would go. I sent and replied to hundreds of emails, answering questions and asking if there was interest. The miracle I needed appeared in an email reply: I was offered a space to meet at Fox Chapel Publishing's building. I now had a place for a night. I needed members. I hit the emails again, this time with a time and date. Come and hear what we are about.

It is said timing is everything. I was trying to start a club in now what was becoming winter in Pennsylvania, but when meeting night came, a dozen people showed up. I welcomed everyone and asked for one thing, "Give me one hour, and at the end I am going to ask for a show of hands. If there is interest we move forward. If not, thanks for your time." I presented my view of what the club could be and what challenges we faced. At the hour point, I asked for a show of hands and twelve hands went up. In January of 2009, the Lancaster Area Woodturners were formed.

The newly formed club held an election, formed by-laws, picked a club name, and proudly requested to be recognized as a chapter of the AAW. We now have two dozen members and have achieved Star status for being 100% AAW members. We celebrated our one-year anniversary by moving into unused space in Fox Chapel's warehouse, where we can store equipment, hold meetings and demonstrations. In exchange, we'll offer turning classes to Fox employees. What a deal!

It has not been extremely easy to start this club. However, we didn't give up and have come a long way from the meeting on the street waiting for some free wood. How do you start a club? Have a vision. Understand that there are many reasons to join a club. Have answers. Have questions. Once the club forms you do things by committee and voting and politics. Someone has to lead initially. Someone has to lead once it is formed. Be prepared. Do not wing it. Remember your turning beginning. Don't lose the newbies. Value everyone's turning ability. Embrace the challenge of new ideas. Don't get lost in the craft. Don't get lost in the art. Do not give up. Many things take time. Do not be afraid to succeed.

POP: Reaching Out to Professional Woodturners

Mark Sfirri

The Professional Outreach Program began in May of 2004. Phil Brennion, the president of the AAW board at the time, and board member John Hill were instrumental in forming the committee. The first members were Christian Burchard, David Ellsworth, John Jordan, Bonnie Klein, Binh Pho, Jacques Vesery, and me. I would characterize the first year or so as being largely unproductive. We didn't have a unified vision of our purpose or a clear sense of what the AAW board wanted from us. The ideas that we did generate required financial support, and the committee had no funds with which to work. Additionally, there was a feeling of opposition between the POP and the AAW, an attitude that we tried hard to address and continue to address. The AAW board's position changed, I think, because of Angelo Iafrate's support of the committee. Angelo, the succeeding AAW president, encouraged our efforts, attended our teleconference meetings, and helped us see things from the board's point of view. Without Angelo, POP would never have evolved to its current state of usefulness.

One successful early initiative was the creation of a series of POP presentations at the annual conferences. We figured that a lot of the professional membership would be more likely to attend a conference if there was programming that would apply more to their level of involvement in turning. As a result, rotations with titles such as Professionalism, Photography, Surface Ornamentation, and Marketing, and a variety of panel discussions began. Conferences currently have a rotation for each time slot to allow participants to attend presentations on such topics.

Past president Angelo Iafrate attended an exhibition of Japanese turning. As a backdrop for the display, there were about fifty small roughed-out bowl blanks. Angelo

asked the exhibitors to consider donating the blanks to the AAW, and then, on receiving them, asked the POP committee to do something with them. That seed became the first of what has become an annual POP themed invitational exhibit. The first was called *Japanese Bowls: A Western Perspective* (page 108). Bowl blanks were sent to turners with instructions to complete them according

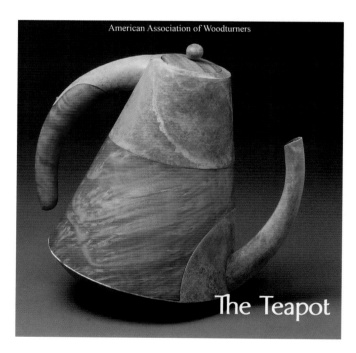

POP exhibitions

In recent years, the AAW's Professional Outreach Program has organized a series of themed invitational exhibitions, with the pieces then being auctioned to raise educational funds.

The series includes *Japanese Bowls: A Western Perspective* (2007, page 108), *The Sphere* (2008, page 114), *The Spindle* (2009, page 115), and *The Teapot* (2010, page 116).

On *The Teapot* cover: Lapsang Souchong, by William Moore, Hillsboro, OR. Madrone burl, patinated copper, 9" high.

to their own distinctive styles and send them back for display and sale. Tib Shaw produced a wonderful catalog. The work was auctioned off at the end of the conference. It was an unqualified success. Since the POP received the proceeds, the committee now had funds to implement new programs. Subsequent themes were sphere, spindle, and teapots. Plans for other themes are in the works.

With *The Sphere* show at the AAW Richmond symposium in 2008, we decided that up to half of the sale price should go to the artist. This incentive made for another great show, and the sales from that were even more substantial.

The great dilemma for POP then became how to spend the money. The committee decided to give away $10,000 in Instant Gallery awards beginning with the 2008 conference. The awards include a number of categories: student, excellence, and purchase for the AAW permanent collection. In addition to the awards, many of these pieces were shown in the post-conference journal, another feather in the caps of the winners. This initiative was an extension of the Instant Gallery critique that was already a part of the programming of the AAW conferences.

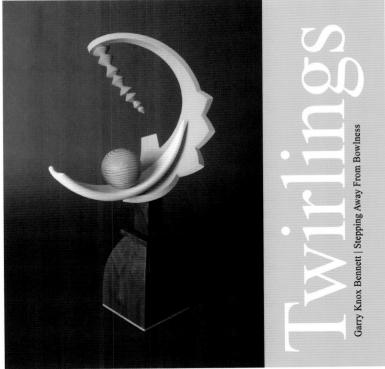

Twirlings

Garry Knox Bennett | Stepping Away From Bowlness

Another initiative was the implementation of the resident artist program. A turner works on a piece throughout the conference so that attendees can see an evolution over the three-day period, providing a contrast to the work produced in a 90-minute rotation.

The POP's biennial fellowship grant, for which application is required, is intended to encourage creative growth, research, or inspiration for new directions in turning. The merit award, for living turners who have made a major contribution to the field with their work, is given out in the alternate years. The inaugural class of 2007 honored Stephen Hogbin, Giles Gilson, and Mark Lindquist. The 2009 award went to Merryll Saylan (page 65).

Mark Sfirri, professor of woodworking at Bucks Country Community College in Pennsylvania and a member of the AAW's Professional Outreach Program, recently won a Distinguished Educator Award from the Renwick Alliance.

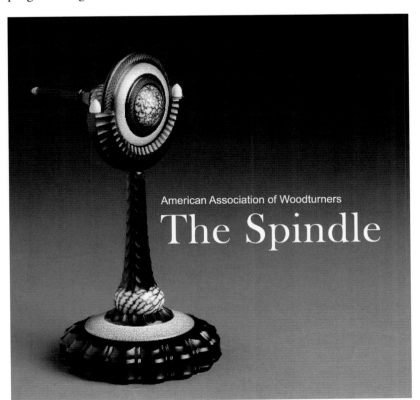

American Association of Woodturners

The Spindle

On *The Spindle* cover: Bamboo Spinner by Jon Sauer, Pacifica, CA.

Chapter Collaborative Challenge

Al Hockenbery

The spirit of sharing among members is pervasive throughout the American Association of Woodturners. Nowhere is sharing more evident than in the chapter collaborative challenge. The chapter challenge is one event in which local chapter members spend months (a few chapters report years) working together to produce a collaborative work which they share with the whole membership at the annual symposium.

The chapter challenge became an annual symposium event when it was introduced at the Akron symposium in 1998. Eleven chapters stepped up. The Chicago Woodturners took home bragging rights with Rough Rider, an antique bicycle made from parts turned by 31 chapter members. Jerome and Deena Kaplan took Rough Rider home with a high bid at the auction. This marvelous beginning set the stage for all the chapter challenges to come.

Each year 10 to 30 chapters accept the challenge, engage their membership, combine their imaginations, apply their individual attention to detail, and wow the symposium attendees with their creations. Using subjects both real and imaginary, chapters have created all sorts of turned works that have delighted and inspired symposium attendees since 1998. These

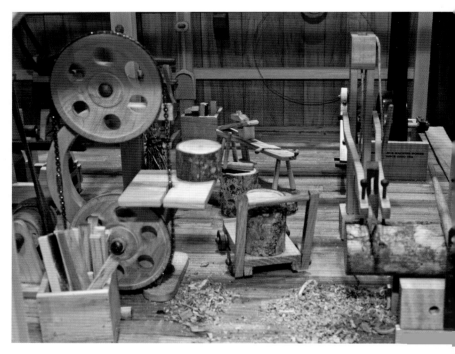

2010: Members of the Wilmington Area Woodturners each made a section of this miniature woodworking shop from an earlier water-powered era. The one-twelfth scale set of moving models fascinated camera-toting visitors at the 2010 Hartford symposium, where the collaboration took the "best in show" award. This was the second year the young club had participated in the challenge.

2010: Thirteen members of the Granite State Woodturners and Guild of New Hampshire Woodworkers created this fascinating array of nesting spheres on display at the AAW's Hartford symposium.

1990: In a precursor to the chapter collaborative challenge, 24 AAW clubs participated in the Unity Totem project for the 1990 symposium at Arrowmont School of Arts and Crafts. The clubs created, assembled, and installed the pair of totems as a gift to Arrowmont, to recognize the role the school had played in providing the venue where the new organization could gather. The 1990 symposium was the last that Arrowmont could accommodate, with ever more members clamoring to attend. Photo by Cynthia Huff.

creations are a highlight of each symposium where the attendees vote for their pick of the Artistic, Technical, and Fantasy categories as well as Best in Show. The announcement of the winners marks the end of a journey for the participating chapters, but the works created live on in private collections, chapter meeting halls, and museums.

Set in the framework of friendly competition, the challenge inspires chapter members to work together. In most cases arriving at the design is the most daunting aspect. Then it is on to dividing up the work and making sure those parts that are intended to join will do so without the big hammer. The meetings, the phone calls, the trips to friends' houses enable the chapters to grow stronger with the spirit of the AAW.

For participants, working together, planning, designing, turning, constructing, packing, delivering, and setting up their collaborative entry is the reward. The collaborative is all about the journey.

Al Hockenbery of Lakeland, FL, is a regular demonstrator at AAW symposiums and a former member of its Board of Directors.

The Art of the Pen

This beautiful array of turned pens includes work by Angelo Iafrate, Ed Davidson, Jay Pickens, Patricia Lawson, Wally Dickerman, Scott Greaves, Kenn Osborne, Emory McLaughlin, and Jim Lambert.

A Gateway to Woodturning

It is rare to find a woodturner who hasn't turned a pen somewhere in their past. There are some, but not many. For a pretty large percentage of the woodturners, the pen is the gateway into woodturning. They saw or participated in the Freedom Pen project, took a pen class at their local wood retailer, or watched pens being turned by an AAW chapter at the county fair. Regardless of their initial exposure, the immediate gratification of taking a piece of wood and quickly creating a functional, personally crafted item is often the hook to a woodturning addiction.

There are some pen turners who are very content to make pens as their main turning projects, continuing to make kits and reveling in turning pens from every wood species that can be found. Others become enthralled by the woodturning craft, move quickly beyond the pen, and never look back. The pen kit, not requiring extensive turning skills, is sometimes looked down on

as a beginner-level project. Explain that point of view to those pen makers who create their own designs, fabricate their own parts, embellish their creations with paintings, pyrography, or piercing, or make their own patterns and cast precious metal components. These makers have created their own art form—one that rivals fine jewelry.

Regardless of your current view of pens, as a low cost and low risk entry or a high-end artform of its own, they have a very special place in the world of woodturning. With several pen turning groups, each numbering in the many thousands, being part of the virtual AAW pen turning chapter, the pen has the unique position of being the single most popular introduction to the joyous world of woodturning. Without the humble pen, many of us who currently enjoy the world of woodturning might never have started.

—*Kurt Hertzog*

Dip pen with stand by Kurt Hertzog, rosewood and abalone.

Fountain and roller ball pens by Colin and Ken Nelsen, laser-cut woods in various species. Photo by Kurt Hertzog.

Fountain pen by Dan Symonds, acrylic.

Pen cap and barrel by Barry Gross, watch parts and acrylic resin, photo courtesy of *Pen World* magazine.

Fountain pen by Rich Kleinhenz in alternative ivory, mammoth ivory, African blackwood, sterling silver, stabilized oak.

Turned Canes Honor Wounded Heroes

It is a simple gesture in contrast to such heroic action. A cane, turned on a lathe and topped with a handle carved in the shape of an eagle's head, is presented to a wounded warrior. "This cane is not to be seen as any sign of weakness," says Hank Cloutier, coordinator of the Eagle Cane Project for the Washington, D.C. area, to the recipient. "It is a sign of respect and honor and thanks for your personal sacrifice."

According to Cloutier, an Air Force retiree, cane presentation ceremonies date back to the Civil War. The eagle carved into the cane is symbolic, Cloutier explains: "Native Americans believed that when a warrior falls on the battlefield his spirit will return as an eagle."

On a cold Sunday in January 2008, the Walter Reed Army Medical Center was packed with wounded warriors, their families, and young children. "We're fighting an enemy you can't see," says David Nieves, who was injured near Camp Liberty in Baghdad. "We are fighting a ghost you don't see." Nieves, like other soldiers in Iraq and Afghanistan, found that his armored vehicle offered little protection against IEDs, or improvised explosive devices. Unfortunately, he adds, "explosives cut through the armor like paper."

The soldiers treasure the eagle canes and feel honored that thoughtful Americans have taken the time to handcraft an object that, like the Purple Hearts awarded them, will stand as mementos of their service and sacrifice. One of the cane recipients, Sgt. First Class Gordon L. Ewell, wrote what he described as a very humble thank-you: "You have given me not only a much-needed tool, necessary for my mobility, but also a constant reminder, as I walk with your cane, of the goodness that lies in the hearts of mankind."

Jack Nitz, a member of the Eastern Oklahoma Woodcarvers' Association (EOWA), initiated the Eagle Cane Project in 2004 to honor wounded warriors at Walter Reed and the National Naval Medical Center at Bethesda. Working with EOWA, the NE Oklahoma Woodturners helped get the program started by turning cane shafts. The project has since spread to woodcarving and woodturning clubs in 25 states and has produced hundreds of handcrafted canes.

—*from* American Woodturner, *summer 2008*

Jeffrey Hudgens, USMC, is honored by the former Boy Scout troop in Tahlequah, OK. Jack Nitz, founder of the eagle cane project, is second from left.

SPC Evan Mettie's mother receives an eagle cane on behalf of her son from Richard Hamilton at the Palo Alto VA hospital in California.

Dawson McLemore: helping wounded veterans learn to turn

Most major military installations host a Wounded Warrior unit where injured veterans are cared for and where resources can be pooled to help soldiers and families adjust. Fort Benning, Georgia, is home to one such unit and Columbus, Georgia, adjacent to the post, is home to the Bi-City Woodturners, a local chapter of the AAW. For the members of the club, many of them veterans themselves, reaching out to help was only natural.

"Our initial goal was to make fifty canes to be given to wounded warriors," said Bob Ingram, vice-president of the club. "Bringing the soldiers in to participate in woodturning was an afterthought, but one that proved to be as rewarding for the club as it was for the soldiers," he said.

Every Monday, club members invite the soldiers to learn the craft of woodturning. They never really know exactly what each individual soldier will get out of the program. "The intent is to expose the soldiers to something that will allow them to forget their injury and learn a hobby that can last a lifetime," said Karen Nichols of the unit's occupational therapy program.

For some soldiers, working with the club is simply a chance to get away "I like the shop because it makes me relax and focus on what I am doing. I am doing something that releases my stress, and it boosts my self esteem," said Sergeant Angel Morales.

In the spring of 2009, members became concerned about soldiers unable to stand at the lathe long enough to finish a project. The club applied for and got a grant from the AAW to help purchase a sit-down lathe. But when the club inquired about the cost and explained its purpose, Tim Clay at Oneway Manufacturing decided to donate a sit-down lathe. Oneway's generosity was tremendous. And, having no need for the grant it received, the club returned the money to the AAW.

Recuperating soldiers can sit at this professional quality lathe that the manufacturer donated to the Wounded Warrior program sponsored by the Bi-City Woodturners of Columbus, GA.

Turners Send Freedom Pens to Troops Overseas

"I had an idea this morning to start making wooden pens and donating them to our troops overseas..."

When he typed that post on the Sawmill Creek woodworking forum on January 16, 2004, Keith Outten of Hayes, Virginia, had no idea what he was getting into. Seven years later, the Freedom Pens project is still going strong (www.freedompens.org).

What started as Outten's desire to share his personal effort became a nationwide effort, with hundreds of woodturners making pens for American soldiers in Iraq and Afghanistan. With woodturning chapters, retail stores, schools, and individual turners taking part, almost 100,000 pens have been sent overseas.

"A pen seems like such a small item to us," says Ruthe Ingram, coordinator for the Orange County Woodturners Association. "But to the troops it is a big thing, because it is handmade and comes from perfect strangers who just want them to know we love and appreciate the sacrifices they are making."

—*from* American Woodturner, *winter 2007*

VOICES

Dave Bowers: encouraged by a pen turner

My journey into woodturning runs parallel to many turners involved today. It is unique in the specific facets of what individuals have taught me and what I've done with that knowledge. The journey itself embodies the underlying culture and spirit that so many others have experienced and provided. The American Association of Woodturners thrives from this one prevailing attitude to help and teach others the art and craft of woodturning.

I still remember the first turning lesson. I had been assisting with a college campus church group. One student's grandfather was a retired Ohio State dentistry professor with a passion for wood. He took the time one Saturday to invite the whole group over for pen making. To my surprise and luck, only two of us showed up that day. After the first hour, I was the only one left. He showed me the first steps in blank preparation and went upstairs. After I stumbled through those steps, he came back down and started my turning lesson. With a gleam in his eye, he knew what he was introducing me to. I wonder if he really knew how far I would embrace this passion for wood. I have to thank Dr. Gus Pappas for that first lesson. To this day, I remember that finished padouk slim line pen—it's the best piece I ever made.

The next evolution in my turning started shortly after that fateful padouk pen with Gus. The newspaper *Weekender* told of a December showing of turned bowls and objects from the local woodturning club. I joined the Central Ohio Woodturners that night and started attending their meetings. Early on, two particular members answered many questions. Freddy Dutton not only invited me to his shop a few times for learning the basics, but also loaned a table-top lathe that was far better than the small lathe I had been using. Floyd Anstaett also invited me to his shop, and soon I was trying to find every reason to go visit and soak in more turning. I heard later on that he told my wife to keep encouraging me and that I should get a larger lathe. Walt, Ron, Chuck, Barb, Jim, Fred, and numerous other members of the Central Ohio Woodturners have also contributed to my knowledge. Beyond the woodturning, I value and respect every friendship within this group of good people.

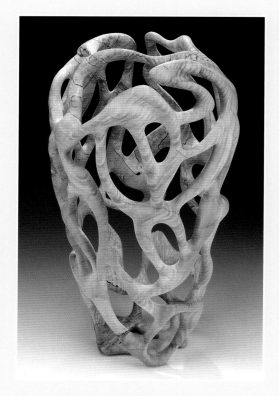

2009: Turned and carved by Dave Bowers.

The most significant step that steered my journey towards its present direction was meeting Harry Pollitt. I consider Harry one of the great wood sculptors and now one of my closest friends. After discovering each other's love of wood, he invited me to his studio. There I absorbed knowledge of sculpting, tools, and finishing. Working on ideas, I learned from both guidance and failures until I had my breakthrough sculpted turning. Harry told me that he sensed there was something different in me. He could see the passion and desire for wood turning and sculpture.

It's still amazing to me when I reflect upon my journey so far—not only the skills I have developed, but more importantly the friendships. I think of everyone I look forward to seeing each year at symposiums. I think about Freddy, Floyd, Harry, and what everyone else has done for me. All of this was made available because one retired dentistry professor took the time to share his knowledge one Saturday morning.

VOICES

Patricia Allen: my gorgeous hunk of metal

When I walked into the free, hands-on, learn-to-turn class at the Klingspor Extravaganza in Hickory, North Carolina, in 2005, I met my first lathe along with a kind woodturner smiling and saying, "So, you'd like to try your hand at woodturning. You can do it. It's easy. …This is your face shield…" Thus, I was immersed in the wonderful world of making shavings. A warning label should have been plastered on that gorgeous hunk of metal. "Warning! Touch me, and your whole world will change!"

I took two classes that day: Weed Pot 101 and Beginning Ornament. As I struggled to finish the tip of my ornament, that kind woodturner showed up and gently asked if I would like some help. Help is possible? Oh, YES. What was I attempting? I wanted to make it pretty on the end and pointed. Honestly, I was near to tears. "Would you like me put a few bells on the

Pat Allen outside her home in Newton, NC.

end of that for you?" Bells? On that tiny broken piece of wood? I nodded. His hands were like fluid motion as the metal gouge kissed the broken wood. Miraculously, the wood submitted to his touch and bells formed—bell after bell after bell all the way to the tip. I nearly wept again for the wonder and joy of such skill.

In some mystical manner, as I left the building, an inner knowing blossomed. I knew I would have a woodturning business and the name would be (and is) Pat's Pens & Treasures.

The next weekend in nearby Statesville, North Carolina, there was a regional symposium. There was a pen demonstration and I had to go.

Pens? Yes! Now I would be able to see what pens had to do with weed pots and ornaments. I had no idea how wood pens were created, I had only seen one. At the symposium, I saw two pens created. I understood very little of what I saw, but I understood parts, sharp tools and gentle touch, glue, and make a nice finish. I squealed and trembled with excitement all the way home. I am not naturally an emotionally expressive person, but woodturning was deeply exciting. I could not have given any logical reason for my reaction. It's pens! Pens. That was all my mind would give me for logic.

Without the American Association of Woodturners' support of my mentors, my suppliers, my friends, and little ol' me, I would have given up on this heart passion of mine. I had never used home shop tools before. Not a drill, nor a miter saw, nor bandsaw, nor hammer. The first year was a vertical learning curve. But now I've my own shop, I am known as a maker of quality pens with a hand-burnished lacquer finish that other woodworkers have told me openly they could never match. Thank you AAW for helping me find my life's work and being good at it.

Pen and vase turned by Pat Allen.

Segmented Turning Comes of Age

Malcolm Tibbetts

Visiting any symposium Instant Gallery is always a huge treat. Nowadays, as part of the display, you will undoubtedly be intrigued by a multitude of segmented woodturnings, that is, assemblies of many small blocks of different kinds of wood.

In recent years, segmenting has enjoyed a very noticeable increase in popularity. In the fall of 2008, the first segmented woodturning symposium was held at the Marc Adams Woodworking School in Indiana, and as a result of attendee discussions, there is now a specialty, web-based, segmented woodturners chapter within the AAW. What has inspired so many turners to tackle the challenges of accurately assembling many little pieces of wood before they approach the lathe?

I'll share my perspective. In 1973, Emmett Brown and Cyril Brown co-wrote *Polychromatic Assembly for Woodturning*, published by the Society of Ornamental Turners of England. Later, in 1982, Richard Sorsky of Linden Publishing made the Browns' work available to all woodturners. For many years, this was the bible for segmenters—there was very little else available.

In 1975, the very first issue of *Fine Woodworking* displayed a segmented woodturning. Paul Roman, the magazine's founder, told me, "I was intrigued by a couple of segmented turnings at a craft show. I was able to borrow them to take a few Polaroid pictures on my kitchen table." Irving Fischman was the maker, and how lucky for all of us that his work grabbed Paul Roman's attention. But segmented work has a way of doing that.

I'll bet that I was not the only woodworker that became intrigued by the possibilities presented by that black-and-white cover image. Ten years later (1985), another *FWW* cover showed two exceptional southwest-style segmented vessels by Addie Draper and Bud Latven. Addie and Bud shared their techniques with the world, just as turners have always shared. Perhaps no other magazine issue has had as much impact on the growth of segmented woodturning.

There are many pioneers and events that deserve credit. Albert LeCoff of the Wood Turning Center, the force behind countless exhibitions, introduced Lincoln Seitzman's work (page 141) to the woodturning community. Lincoln was an innovator, and with Albert's support, he inspired me and hundreds of turners to pursue segmenting. At the First Segmented Symposium, Lincoln was honored for his pioneering innovations.

Current-day segmenters, whether they be hobbyist or fulltime professionals, owe a huge debt of gratitude to the segmenting pioneers. In the 1940s, long before Bud Latven started to make miter cuts, people like Howard Wipple were pushing the art form. Wipple very successfully incorporated intarsia techniques into his segmented pieces. His work made people stop and look. In the early 1970s, Canadian Stephen Hogbin (see page 39), someone not typically associated with segmenting, produced an amazing set of chairs and tables from a huge six-foot diameter laminated turning. Hogbin's work definitely caught my attention, and it opened up all sorts of possibilities. As if six feet was not big enough, years later, two Austrian turners stunned the turning world with a world record, 14-foot diameter segmented bowl—once again bringing attention to segmenting.

In 1975, Rude Osolnik, the grandfather of American woodturning, started experimenting with laminated material (plywood) (see page 55). Rude gave respectability to the use of glue. Then, Virginia Dotson (page 153) took inspiration from Rude's work and continued pushing the use of laminations. Early books by Dale Nish (page 45) offered many pages of segmenting instruction. Dale's books inspired people like Mike Shuler of California, who started from Dale's angle-cut ring instructions and spring-boarded to his distinctive style. Mike shared his technique with the AAW symposium attendees in 1995. Ray Allen also read the Latven/Draper article, and he found what he was looking for—a challenging hobby that allowed him to

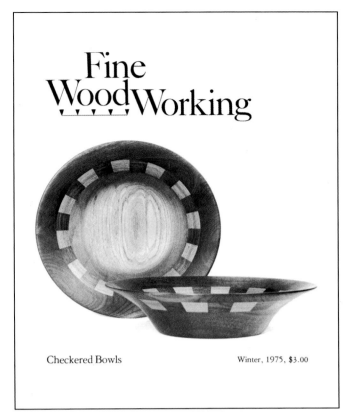

Checkered Bowls   Winter, 1975, $3.00

1975

2006

use his prior woodworking skills. Ray perfected his art quickly and then began to share. In a conversation with Curt Theobald, I found it interesting that we both met Ray at the same time—at the 1994 AAW symposium in Ft. Collins, Colorado.

In 1993, another eye-opening book, *Beyond Basic Turning* by Jack Cox, detailed segmenting techniques that were far more advanced than anything previously documented. More recently, Dale Nish wrote a segmenting how-to that profiled his friend Ray Allen. As turners, we now have ultra-specialty books such as Bill Smith's *Segmented Woodturning*, which details "open" techniques, and my own book, *The Art of Segmented Woodturning*, which introduces ribbon and tubular constructions. Everyone shares and everyone benefits as they push the art form into new areas.

Today's novice segmenter has so many more learning opportunities that simply didn't exist just a few years ago. There are now numerous how-to books, DVDs, computer design software, club mentoring programs, Internet discussion forums, magazine articles, and YouTube videos. A quick Google search for "segmented wood turning" reveals over 62,000 items—that's a lot of information. A segmented/laminated turning by Ted Hodgetts has even been featured on a Canadian postage stamp.

The AAW's journal, *American Woodturner*, has contributed tremendously to the advancement of segmenting. Since its inception, there has been a segmented turning on an *American Woodturner* front cover every year (and countless back covers). There have been frequent how-to articles, but two issues particularly stand out. The December 1989 issue displayed a piece by Virginia Dotson on the cover, and inside there were nine different articles all on segmenting, and in the fall issue of 2006, eight pages were devoted to a photo gallery of current segmented work. And to add to the information pool, in 2008, the journal included a three-part series on segmenting by Jim Rodgers. With all this attention and exposure, how could the popularity of segmenting not flourish? Segmented work has a way of grabbing people's attention. Perhaps that's why a recent AAW membership promotional flyer displays one of Bill Smith's segmented pieces on its cover.

This has all led up to the formation of Segmented Woodturners, a specialty web-based chapter within the AAW. The future of polychromatic assembly has never looked so good. If you would like to view the current state of segmenting, I invite you to visit www. segmentedwoodturners.org.

VOICES

Phil Brown: mapping the membership

The first chapter location map I prepared for the American Association of Woodturners was published in the 1992–93 *Member Directory*, and the first membership map appeared in the 1994 *AAW Resource Directory*. Included in annual issues since then, these maps were not initially designed for the directory. From this beginning, they have evolved a bit like a vessel evolves on the lathe from a burl or flitch of irregular-growth wood. I have watched the AAW grow from 20 chapters in 1992 to 309 chapters in 2009 and watched membership grow from just hundreds in the beginning, and from about 4,200 in 1994 to nearly 11,500 at the time the 2009 map was prepared.

My interest in mapping our membership began in 1991 when Capital Area Woodturners (CAW) was meeting at the Bryant Adult Education Center in Alexandria, Virginia, a former junior high school. The building had a wood shop with eight lathes, other industrial arts class rooms, an auditorium, and a kitchen next to a gym with portable seating—all rentable. There were a half-dozen low budget motels within a few miles on Route 1. With such facilities adequate for a mini symposium, and recalling Albert LeCoff's weekend symposiums from the late 70s, I wondered how big the turning population was within a one-day drive.

I made an approximate membership count by state from the AAW membership directory, put the numbers into a U.S. map, and printed it using Harvard Graphics. To identify AAW chapters as potential co-sponsors of a symposium, I also put their initials on a map and did the same from the demonstrator list. On a whim, I sent copies to Mary at the AAW to demonstrate what could be done with their data. She showed the maps to the board, which requested the chapter and membership maps for the Resource Directory.

The production process for these simple maps became more difficult after the former 1985 vintage DOS software was abandoned and new printers no longer supported DOS drivers. But I haven't given up making the maps. The most recent DOS version maps loaded into an old Windows version of Harvard Graphics for printing. Fortunately, good lathes don't pass away like the latest digital technology. And, I never did organize or prompt CAW to organize that mini-symposium.

Phil Brown turns wood in Maryland and has been a supporting member since the AAW began.

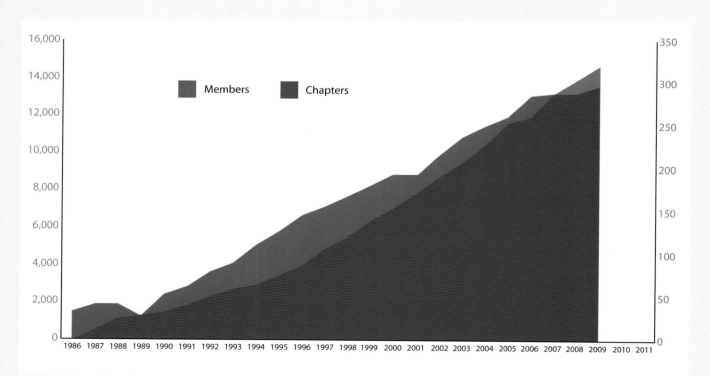

Local Chapters
American Association of Woodturners

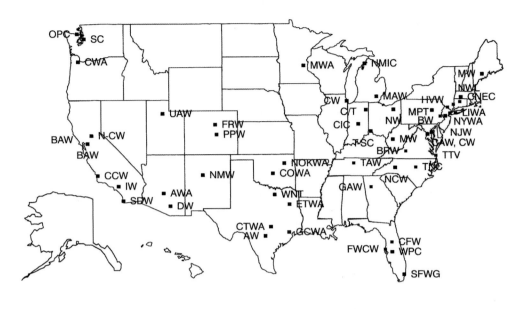

9-24-92, Phil Brown

1992: The AAW was just six years old when Phil Brown began mapping chapter locations.

Local Chapter Locations

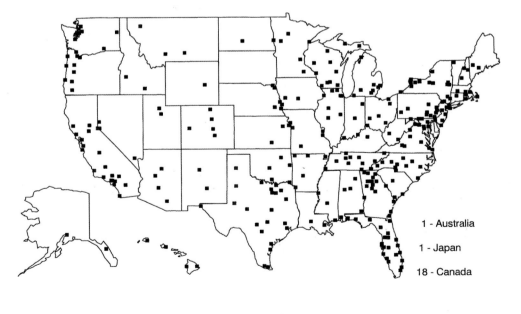

1 - Australia

1 - Japan

18 - Canada

January 2010

2010: After 25 years, more than 300 chapters fill the map.

Collectors of Wood Art

The first time you buy a piece of turned wood art, you are a collector. If you are an artist, when you make your first piece of art you are also a collector. Collectors of Wood Art members explore such topics as how to discover a magnificent piece of wood art, where artists get their inspiration, how to care for a wood art collection, and how to insure, document, and appraise wood art. CWA programs include forums, studio tours, exhibitions, and a newsletter.

The images on these pages are from the juried exhibition, *Turning to the Future: A Fresh Look at Wood Art*, held at the Grovewood Gallery in Asheville, and from a concurrent invitational exhibition of wood artists at Blue Spiral 1 art gallery in Asheville. Both shows were organized to coincide with a Collectors of Wood Art forum in April 2009. Photos by Jim McPhail.

Full circle
Woodturner Norm Rose, right, laughs it up with Collectors of Wood Art founder Arthur Mason (left) and del Mano Gallery co-founder Ray Leier. Each member of the circle relies on the other two. Photo by Andi Wolfe.

Influential people

Dave Long

Masters of the lathe they are not, but Ray Leier and Jan Peters make any list of the most influential people in woodturning over the last 25 years.

Their uparalleled expertise along with aggressive marketing of artists represented in their del Mano Gallery have been vital to growth in the wood art field and the AAW. Since founding their Los Angeles gallery in 1973, they have challenged turners to develop into artists and casual buyers to become educated, passionate collectors. They have helped make wood an acceptable medium in high-end galleries, on the same level as decorative objects made from glass, ceramics, fiber, or metal. With their proactive approach, they have built del Mano into the world's top gallery carrying wood art.

From the beginning, Peters and Leier traveled nationally to almost every venue where the medium is displayed, looking for new talent. In 1985, Leier and Rick Snyderman (Snyderman Gallery in Philadelphia) helped provide the initial funding to launch the AAW. They helped grow awareness of the field to the public and clients by marketing through various visual media—books on turned objects featuring outstanding photography, color catalogs, tapes, and DVDs of numerous shows. They curated national exhibitions and promoted objects on the secondary market. When the Collectors of Wood Art was formed, they were among the first members.

With the advent of the Internet, they constructed the best website on the net to see both past and current work of the almost 200 artists from 14 countries they represent. That Internet presence was coupled with aggressive advertising campaigns in publications geared toward art patrons rather than turners. They are among the few galleries with wood art in the SOFA art fairs held yearly in New York, Chicago, and Santa Fe.

"We're doing what we love, representing the best people in the world," said Leier. "What more could you ask for?"

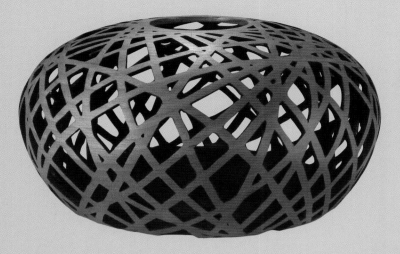

Bird's Nest, Tucker Garrison, cherry, 7.5" dia.

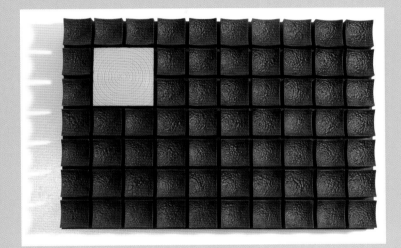

Harvest Moon, Darrell Copeland, maple, acrylic, MDF, 27" wide.

Aspen Grove, Paul Stafford, wood and acrylic, 10" tall.

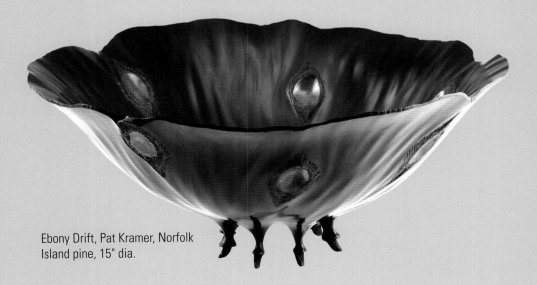

Ebony Drift, Pat Kramer, Norfolk Island pine, 15" dia.

30 Years of Turning Symposiums in Utah

Kip Christensen

In 1975, the book *Creative Woodturning* by Dale L. Nish was published and soon became the most popular book on woodturning in America. As a result, Dale was asked to demonstrate and lecture at the 1977 symposium organized by Albert and Alan LeCoff, held at the George School (see page 46). Dale was very impressed by the experience, and the ideas he encountered were to be life-changing. He immediately began making plans to host a series of woodworking symposiums, hoping to broaden the instructional base for the woodworking program at Brigham Young University (BYU) where he taught industrial education.

In the fall of 1979, Symposium West '79, Utah's first woodturning symposium, was held at BYU. Demonstrators included Albert LeCoff, Frank E. Cummings III, David Ellsworth, Dale L. Nish, and Bob Stocksdale. The format allowed participants to select demonstrators of their choice for sessions lasting about two hours. This set the basic format for future events. Thus began the Utah Woodturning Symposium, which has become the longest running woodturning symposium in the world.

During the 1980s and early 90s, Dale traveled extensively and visited many excellent turners in the British Isles, Canada, New Zealand, and the United States. He invited many of these turners to demonstrate at subsequent Utah symposiums. Dale also made an effort to identify young turners who he felt had the potential, temperament, and skill to become future demonstrators. He would encourage them to attend the symposium, waive the registration fee, and provide housing. Many of today's best-known turners first demonstrated at the Utah symposium.

Dale coordinated the symposium from 1979 through 1998. Upon Dale's retirement, I became the symposium director. I had been a student at BYU and a teaching assistant to Dale during the first four symposiums from 1979 through 1982. In 1988, I returned to BYU as a new faculty member and continued as symposium director for nine years between 1999 and 2007. During this time, the symposium attendance was generally between 450 and 500 participants, which was at capacity for the facilities at BYU.

In 2008 Mike Mahoney (page 2), who had previously given many hours of volunteer service to the symposium, took over as director, and the event was moved to Utah Valley University in nearby Orem. This allowed for increased flexibility in scheduling and for room to grow. Beginning in 2010, the directorship was restructured to consist of a board (Dale, Kip, and Mike) with significant help from local turners and members of the two Utah woodturning clubs.

The goals of the Utah symposium have always been to provide a unique educational opportunity for those in the world woodturning community, to contribute to the educational offering of the campus in general, and to support students in their educational goals. Each year, after financial obligations have been met and a modest sum withheld to seed the next symposium, the remaining funds have been used to establish and build scholarship accounts, which by 2010 totaled nearly $750,000.

Utah Symposium events

Since it spontaneously emerged at that first symposium, the Instant Gallery has been a focal point, recently including as many as 800 turnings. The symposium also

While there may be a few accomplished woodturners who have not yet presented at the Utah symposium, those who have include hundreds of leading turners from around the world. Many of them returned in 2004 for the event's silver jubilee (right). At the 2001 symposium, the 26 presenters together had a total of 718 years of wood turning experience.

has sponsored four special exhibitions, including in 2004 a 25-year retrospective of work by more than 140 leading turners from 15 countries, all of whom had presented at the Utah event.

The Great Egg Cup Race was introduced in 1996. Pairs of competitors race each other and the clock to turn an egg and an egg cup. A team competition adds to the commotion: two toolrests on one lathe, one turner hollowing the end of the cup while his companion turns the spindle. As the English ornamental turner Bill Jones wryly noted, "You can watch heaps of really good wood being totally ruined by the world's finest turners." Symposium presenters also entertain in another way, demonstrating their specialties by turning completed projects in only 15 minutes each.

Woodturners love to swap stories, ideas, and, almost always, wood and tools. In 1986, Dale added a Swap Meet to the program. Somehow, everyone seems to return home with more items than they came with.

Published in 2004, *Beneath The Bark* documented the major international invitational exhibitions representing the work of more than 140 leading turners from 15 countries who had presented at the Utah Woodturning Symposium during its first 25 years.

The View from Afar

The AAW and Its Influence on World Turning

Terry Martin

The American Association of Woodturners is well known among turning communities around the world. In fact, there are over 800 non-American members of the AAW in more than 25 countries, and they are kept well informed by regular deliveries of *American Woodturner*. In a time when the number of magazines catering to turners is in decline and when many of the surviving magazines look like they might sink under the weight of advertising pages, the *AW Journal* is a non-commercial alternative with wide appeal. Equally, the AAW website keeps overseas members up to date with its online forums, news updates, and directories.

The annual symposium is a major focus of attention. For foreigners from a more modest local scene, this symposium can be a mix of the Oscars and Disneyland. A journey to a symposium can become a trip of a lifetime and something to tell stories about when they return home. Also, some wannabee superstars travel to America to strut their stuff in the hope of becoming famous, while others are lured by dreams of the pot of gold. How often have I heard, "If only I could crack the American market...."

Some of these visitors suffer a rude awakening when they find they are invisible in a sea of talent, and a few days is not enough time to build a reputation. I have enjoyed seeing some very confident overseas visitors put their work out at the Instant Gallery, only to quietly pack it away at the end of the weekend. More gratifyingly, I have seen others sell their work immediately and have heard them mentioned as someone to watch. Occasionally, a superstar is recognized, and they become regular and well-known symposium guests year after year.

The AAW also offers an alternative way for turners to tap into a wider market by allowing them to sell their work through the AAW website and the AAW gallery in Saint Paul. In a time when reliable wood galleries are rare, if not extinct, this is another way for international turners to reach American customers.

Of course, it's not a one-way street when foreign turners visit AAW events. By demonstrating at the symposiums and at local chapters across the country, they have also changed the way Americans turn. Who can deny the influence of people like Jean-François Escoulen, Eli Avisera, Alain Mailland, Louise Hibbert, Hans Weissflog, Hayley Smith, and Rolly Munro? These are now established names, but every now and then a relative newcomer arrives at a symposium and makes an instant impression. A recent example of that is the young Swiss turner Jérôme Blanc (page 205), who is creating beautiful and unique pieces.

Although there have been other influential symposiums, because of its size and longevity the AAW has served as a major role model and it is reflected in other events, both big and small, all over the world: one long weekend of rotations by visiting turners, instant galleries, critiques, and sometimes accompanying trade shows. It's now a tried-and-true formula, but occasionally it has been transformed into something quite different.

Redefined by French vision

In 1996, I was with Jean-François Escoulen at the AAW's 10th anniversary symposium in Greensboro—the first for both of us. As we wandered the vast air-conditioned halls where the event was being held he said, "This is

People gather in the square in Puy-St-Martin waiting to enter the village church to see the exhibition of woodturning. Photo by Terry Martin.

Symposiums in Puy-St-Martin

Visitors throng the tiny town of Puy-St.-Martin, amazed by the exhibition of woodturning from around the world. It's a revelation for most who visit. Photo by Terry Martin.

wonderful, but I can't get any sense of where we are."
Later he told me he'd like to organize a symposium where people could really feel a sense of place. He went on to organize the two famous symposiums in his village of Puy-St-Martin in the south of France (2000 and 2003), still spoken of by many as the best ever—inspired by the AAW, but redefined through French vision. It was amazing to see that on the last day of the first symposium, an open day for the general public, more than 10,000 visitors came to the village, which has only a few hundred residents. It was perhaps the best single day of publicity that woodturning has ever had.

Ring-turning: a German twist

Another example of a symposium with distinct local character was the one-off Drechseln Symposium held in 2000 in the town of Olbernhau in the Erzgebirge mountains of eastern Germany. Olbernhau is a small community in a region with a tradition of turning going back to the 1600s, including their world famous ring turning. In some nearby villages, hand-turning is still the major industry, something that is only a memory in most of the world. As it was largely funded by the European Economic Commission, it was a fascinating example of how government funding can be adapted to the American model of private enterprise. Inevitably, the weekend was opened with many speeches by bureaucrats and politicians who wanted to take credit for what was happening—the price you pay for government help. A very German band started proceedings, and then everybody rushed to the demonstrations they had chosen. Just like in France, many of the activities were open to the public and the cobbled town square was turned into a kind of carnival of turning with demonstrators showing different traditional techniques such as the bow lathe, pole turning, and more. For the paying attendees, there were 35 demonstrators from 10 countries, teaching their techniques in exactly the same kind of rotations as we see at AAW events.

In the Australian bush

Turnfest, which has been held in the Australian state of Queensland every year since 2003, is another variation on the AAW model. It is the only annual Australian turning symposium that features overseas demonstrators, and in a climate that is nearly perfect, there is a genuine outdoor feeling to much of the event. As well as the usual air-conditioned venues, demonstrations are often given

This traditional Erzgebirge ring turner cuts a ring that is shaped in the profile of an animal. Amazingly, he doesn't use a template. When the ring is removed it is cloven into dozens of little figures. Photo by Terry Martin.

under open-sided marquees with gentle breezes wafting away the sawdust. Hans Weissflog, a regularly featured demonstrator, says, "I've never enjoyed myself like this at a woodturning symposium!" The event is always held in a holiday resort, and that creates a relaxed atmosphere with beaches, forests, swimming pools, outdoor bars—and turning! What else could you ask for?

The AAW model is also obvious in Britain, although it can be hard for the British to recognize that recent developments in woodturning are largely driven by another country. However, the biennial Loughborough symposium run by the Association of Woodturners of Great Britain shows the unmistakable influence of AAW events. Some American turners are usually invited, as well as other internationals. After watching Frenchman Christophe Nancey work, one comment from a local club newsletter gives a sense of the sometime xenophobic attitude of British turners: "Very clever, very artistic, very innovative, very very French, but not really my cup of tea."

The pattern is repeated in Ireland and on the other

2007: The annual Turnfest tradition, where demonstrators (in yellow) and attendees gather for a group photograph outside the conference venue. When this was taken in 2007, Turnfest was held at a mountain resort. Nowadays it is held at a major seaside resort. Photo by Terry Martin.

Turnfest in Queensland, Australia

2007: It's a shoes-off event! Terry Scott of New Zealand demonstrates pyrography in a marquee among the trees. Photo by Terry Martin.

2007: Neil Scobie demonstrates to a turning audience like anywhere in the world, except that it is under shady trees in Australia. Photo by Terry Martin.

side of the world in South Africa and New Zealand, both countries with relatively small turning populations, but with remarkably strong and innovative approaches to turning. I have been particularly interested in how turners in both countries have acknowledged the material cultures of their indigenous populations and tried to incorporate these influences in their work.

I suspect that many of the turners who attend these international events don't even know where the influence began as it has become received wisdom that this is how you run a turning event.

These events and others show that not only has the AAW had a huge influence around the world, but also that the model can be changed to offer new ways of doing things. Fourteen years after my first AAW symposium, I still enjoy them immensely, but sometimes I feel that an "if it ain't broke, don't fix it" attitude can produce predictable and boring results. Maybe the AAW could look abroad for some new ideas.

Another way non-Americans offer input to the AAW membership is via the demonstrators who tour the country strutting their stuff for local chapters. Following in the footsteps of some amazingly itinerant American demonstrators, a few outsiders also have created almost full-time careers as touring hucksters. It may seem like a great way to live, but most will admit privately that it is very hard work. What the local chapters usually see is an enthusiastic turner with an interesting accent offering new insights and stimulus for their chosen hobby. What the visitors see is invariably kind people who generously offer their homes and hospitality, but there is an energy-sapping sameness about the experience that means few of these travelling turning wizards last more than a few years. Home and family responsibilities usually win out.

Good will, generous welcome

So what is it like for a foreigner to be at an AAW symposium? The overwhelming impression is of good will and generous welcomes, in a well-run environment. Americans are invariably kind to visiting turners and it is this, more than anything else, that always makes it a good experience. For me, the most important thing is the networking. I've learned that if you sit in one place long enough, every person you know or have ever wanted to know will probably pass by. Of course, the best place to meet and greet is in the bar after every day's events,

and foreign visitors tend to make the most of that. Even the newest of newcomers can find themselves sitting with their heroes, and I am sure many far away woodturning clubs are treated to snapshots of, "me and my friend David Ellsworth."

Just like the majority of American delegates, foreign visitors go home with notebooks overflowing and digital cameras overloaded with new ideas. Also, as a practicing turner, the trade show is as much a magnet for me as everybody else. I often think I should bring an extra suitcase to carry home the toys that are much cheaper in America. Seeing new ideas and then the tools with which to create them with is a real wallet-opener and I have to fight to control myself every year. Luckily, excess baggage rates help put a realistic ceiling on what I can spend.

For me, the AAW is a wonderful extension of my woodturning family. Each year as I travel to the U.S. for the annual gathering I know I am going to compress an outrageous amount of social value into the few days I am there. I will meet amazing new turners and refresh distance-strained old friendships. In the Instant Gallery and associated shows, I will see wonderful pieces of both turned art and traditional turning in what remains the largest single exhibition of woodturning in the world. Sometimes, I am even able to buy a rare piece of turned wood during the banquet auction. Once, I ended up taking home a piece I didn't want when I got caught trying to bid a piece up! I consoled myself with the thought that it all goes to a good cause. Every year I am particularly impressed with the army of volunteers who make all these wonderful things happen, both locally and nationally. They can never be thanked enough.

For those who are familiar with that wonderful film classic, *The Wizard of Oz*, you may recall that at the end of the film the Wizard says he is going to leave, "to confer, converse, and otherwise hobnob with my brother wizards." We all have something of the turning wizard in us, and this pretty much sums up my reasons for being a member of the AAW. Along with many other non-American members, I am eternally grateful for being accepted as a guest.

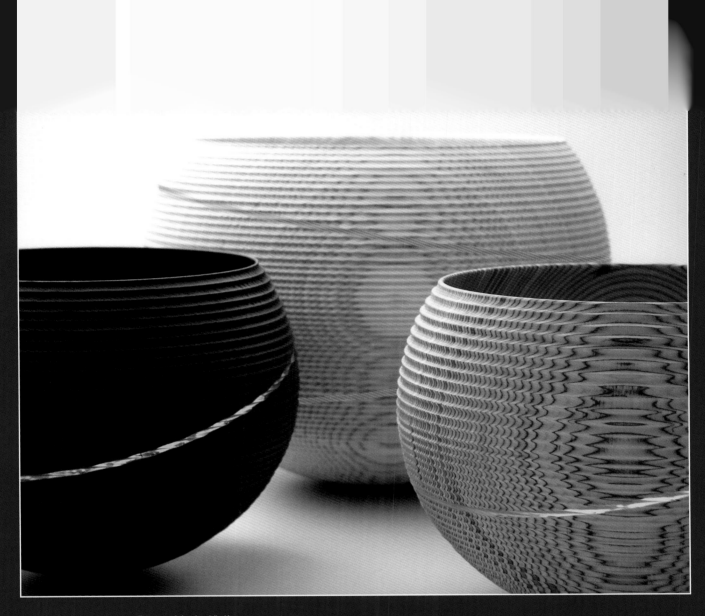

2007: Bowls, Jérôme Blanc, birch, 8" dia.

The annual AAW symposium is a kind of Mecca for woodturning artists from around the world. They come to learn, to gawk, and to meet colleagues, and every now and then a relative newcomer brings work that makes an instant impression. A recent example of that is young Swiss turner Jérôme Blanc, who is creating beautiful and unique pieces.

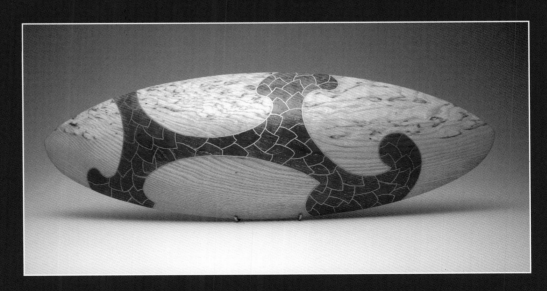

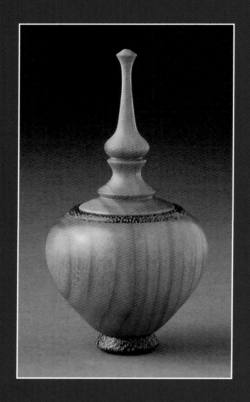

Kids can do it

Eric Johnson of Stillwater, Wisconsin, began turning at age 11 and was 13 when he made this beautiful lidded box, just 3.5" tall. Eric entered his work in the 2007 juried exhibition *Turning for the Future*, held at the American Association of Woodturners Gallery of Wood Art in Saint Paul. Kids who take up woodturning are an important part of the organization's future. Perhaps more important is the fact that training the hand also trains the mind. Kids who learn how to work with their hands grow up to think better than those whose manual training ends at the computer keyboard.

The Future: Introducing People to the Fun of Woodturning

Where do new woodturners come from? In the first half of the 20th century, many people were introduced to the lathe in middle school woodshop classes, and many of them are senior members of the American Association of Woodturners today. The association, in turn, sponsors and encourages ambitious efforts by local clubs to teach young people the woodturning craft. There's also a great thirst for instruction among younger adults who were not introduced in school and who through club membership are now experiencing, for the first time, making something by hand.

Lessons Learned

Coaching high school turning students

Jim Rodgers

For the last three school years, five members of the Bay Area Woodturners Association (BAWA) have been coaching woodturning at two high schools in our area. Although many of us have taught introductory lathe and turning classes to adults and young students, helping teach in a high school shop is another story.

The high school environment requires different thinking. We learned that chopping lathe time into small bites—about 35 minutes for each class period, spread over six weeks—requires a lot of organization.

From our experiences, we have developed guidelines for what our chapter members may expect with most students.

Even though we teach knowledge and skills, our target is a completed project. Regardless of how the first project looks, we celebrate the successes and evaluate the positive aspects. We invite student input on what they might do differently the next time.

The positive experiences throughout the year conclude with successful open houses at each school. During the day, school is dismissed early so shop students can show their projects to classmates. Then in the evening, parents come to the school to view the student work. Proud? You bet!

One step at a time

When teaching new students, we always start with spindle work to give them a basic understanding of the lathe, tools, and body motions. This engages the new turners safely while assessing their abilities to assimilate new techniques.

We get right to a project—no practice pieces. First up: a bud vase. Each student selects a pleasing profile from several models and begins turning down a square with a spindle roughing gouge. For the first week, the coaches sharpen the tools.

We provide basic, simple, and brief instructions with a little background suitable for the students' attention spans and desires to "get on with it." We resist the temptation to provide more turning information than they can absorb.

We give instructions for one step, allow the student to practice, deliver new instructions, and start again. For example, all instructors agreed in advance to teach just one method of turning a bowl interior (a simple three-part process to avoid catches). We don't reveal advanced methods of using a tool until the second or third project.

Defined work process

Being clear seems easy, but there are several aspects that must be managed, starting with the coach's role in the classroom. This is clarified with the school's shop teacher before the semester begins. For example:

- What should I do if I see a student in another area creating a safety issue?
- What is my role in the cleanup at the end of the class session?

Before we started a new program last fall at Las Lomas High School, Jacques Blumer, Brad Adams, and I had four planning meetings (about 10 hours total) with Pat Blank, the shop teacher. During an additional work session, Pat turned a bowl with us.

Since all school students must receive a letter grade, we discussed how the turning unit would fit into the semester grades.

We also got the students' buy-in to complete the six-week turning rotation. (The shop teacher selects the students based on interest).

Because two turning coaches work with the same students, we assured the school district and shop teachers that we would be in concert on how we described activities, which techniques would be demonstrated, and the specific steps in a project.

And to make sure we were on the same page, Brad and I spent four hours at the lathe on the bowl project to make sure we didn't confuse students with conflicting instructions and techniques.

Be flexible

We schedule two coaches at each school: one at the beginning of the week (Tuesday and Wednesday) and one later in the week (Thursday and Friday classes). The first member sets up the activity and expectations for the week, and the second corrects, adjusts, and supports. Although we don't see each other at the schools, Brad and I talk at least twice a week about our students.

Our experience has taught us to roll out new information, behaviors, and techniques in small, repeatable segments and only at the specific time that the information is needed. Because students can forget information over a weekend, we introduce new skills on Monday or Tuesday.

Projects rarely go as planned. Holidays, teachers' meetings, and special assemblies interrupt the schedule. Equipment breaks or is not available, and students

may choose to focus on another, more urgent activity. Flexibility within the process is a must and requires constant communication between the shop teacher and coaches so everyone stays on schedule.

The planned activity must fit into the available time frames. In a 50-minute class, the time needed for attendance, announcements, and cleanup leaves about 35 minutes in the average class period. This is worth repeating: Plan on 35 minutes of actual turning in each class period.

We've been reminded that all students will not progress at the same rate. The more advanced students may need to be redirected to another activity while others catch up. We've worked around this by providing advanced students with the opportunity to help with sharpening and equipment maintenance.

Brad and I feel fortunate. Some students spend their lunch hours in the shop, and the parents have embraced the lathe program with fund-raisers and contributions.

Pat Blank, the shop teacher, couldn't be happier. Although he knew little about woodturning when he met us, he's eager to expand the program. This summer, he completed a one-week class for woodturning instructors at Craft Supplies in Provo, Utah.

Jim Rodgers was president of the Bay Area Woodturners Association. He lives in Martinez, California. From American Woodturner, *Winter 2006.*

Back to School

Tips for introducing turning to your local school

Jacques Blumer

As many woodturners and woodworkers are keenly aware, high-school shop programs are disappearing for many reasons, including lack of equipment, lack of funds, space demands, or lack of turning knowledge by shop teachers. Indeed, some schools have closed their woodworking programs altogether.

In 2002, the AAW awarded a $1,000 Educational Opportunity Grant (EOG) to the Bay Area Woodturners Association (BAWA) to develop a turning program at Campolindo High School in Moraga, California. The program was a great success. As the word spread, the BAWA was invited to set up a similar program at Las Lomas High School in nearby Walnut Creek.

Here are some of the lessons we have learned from our youth training programs:

- You don't need to be your chapter's best woodturner or the best instructor to teach young students. You do need to be a competent turner and teacher, but other qualities are far more important. Working with and relating to young people requires an easy-going personality, flexibility, a sense of humor, and lots and lots of patience. Being structured and consistent is important.

    When more than one instructor is participating in the program, constant communication between teaching sessions is essential for continuity. "Winging it" isn't an option for these classes.

- Every program needs someone who has the vision, drive, and enthusiasm to make it succeed. Your chapter may have many willing participants, but you need at least one leader to assume responsibility.

    Coordination, planning, scheduling, and other support activities will demand as much time as teaching the students. There will be critical decisions to be made or occasions where a leader needs to take charge and provide direction or develop a consensus among members.

Many certified industrial arts (shop) teachers are skilled wood workers, but few we've met have lathe experience. Take time to train the teacher in private sessions. Encourage him or her to attend chapter programs (many chapters waive dues for high school students and instructors). Also remember that the AAW waives the registration fee for the annual symposium for all youth instructors. And if your mini- or regional symposium isn't already making a similar offer, it should.

Many schools around the country have turning programs with lathes and tools that are 30 years behind the current technology. These programs need financial support so that instructors have the right equipment with which to teach and students have the right equipment to complete projects.

At our two high schools, more than $20,000 in lathes, tools, and supplies has been invested in the last three years. Think about the combination of resources available: EOG grants, general and special school funds, parent clubs and individual parent donations, holiday fund-raisers, support from your local turning club, and grants from outside organizations. Be creative and think big.

I recently spoke to Christian Burchard, who volunteers at a local school in Ashland, Oregon. He said that he gets back so much more than he puts in that he can't understand why everyone is not doing something to prepare the next generation of turners. (On page 211, read Christian's story about one of his students.)

When we started our program in the Bay Area, Jim Rodgers said, "If we make a difference in one teenager's life, I will be satisfied with our effort."

Jacques Blumer is a studio turner, instructor, and demonstrator in the San Francisco area. From American Woodturner, Winter 2006.

VOICES

Christian Burchard: teaching Dan to turn

I live in Ashland, a small southern Oregon town. When my own kids entered high school, I volunteered to help in the shop classes. I was received with open arms and started coming into the shop two to three times a week.

Most of the kids will just turn one or two bowls and then return to their other wood projects. But a few of them get hooked. Dan was one of them.

A couple of years back, when I first met him, Dan seemed a bit hard and angry—troubled, I assumed. He was not easy for me to work with. Dan demanded a lot of time, and I couldn't keep him off the lathe.

He began spending more and more time in the shop. Then Dan actually started showing up on time for class!

The technical skills he acquired within that first year were amazing—salad bowls, balls, and hollow forms.

In an article for a local newspaper, Dan admitted that he had been close to dropping out. Today, he seems so much happier, and to watch him working on the lathe is a delight— all intent and so much willingness to learn. Oh, you should have seen that glow of pride after selling his first piece!

Dan's requests to be challenged and his acceptance of failure are mature. I can now ask him to help others when they need help. And I can see how much respect he gets from the rest of the class. He even stands taller now.

Last year, Dan's parents bought him a small lathe, and he adds tools as he goes along. His senior project for graduation was entirely turned work.

Will he become a woodturner? Who knows? It doesn't really matter. Dan is learning things that will not be reflected in grades or SATs. The ability to envision an object, then create it. The pride of knowing how to use a tool well. The satisfaction of making something with his own hands.

There are a few more students like Dan in these classes, and we have become friends. We have something in common.

For more of Burchard's work see pages 138 and 151.
From American Woodturner, *Winter 2006.*

2006: Kids rough-turn green-wood bowls during one semester, then after the wood dries, the next class turns the blanks into finished bowls.

Twenty of Everything

John Hill

For many years, the constant worry expressed by AAW members and chapters was, "We are just a bunch of retired people. Where will our future turners come from? How can we get kids involved?"

While on the AAW board and as chair of the chapters and membership committee, I had persuaded several lathe manufacturers to offer special deep-discount pricing on lathes sold to chapters that would use them for demo or teaching. In a conversation with John Otto, the marketing manager of WMH Tool Group, the U. S. importers of JET and Powermatic lathes, I mentioned that our members would love to get kids involved in turning, and John said he would be interested in some program if we could put it together. We proposed having kids invited to attend our symposium for free and setting up a room just for them. We would need about twenty lathe stations. I said that the AAW did not have anything in the budget to purchase the lathes and that storing them from year to year and continued shipping to new symposium locations would present a problem. I asked for a really deep discount. John said he would talk to his managers and get back to me. When we next spoke, John said that WMH Tool Group would donate the lathes. He said that it would be more economical to give the lathes to the kids than to take them back and hold them till next year and re-ship to another symposium.

I was super excited with this prospect, and armed with this proposal from WMH, I contacted Teknatool International and asked for Nova midi-chucks. They said sure, they were on board. Then Brian Gandy of Crown Tools offered twenty tool sets of seven tools each. Woodcraft Supplies agreed to furnish twenty face shields. Now I was like the little dog that chased the garbage truck. Once he catches it what does he do with it?

We needed a famous turner to teach the youth classes. I called Bonnie Klein, since I knew that she had long been teaching kids on her small Klein-design lathes. When Bonnie answered the phone, I told her about the concept of a youth room and told her of the donations,

and I wanted to know if she knew anyone that could teach kids on small lathes. She burst out laughing and said that was the most subtle question that she had ever heard. She said of course she would do it. Bonnie needed a co-teacher, and Nick Cook agreed, saying he was excited to be on board.

Now I had to present my proposal to the rest of the AAW board for approval. I proposed that all kids age 10 through 17 be admitted to the symposium free ($245 value) if they were accompanied by a registered adult. The board voted unanimously to proceed with the youth program at the Overland Park symposium in 2005. Gary Lansinger was the board person in charge of the room. We asked the Northland Woodturners to help as teacher assistants in the youth classes. They did a great job and loved it. They even received and set up the lathes. For the first couple of years, Bonnie stayed up till the wee hours sharpening the tools. For the past couple of years, the tools have been sharpened by the local clubs.

We put out the call for kids in *AW Journal* and in emails to the chapters. Bonnie saw that we needed to be really organized so that each kid would have an equal chance to be in their classes of choice, so she had all registrations sent to her, and she completely organized the classes on her own. We had 55 registered kids attend and every rotation was packed with a waiting list. For each rotation, we had a project taught by a designated teacher assisted by many volunteers—nearly enough for one-on-one with each student.

We had the drawing for the 20 complete lathe/chuck/tools/face shields stations, and 20 of the kids went home with free outfits. All of the donor vendors were very excited about the program and wanted to sign up again for the next year. They have been doing it ever since, with 25 lathe stations, and it looks like it has become a an ongoing event at every symposium. In 2007, Paulo Marin of CET, Inc., gave a complete tool roll containing six tools to each youth registered, not only the lathe winners. Now we know where the future turners will come from!

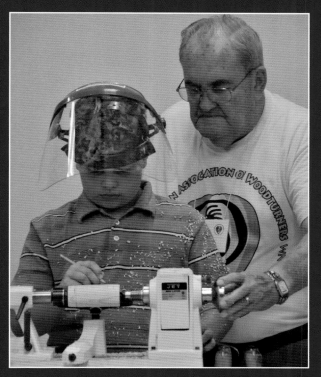

The grandfather experience

It would be difficult to say who has more fun at symposium youth turning events—the kids, or the instructors.

Turning for the Future

In 2007 the AAW organized an international juried exhibition of work by turners younger than 22. The jurors selected 64 pieces by 48 young turners for display at the AAW Gallery of Wood Art in Saint Paul.

Jason Mast, age 20, Pacific Rim, big leaf maple. Mast lives in Reedsport, OR, and plans to become a professional woodturner.

FAR LEFT: **Stephen Nachreiner, age 20, Cherry stool.** A class project at Indiana University of Pennsylvania.

LEFT: **Lara** and **David Lutrick**, a father-and-daughter collaboration featuring Lara's beadwork on her father's madrone goblet.

VOICES

Dave Bowers: the Young Turners program

About a week after the Overland Park 2005 symposium, I was on an airplane, flying home from work. As the peanuts and drinks were passed out, I was thinking about the youth turning room and how big a success it was. Nick Cook and Bonnie Klein had led the charge of numerous volunteers exposing kids to the joys of woodturning. It was a shame this large of an effort happened only once a year.

I also thought about many school systems that were losing their industrial arts, art, and music programs in the wake of tighter budgets and failed school levies. I truly believe this type of education leads to better-rounded adults. There had to be a way to teach more youth these skills. The rest of the flight home I brainstormed and ended up with a two-part system. The first phase was to attract the students to woodturning, get them excited about it, and have a completed project at the end of the day. Phase one would entice students to complete four more projects in phase two.

Although I met a few skeptics who thought kids were only interested in computers and electronics, most AAW members I talked with were very excited. Al and Sherry Hockenbery have many years of experience teaching youth to turn. At the time Al was on the AAW board and I worked with him to develop the Young Turners program. We decided to run the program through local chapters, and we invited other AAW members to participate by writing project tutorials, creating a teaching aid for each lesson.

The mission of the AAW is to provide education, information, and organization to those interested in woodturning. Many chapters have taken up the challenge of starting and maintaining youth woodturning programs. The ultimate goal would be for every AAW chapter to run a Young Turners program. This program is only a start. It is the cornerstone upon which to build and develop even more outstanding youth education opportunities.

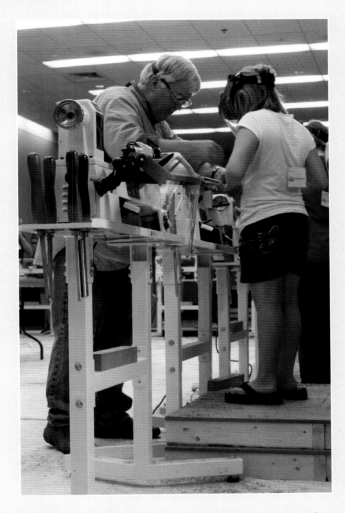

Nick Cook of Marietta, Georgia, helps a girl during youth turning at the AAW Richmond symposium, 2008. Sixty-six youngsters and forty-nine adult volunteers turned out for the event, allowing a 1:2 teacher-pupil ratio on twenty donated mini-lathes.

The kids catch on...

"One of the things I enjoy most is when the kids catch on to the idea that they can come in and fill the empty lathes during a rotation. Several of them attended many extra rotations, and one boy had a whole bag full of items he had turned. He was so-o-o excited!"
—*Bonnie Klein, youth turning coordinator, Richmond, VA, symposium, 2007. Photo by Andi Wolfe.*

VOICES

Sam Scalzo: youth classes are free

On a strictly volunteer basis, in the past few years, I have been involved in two woodworking high school classes teaching students how to turn on the lathe. This semester, the students have turned 100 pens for military men and women serving in Iraq. The local Woodcraft store has supplied all the parts for this project, so it has become a community effort. The students will soon start on another 100 pens. In addition to the pens, they have made bowls, keepsake boxes, and goblets. One of my future projects I want to accomplish will be to teach them how to turn Christmas ornaments as we get closer to the end of the year.

My experience is that I have been turning for 18 years with my first lathe being a Shopsmith. I now have two JET lathes with one being a mini-lathe which I take on my travels in a fifth-wheel camper. Each year I sell my turnings at craft fairs.

I am currently serving as president of the Southern Arizona Woodturners Association (SAZWA) in Tucson, Arizona. Our club makes toys for needy children at Christmas time. For many years we have made 1800 to 2000 toys. What a great joy we all receive to see the children when they receive one of our toys. Two years in a row, I made 85 keepsake boxes for a school to give to students going from fifth grade to sixth grade. When they say it is more blessed to give than receive, it is true.

Another pleasure I have is teaching classes in my shop—youth are free. Giving back to the community is very important to me, and this is my goal. Woodturning is becoming a lost art, and in my own small way I am trying to keep it going for the next generation.

Sam Scalzo teaches kids to turn at his shop in Tucson, AZ.

Starting a New School for Woodturning in New Jersey

Steven Butler

I love turning. I don't know much about it other than how to turn a basic spindle for a table leg, but I love it. I love the community woodturners have formed. I'm a studio furniture maker—a flat worker. I'm active in the field, I exhibit my work regularly, I go to most of the furniture conferences, and I occasionally teach at other craft schools. I am currently the department head of the wood studio at Peters Valley Craft Center, and as such, I set up a new woodturning program.

It is by teaching at other craft schools, such as Arrowmont School of Arts and Crafts, that I first became aware of just how tight and close the turning community is, much greater than is true of the furniture-making community. Or, at least it's different. I wanted to bring this feeling of community and enthusiasm back to Peters Valley. But like many schools, we suffer from government cutbacks to arts organizations and rely heavily on grants and donations.

In the summer of 2006, I had just moved from Worcester, Massachusetts, where I had spent the last year as department head of the wood studio at the Worcester Center for Crafts, to Layton, New Jersey, to work at Peters Valley. Both craft centers are not-for-profit organizations specializing in multi-media craft education. The Worcester Center for Crafts is all under one roof and located in a once-thriving industrial part of Massachusetts. Peters Valley sits in the serene Delaware Water Gap Recreation area with its campus spread over many miles. We offer workshops from mid-May to mid-September.

Peters Valley Craft Center

In 2006, when I moved into my home at Peters Valley, I literally dropped the boxes onto the floor and proceeded to teach the first workshop of the season. A month later, I drove to Gatlinburg, Tennessee, to teach a week-long woodworking class at Arrowmont. The facilities at Arrowmont are excellent. The woodworking studio and the woodturning studio are in the same building next to each other, separated by a gallery space. Everyone I met there was excited at what they were learning, and most couldn't wait to get back into the studios, especially the woodturners. Long after each day's class had ended, the students in the turning class would still be there practicing. There was a lot of infectious energy coming from the studio, and I caught it.

What a great community. I must admit, I was a little jealous. Michael Mocho, a wood artist from New Mexico, was the turning instructor that week, and Graeme Priddle, from New Zealand, was an assistant. Graeme had taught the week prior and stuck around an extra week to help out. No wonder there was so much fun and energy coming out of the studio with those two at the helm. I remembered in Worcester how well the adult education woodturning classes did compared to all others: they always seemed to fill. Turning is not only fun, but is also good business.

So there I was, only a month and a half into my new position at Peters Valley, and I'm wondering what I can do to increase enrollment. That's it! I'll start woodturning at the Valley. It seemed easy enough. All I needed was to get some lathes and hire a teacher.

I said to Graeme, "Why don't you teach a workshop at Peters Valley next summer?"

We talked about it for a bit, shook hands, and it was a done deal. I taught my class, drove back to New Jersey and continued on. Late fall, I got an email from Graeme: "Listen—I just realized you hired me to teach a turning class, but you don't have any lathes. Oh well, we'll make it work." Graeme was right. I don't know if I was confidant, cocky, or crazy, but I got caught up in the energy, and it hasn't stopped since.

In 2007, we were generously given six JET mini-lathes and borrowed two more to make Graeme's class run. His class filled in the first week registration opened: a great compliment to Graeme and also a testament to the popularity of woodturning. Each evening of Graeme's five-day workshop, the studio was full of eager and energetic students. The sense of community was terrific, each student helping and encouraging the other, creating a great learning environment.

In the fall of 2007 Peters Valley received a generous donation of equipment, including nine new Oneway lathes and accessories. It has been my vision to create a separate woodturning center at Peters Valley, operating on its own, offering a full curriculum of workshops. This was a great start.

In the spring of 2008, we started a local chapter of the AAW, Watergap Woodturners. We meet the first Wednesday of each month at the wood studio at Peters Valley Craft Center. I joined the AAW myself, even though I'm not much of a turner. I used the resource directory to get in touch with members from New Jersey to spread the word about our new club. The club is already thriving because turning is popular, and there wasn't another group close to this area of northwest New Jersey.

I must admit, I'm hooked. I look forward to each meeting, the show-and-tell sessions, the demos, the camaraderie. This energy is what first engaged me at Arrowmont and still engages me now. It's all about the lure of woodturning and the sense of community it creates. I can't wait for next season, to see old friends and make new ones.

Back to summer school...

Anderson Ranch Arts Center
Snowmass Village, Colorado
970-923-3181 or www.andersonranch.org

Appalachian Center for Craft
Smithville, Tennessee
615-597-6803 or www. tntech.edu/craftcenter/

Arrowmont School of Arts and Crafts
Gatlinburg, Tennessee
865-436-5860 or www. arrowmont.org

Canyon Studios
Copper Canyon, Texas
940-455-2344 or www.canyonstudios.org

Center for Furniture Craftsmanship
Rockport, Maine
207-594-5611 or www.woodschool.org

John C. Campbell Folk School
Brasstown, North Carolina
800-365-5724 or www.folkschool.org

Maine Woodturning School
Damariscotta, Maine
207-563-2345 or www.woodturningschool.org

Marc Adams School of Woodworking
Franklin, Indiana
317-535-4013 or www.marcadams.com

Peters Valley Craft Center
Layton, New Jersey
973-948-5200 or www.petersvalley.org

...or for a college degree

Center for Turning and Furniture Design
Indiana University of Pennsylvania,
Indiana, Pennsylvania
724-357-2530 or www.iup.edu

VOICES

Al Tingley: EOG grant helps turn kids around

I applied to the AAW in 2005 for an Educational Opportunity Grant (EOG) to fund a woodturning program at the Johnson Youth Center (JYC) in Juneau, Alaska. The JYC houses juveniles who are experiencing difficulties in their lives.

I had some difficulties in my own life that resulted in my early departure from the public school system. My desire to take shop classes was one of the major influences in my dealing with my issues. Fast forward to 2005 in Juneau, Alaska, and

Kids learn to turn tops and bowls at a juvenile facility in Juneau, AK. From American Woodturner, *Fall 2009.*

the Johnson Youth Center. The kids housed there also have had difficulties in their lives. Their opportunities for shop or any other hands-on classes are limited. Knowing that woodworking provided me with the resolve to improve my situation, I approached the teachers and staff to get their thoughts on bringing sharp pointed objects into the facility to teach woodturning. They welcomed me with open arms.

The true benefit from this grant is providing young men an appropriate adult male role model. On the surface that may not sound like much, but these kids have not had the same opportunities as youths whose families are doing well. Some have no active father figure in their life, some struggle academically because of learning impairments, and some have

little sense of self-worth. By volunteering my time and talents, I demonstrate my belief that they are worthwhile.

This isn't a project for the everyday woodturner. Working with kids is a challenge, and working with troubled kids compounds that challenge. Working in a locked facility can be intimidating for the uninitiated. I have gone into the local adult prison here for years to referee basketball and play softball, so I was familiar with the sound of that metal door closing behind me.

I used the EOG grant to buy the equipment for the project. Like all woodturners, I enjoyed the thrill of buying new tools! I quickly burned through the $1,000, but fortunately a grant such as the EOG provides a strong base from which to approach other sources for funds. The Rotary Club of Juneau provided $450 and the teacher at JYC has been able to fund materials.

I've had teaching experience, so I understood the saying, "a person quickly finds out how well they know a subject when attempting to teach it." I made sure my instruction was project-orientated, and I picked projects well within my comfort zone: a top and a small bowl. The boys have to pass a written test on the parts of the lathe before they are allowed to actually start turning.

Recently, Bob Winter, a fellow member of the Tongass Turners, joined me for a pen-making day at the JYC. It was early December, so the timing was good for the boys to make something to send home. We kept the three lathes humming, and all of the participants were able to complete a pen. The boys spent the rest of the day showing off their pens to the staff. It was a highly successful day.

So far, I have had 57 boys go through the woodturning program. They have each completed a top and a bowl. It would be nice to give the boys more turning opportunities but time, both theirs and mine, is limited. And frankly, it is good to see most of them leave the facility before their turn comes up again. This project proves that a lot can be accomplished with minimal overhead and a little determination.

Al Tingley is a fisheries biologist with the Alaska Department of Fish and Game. He and his wife have four kids of their own.

VOICES

Rick Orr: KidSpree is summer's hottest weekend

Pete Holtus got the Front Range Woodturners Chapter of the AAW involved in KidSpree five years ago, when he was contacted by the city of Aurora, Colorado. Since that time, the group has turned, colored (actually the kids do the coloring), and given away over 5,000 turned wooden tops. That number includes the July 2009 event at Bicentennial Park.

KidSpree is Colorado's largest outdoor festival just for kids. Admission and all activities are free to the local kids. KidSpree focuses on the local kids from Aurora, but keys in on those families that are less privileged.

Our club, which is based in Denver, begins preparation of top blanks in February each year, followed by the volunteers pre-turning the tops in advance of the festival. 1300 tops were "pre-turned", and another 250 blanks were turned at KidSpree in 2009.

Top blanks are made out of birch dowels with scraps of poplar, soft maple, or alder. Once the blanks are all glued up, the turning begins using a mini-lathe, a small dowel chuck, and a revolving cup in the tailstock. A small roughing gouge plus a spindle gouge is all the tools needed for the actual turning.

The kids then color the tops with art pens while the tops are turning on the lathe. To keep the kids moving along, they are limited to the choice of three colors. This is all done under the close supervision of the AAW chapter volunteers.

The KidSpree is scheduled each year in mid- to late July. Members of the group are often asked, "When is KidSpree?" The reaction is always the same. "It's the hottest weekend of the summer."

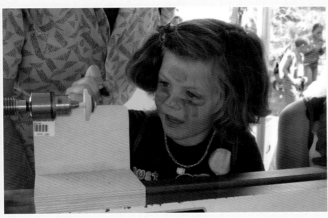

Turning became my passion...

I have long been an avid woodworker and when my wife and I bought our first house I began amassing tools for my shop. In January 1999 I acquired a lathe, about which I knew almost nothing, but I thought it would be useful for making table legs, and as a musician I thought I might even be able to make my own drumsticks. Turning soon became my passion as I watched shapes in wood transform before my eyes. This was totally unlike any other experience I had had working in wood. Furniture projects required measured cutting and assembly, and it took a long time to see a finished project. With woodturning I could see a finished project within a single session! How great is that? I soon discovered the AAW and joined Silicon Valley Woodturners. Woodturning has become a big part of my life. It isn't just a hobby, it's an entire community. And by the way, I finally did turn some drumsticks.

—*Jim Gott, San Jose, CA*

SECTION VII

Our Stories

While preparing this book, the editors invited members of the American Association
of Woodturners to write short essays telling about their adventures in woodturning,
how they came to the field, and what it means to them. The project closes with
a representative selection of those stories.

Binh Pho: dreams and mentors on the journey

It was February 1992, and destiny had led me to a new life in the United States. It was a dream come true, or the culmination of many dreams, as I was reunited with my family, living in a land of freedom and limitless opportunity. As an amateur woodworker, I attended a local woodworking show and wandered into a slide presentation showing how the lathe could be used to create vessel forms. I watched as John Jordan discussed his work and for the first time, I saw the potential of woodturning as an art form. I purchased a lathe, took it home, and began working with it.

I soon realized it wasn't easy and that the lathe hadn't turned those beautiful vessels. John Jordan had. Seeking to learn more about woodturning, I attended a four-hour introductory class taught by the late Leonard "Fletcher" Hartline at a local Woodcraft store. Soon after that initial course, I was taking private lessons from Fletcher. As the years passed, we spent a great deal of time working and traveling to symposiums together—I had traveled halfway around the world to meet my best friend.

Like a maestro who instructs his students to practice scales for months, Fletcher had me practice the same processes again and again on the lathe. He never claimed to be an artist, but had taught many artists the craft. The technical abilities I gained have served me well, and I was inspired by the work of other wood artists to seek out new approaches. The process of learning to work with wood took me to symposiums across the U.S. Fletcher had learned the craft from Del Stubbs, and we traveled to Akron, Ohio, to attend Stubb's last mini-symposium. I spent the whole day learning from Stubbs and feel very fortunate to have had the experience.

John Jordan (page 50) is the reason I wanted to become a woodturner, but Fletcher Hartline and Del Stubbs are the ones who trained me as a craftsman. In my opinion, they are the two best teachers I could have had in the woodturning world.

Binh Pho power-carves a thin-walled vessel.

My path took another turn when I met Michael Hosaluk in 1995 and the late Frank Sudol in 1996 (page 139). These two Canadian artists prompted me to explore color on woodturning and to pierce the vessel with a dental drill. In 1998, I was in the same ACC show with Michael Mode, and he pointed me toward finding my own voice. Ultimately, these three led me down the path to becoming an artist. I also made what turned out to be an important decision in not becoming a full time artist, but instead maintaining a professional career that guaranteed I would never have to compromise my artistic vision to satisfy the market.

The American Association of Woodturners and its mission of sharing knowledge has been an important part of my journey. I joined the AAW in 1993 and my first national symposium was in Purchase, New York. I have had many teachers and mentors, and my journey has led me to become a mentor and teacher myself. Beyond techniques and creative approaches, there is something I seek to share with those I meet on my path—that they must dare to dream and then to follow these dreams. It is what I have always done, and my dreams continue to lead me along my path as a woodturner toward my destiny.

2008: Secret Garden, box elder, maple, acrylic paint, 11" high.

Joey Richardson: my journey

I grew up surrounded by trees on a small farm within the heart of Twigmoor Woods in Lincolnshire, England, where my love for wood, nature, fauna, and flora developed. I started turning in 1993, taking classes with Chris Stott and Stuart Mortimer. In 2002, my passion for woodturning evolved into a full-time profession, and I was accepted onto the Register of Professional Turners, which is supported by the Worshipful Company of Turners of London*. In 2005, I was fortunate to be awarded the company bursary.

Being a woodturner can be a very lonely life, especially in England where wood is not readily accepted as art. Winning the bursary award altered that by giving me the opportunity to travel to America and train with Binh Pho. Unbeknown to him, I had been inspired by his work for many years.

My journey, kindly sponsored by the AAW, started with the AAW symposium in Kansas City. I was blown away by the sheer size and diversity of the whole event. I then spent two days with Trent Bosch and two days with David Nittmann. Just when I felt I was overflowing with inspiration and technical details, my three intensive and most inspirational days with Binh Pho arrived.

Binh taught me to refine my traditional methods by combining new, exciting innovative techniques: piercing, color, and texture. More importantly he taught me the importance of creating from my inner self. He showed me how to add my story and my heart into my pieces, transforming my craft into art, giving me the confidence to be free and spontaneous with my work.

Dreams, memories, and passion are now incorporated into all of my work, I feel excited and fulfilled as each unique piece of turned wood comes alive under my hands, allowing the viewer to see into the life of the piece. Each piece tells its own story, has its own heart; all are created with passion. The strength of my feeling for my family is integral with my passion for my work: we are interdependent, each inspiring the other.

Woodturning is one of our oldest and most traditional crafts, which I feel passionate to keep alive. I now teach and give demonstrations of turning, piercing, painting, and texturing, hoping to inspire others eager for turned wood art and utility items, raising each other's profile in a symbiotic relationship. This also fulfills the AAW mission statement that we should help each other grow through sharing technique.

Binh has given me lots of encouragement over the last few years as my work has been exhibited at major exhibitions, schools, symposiums, and galleries in both the UK and the U.S.A. Each year I try to attend the AAW symposium which continues to stimulate me, especially as I have been fortunate to be included in three of the AAW exhibitions.

2009: Kismet by Joey Richardson.

Joey Richardson pierces the turned shell.

Del Mano Gallery has been very supportive, taking on the risks of new unknown artists, giving me the chance to exhibit my work in their gallery, and in the prestigious SOFA expo in New York and Chicago.

The bursary award has turned my dreams into reality and reality into dreams.

*The Worshipful Company of Turners is 51st in order of precedence of the 107 Livery Companies of the City of London. Receiving its Charter in 1604, the Company succeeded the Guild of Turners whose origins are believed to date from late in the 12th century.

More information at www.turnersco.com.

Richard Raffan: I was never a hobby turner

When I decided to turn wood for a living, I reckoned that if I enjoyed the craft, all I had to do was develop good technical skills and marketing, and then I'd earn a decent living selling what I enjoy making. And that's what I've done since mid-1970, first in England, then, from 1982, Australia. Being the only turner juried into *The Craftsman's Art*, a seminal exhibition in London in 1973, was a great boost to my career as that led to my bowls being in a lot of major British exhibitions. I've been fortunate to have been in the right places at the right times.

Richard Raffan.

However, in 1970 I had to create a market for the one-off bowls I inevitably produced as a novice, but after two sales trips I got repeat orders and other retailers sought me out. I was turning utilitarian bowls, scoops, and plates that sold to kitchen shops, and I also sold a lot of delicate bowls, scoops, and boxes to craft galleries. I never needed to consign work, and that's why I've seldom had work in American galleries. Emigrating to Australia was risky business-wise, because I had to start over in a new environment, but fortunately that didn't take too long.

I began teaching in 1978 advising embryo craft businesses, but requests for turning workshops increased once I became a regular presenter for Dale Nish at the Utah Symposiums in 1983. Then after my *Turning Wood* book and video (Taunton Press) were published in 1985, demand took off. Teaching has only ever been ancillary to my woodturning business, but it's good to get out of the workshop for a few days or weeks every few months. I enjoy the teaching, and it's taken me to Kodiak Island, Finland, Norway, France, the Grand Canyon, and a lot of places in between. I've met a lot of very interesting people along the way.

In 1970 locating woodturning tools was difficult. There was no support, no peer group, nothing like the AAW. I had to develop my own techniques when the help available through an organization like the AAW would have been enormously beneficial.

Now, at a time when so much turning seems to rely on the wood or some technical gimmick for impact, I continue to regard turning simple forms the greatest challenge, because simple is never as simple as it looks.

2003: Boxes of African blackwood, Tasmanian leatherwood, Queensland rosewood, 3" max dia.

2008: Small bowls of gidgee and African blackwood, approx. 2.5" dia.

Michael Stafford: thank you, Richard

I started turning because of a picture of a turned box on the cover of a book.

The majority of my life in woodworking has been without a dedicated lathe. Flat woodworking was my sole interest until just a few years ago. I turned one bowl in shop class many years ago, a few spindles on my father's lathe, and turned some simple toy parts when my son was little.

I made jewelry, decorative, tackle and all manner of flatwork boxes until I discovered turning. I was enthralled with making boxes and entered my decorative boxes into art contests. Wanting to create artsy handles for some of those boxes is how I discovered turning.

I had a multi-purpose tool which had a lathe function, and I was trying to turn little decorative handles and finials with it and some clumsy oversized chisels better suited to roughing table legs. I decided to find some smaller turning chisels and while in a woodworking store came across the book *Turning Boxes* by Richard Raffan, with a most beautiful turned wooden box on the cover. It was the most beautiful thing I had ever seen. I bought the book and have been devoted to woodturning ever since.

Once I had a real lathe and chuck, I started turning boxes and I haven't looked back. I turn boxes almost exclusively and work toward the goal of turning as many different woods as I can into boxes. I also strive to turn as many different box forms as my skills will permit.

This hobby has provided me with opportunities that I would never have had in any other form of woodworking. I have been able to teach turning boxes at a woodworking school and at woodworking stores and have shared my love of wood turned boxes with many people. In 2008, the Richmond AAW Symposium provided the highlight of my turning life. I was able to meet Richard Raffan, whose little box pictured on the cover of a book changed my woodworking life. It was also in Richmond that for the first time I actually saw someone else turn a box except for those students I taught. Thank you, Richard.

Michael Stafford turns wood in England.

Lidded jar, koa, 3" dia.

Domed box, cocobolo, 3" dia.

Andi Wolfe: my neighbor Walt got me started

"What kind of woodworking are you doing?" my new neighbor asked my husband, Steve, as we were unloading a table saw from the moving van.

"I'm just the hired help, you'll have to ask my wife what she's into at the moment," he replied.

That was the beginning of my trajectory into woodturning. I live across the street from Walt Betley, a retired Army colonel who has been woodturning since he was 11 years old. He's now approaching 90 and still going strong. I had been learning how to make furniture. For the first couple of years in our new house, I was busy making bookcases, chests of drawers, side tables, and chairs. Walt introduced me to the local woodworking club, and I attended the half-day meetings with him every other month.

A couple of years later, a new woodworking store offered shop rental time and hands-on classes. One class project was a Shaker-style candle stand with a turned pedestal. The instructor was worried about novices using dangerous gouges or a skew, so I turned the pedestal using a round-nosed scraper. Not the most auspicious introduction to woodturning, but the project was a huge success nonetheless. I really enjoyed watching the shape emerge from the wood, and I decided, right then and there, to learn everything I could about turning. Walt thought that was a good idea. "You have a great eye for design—you'll be very good at it."

Walt became my go-to guy. He gave me a quick tutorial in his shop, convinced me to join the Central Ohio Woodturners, and pointed me toward information. I received a mini-lathe for my birthday in October 1999, which sat in the box until Christmas morning. There was a clunky, oversized package under the tree, and I imagined it was a rack of some sort for the kitchen. I wasn't real keen on opening it, but to my pleasant surprise, it was a starter set of turning tools. I rushed off to my basement shop, pulled the lathe out of the box, put a soft piece of wood between centers, and started practicing. It was love at first cut.

I took all my turnings across the street to let Walt see what I was making and to get his honest feedback. "You have some tear out here where you turned the corner." "You could do a bit more sanding there." "Don't be afraid to waste some of the wood—a bowl doesn't have to be shaped like a dog dish."

And so it went, week after week for several months until one day Walt handed back my bowl and said, "I don't have anything to say about this one. It's very nice."

Good neighbors are priceless.

2010: Acer Embrace, ambrosia sugar maple, 10" tall. Photo by Jerry Anthony, collection of Elizabeth York.

Rick Crawford: very open about sharing

After moving back to Florida, I got serious about woodturning and attended a hollow form class taught by AAW member Emory McLaughlin at Woodcraft in Jacksonville. I didn't finish my piece that day, because Emory started talking and showing me many different things well beyond what I came there to learn about. That piece sat unfinished in my studio for a couple of months until I came across AAW member Lynne Yamaguchi's website one morning. Her use of epoxy-encapsulated coffee grounds caught my eye, and I emailed her about the process.

She was very open to sharing the needed information, and I used that new-found knowledge to finish a hollow form piece. This piece, which I named Caffeine Series #1, has garnered lots of attention, and I will continue to use the process in various ways on successive pieces.

Caffeine Series by Rick Crawford.

Ken Dunlap: lifelong ambition for wood art

When I was contemplating retirement as a nuclear mechanical maintenance supervisor I decided to become a woodturner by using books, videos, and hands-on workshops. Wanting to go beyond turning functional items and working toward gallery quality and design, I attended workshops with some of the premier master turners of our time: Ray Key (boxes & bowls), André Martel (end grain lamps), and JoHannes Michelson (range rider wood hats).

I have been working with wood for over 45 years and now have the opportunity to work full time with one of five wood lathes in my studio. It has been my lifelong ambition to become a professional wood artist and wood designer, utilizing the versatility of wood as a medium.

Ken Dunlap with box elder vase at Anderson Art Center's juried show. Ken is wearing a wood hat he made of outback ambrosia maple, with a fish gel brim.

Mark Sfirri: candlestick turned on two axes

I began turning in college in 1974, using the lathe to make sculptural parts for furniture. In 1981, I accepted a teaching position in the Fine Woodworking Program at Bucks County Community College in Newtown, Pennsylvania, and it was there that I was first exposed to the larger world of turning. Several weeks into my new job, Albert LeCoff staged a major turning conference there. Turners from all over the world descended upon the college. Lathes were carted in, and the art department was transformed within a day. It was a Who's Who of presenters and participants.

The first AAW conference that I attended was in Philadelphia in 1988. That was a significant experience for me on several counts, including the exhibition of three of my pieces in the companion International Turned Objects Show and my introduction to Michael Hosaluk. Michael invited me up to Saskatoon in 1992 to be part of a conference that included Del Stubbs, Giles Gilson, and Richard Raffan. Michael and I began a series of collaborative pieces that resulted in a group exhibition the following year. Meanwhile, I was trying to figure out how I could be a part of the programming of an AAW event. I knew that building a piece of furniture was a laborious process and in no way fitted into the 90-minute format of a rotation. Upon my return from that conference, I was inspired to try something new. I thought that maybe I could turn a piece of wood on two axes and have the result look bent. It worked! The next step was to try to figure out what kind of functional object could utilize this concept. I decided on a candlestick and had a pretty good result on the first try. I had successfully (in my mind) created a totally turned piece that could be demonstrated and explained in the time span of a rotation. My plan was successful, too. In 1993, an image of the candlestick was displayed on the cover of the *AW Journal* and I was a featured demonstrator at the next conference.

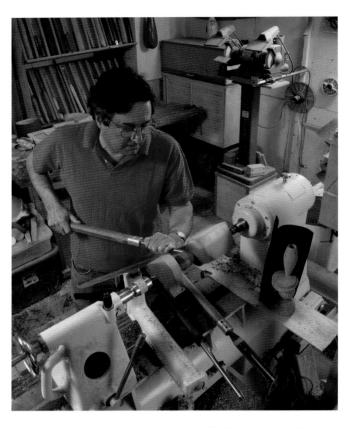

Mark Sfirri at the lathe in Bucks County, PA. Photo by John Carlano.

1993: Candleholder, multi-axis turning. Photo by Randl Bye.

JoHannes Michelson: my wood hats

I first had the idea to make a hat of wood in the early 1980s when I learned about water and wood movement and different shrinkage rates depending on how the log was sawn. I was reading a new book called *Understanding Wood* by Bruce Hoadley. In viewing the illustrations, it became clear that in turning an entire half log into a basic hat form, not only would the crown dry into an oval shape, but I would also enjoy some lifting of the brim at the sides. These facts caused me to think, "Hey I could turn a hat," but my immediate reaction was to dismiss the idea because my next thought was, "Who wants a wood hat?" It seemed all too ludicrous. But the seed was planted and seeds do tend to grow.

Almost ten years go by and I'm busy with my life as woodturner of more common items from the lathe, mostly spindles, because I am a professional stair builder and furniture maker, but also some bowls and vases which I sell at craft shows. All the while this seed grows in my head. The more I thought about this hat thing the more real it became, and it wanted out. Then came the kick, the catalyst, the reason to finally do it: Late in 1990 I received a wedding invitation from Albert LeCoff. He and Tina planned to enjoy a western wedding. It was like the big hand coming down out of the clouds and saying, "Turn the hat, stupid." So I made Hat #1 for the occasion and wore it to the reception, where it received rave reviews to say the least. That's when I knew I was on to something. That hat became their wedding gift and is now part of the permanent collection at the Wood Turning Center.

Wood hats have taken me around the world—several times. I've been around the U.S.A. and Canada many times and to Europe at least thirty times, down under twice and all I can say to that is, "Who knew"?

I have made 1685 numbered recorded hats, 2231 mini-hats, 497 sub-mini-hats, and 396 micro-hats. That's not counting the hundreds of hats made teaching, which I don't number. In all that teaching, I unavoidably created some new wood-hat makers, all of whom were told to go home, make hats, be happy, but please don't compete, "Hats are my thing." Lately I've changed my tune. I now feel that hats have become part of the public domain. I want to see this thing grow and prosper as a statement that "Almost anything that you would like to have a discourse about can come from the lathe."

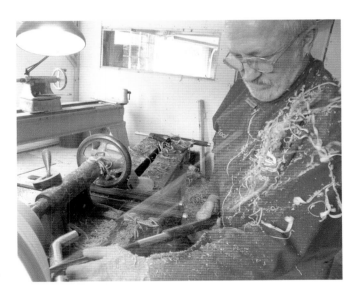

Michelson at the lathe.

1995: Breakthrough—first hat-band.

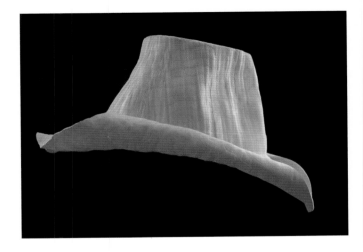

2009: Ghost Rider, bleached maple.

Joshua Salesin: ornamental turning resonated

I've always enjoyed making something from nothing: a song from an idle piano, an origami bird from a scrap of paper, and more recently, a bowl from a firewood log. I've always been attracted to unusual crafts and intriguing designs. And I've always been a hands-on kind of person. Woodturning, and specifically using antique ornamental lathes, brought all of these together for me in an alluring, challenging, creative outlet.

When I first discovered woodturning, I was exploring an urge to move from the two-dimensional field of computer programming to the hands-on three-dimensional realm of a creative crafts person. I was enthralled by simple tools that enabled turning a scrap of wood into a beautiful and perhaps useful object. Meeting other woodturners at my local AAW chapter provided vital resources and experience to hone my skills and realize this transition.

From my earliest woodturned pieces, I have been fascinated by surface design, experimenting with dozens of ways to affect texture, line, and light. When I discovered ornamental turning, I viewed it as just another technique for surface treatment. But with further exploration, I quickly realized it held much more—both the staggering array of promising embellishments as well as the potential for design of the objects themselves.

Ornamental turning resonated strongly with me as it combined a creative, hands-on endeavor of endless, intriguing possibilities with my interest in history, curiosity of how things are made, attraction to antiques, appreciation of fine workmanship, fascination with tools, and more. But I also credit the experience of attending the national AAW symposiums—not just the insightful lectures, instructive demos, and exciting exhibits, but also the interaction with a community of woodturning enthusiasts at all levels—for truly inspiring and challenging me to grow beyond the craft toward an artist with a unique vision.

Joshua Salesin at the ornamental turning lathe.

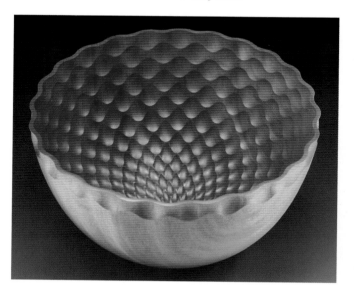

2008: Cosmic Burst Patternbowl.

Arnold Anderson: segmentation was new to me

I would call myself an ordinary woodturner. One needs to remember that your work needs to only satisfy yourself and that you strive to do the best that you can. That is the nice thing about this experience. Many woodturners do work far superior to the work that I do.

My woodturning experience began when I was 14 years old. We were fortunate to have industrial education in school. During that year we as students were introduced to the lathes, driven by line shafts. We were given a series of projects to turn and then as our final project, we were given the "ship wheel clock" project.

Segmented bowl by Arnold Anderson.

After high school, college and through my working years I never had the opportunity to turn again. It was not until 2002, unknown to me, that I would get back into turning. My wife and I decided to become snowbirds, and we traveled to Arizona and stayed at Mesa Spirit RV Resort. At the resort, one of the amenities was a wood shop. I became a member of the wood shop and was introduced to segmented turning, something completely new to me. The method used there to create segments was to laminate material together, alternating light-dark-light wood in one glue-up and in the other alternating dark-light-dark. Most of the bowls were made with twelve segments, so six segments were cut from the laminate of light-dark-light and six segments from the dark-light-dark. Vertical pieces were placed between the segments and a solid base was glued to the segment ring assembly. Shown here is the first segmented bowl that I constructed.

The equipment that we used to cut segments was crude compared to what I now have in my shop at home, although we were able to create bowls. I still have one of my first segmented turnings. Of course there were no chucks, just faceplates and screws. This experience got me hooked on segmented turning, and once I got home, I purchased my lathe, turning tools and the necessary equipment. Since my first bowls, I graduated into bricklay segment construction and began creating design rings.

Since 2002, I have turned over a hundred bowls and vessels, some of which have been sold, some given as gifts or to charity, and some are sitting on display in our home. Woodturning is a hobby for me. If I create one or many turned objects in the six months that we are home in Oregon, I am happy. Since I have my shop at home, I do not turn as much in our winter park, leaving the lathes open to new members who want to get involved in segmented wood turning. I keep on the lookout for new design ring opportunities. My current design is patterned from the design used in the sound barrier walls along US-60 between Mesa and Apache Junction. A definite line continues from one segment to the other. I am using a twelve segment ring for the design.

During the summer of 2007, I attended my first AAW symposium, in Portland, OR. I took in many of the presentations and participated in the Instant Gallery by having three segmented works there. I continue to keep up my membership in this organization and look forward to reading *American Woodturner*. I keep busy in my shop designing, building, and turning segmented work. Once in a while though, I have to put a solid piece of material in the lathe and turn something from that.

Ron Sheehan: neighbor gave me a small lathe...

I am currently president of the Susquehanna Woodturner's Club of Harrisburg, PA. Like many members, I was introduced to general woodworking and woodturning in high school shop class, in the mid 1950s. This is a path of introduction that I fear is being lost for our current young students. Many schools are cutting back on shop and other technical programs.

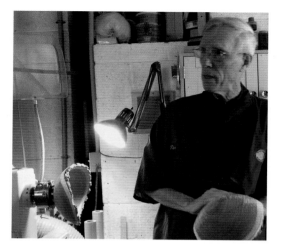

Over the years as my family grew in numbers, four kids, and size, I built many toys, tables, desks, and shelf units. I did not have a lathe and did no turning until 1997. My neighbor gave me a small lathe to thank me for doing him some favors.

This lathe had a 6-inch swing and 24-inch length. I used a spur center and small faceplate, and I turned some goblets and small ornamental items. It was quite a learning experience to try to teach myself tool technique, work-holding, and finishing.

The more I worked on the lathe, the more interested I became. I bought a used Ridgid lathe with 12-inch swing and 36-inch length. I began working on larger, more complex items.

I joined the Susquehanna club in 2003 and became hooked on turning. I have been able to greatly expand my knowledge and understanding of the woodturning process since then. All of our members are willing to share their processes and ideas.

In June 2007, I purchased a Powermatic 3520B lathe with 20-inch swing and 35-inch length. This is a very capable machine. I have been able to greatly expand the scope of the work I can produce.

Judy Ditmer: the bowls I make now...

When I began to turn, it was like coming home. The process captivated me from the first time I used a gouge. The wood peeling off of the spinning piece was as magical as anything I'd ever known. To this day, the thing I love most about turning is how direct it is and that it allows me to design and make a piece at the same time. I love how simple it is on one level: a piece of wood spins, and I cut it. I love how complex it is at another level: many years of experience leave me with very nearly as much to learn as when I started.

Bowls were my first love in turning, and I have never tired of them. Like turning itself, the form is fundamentally simple, and yet as complex as human understanding. To my mind, such a basic object, one we use every day without notice, has great authority. In its simplest form, two human hands cupped together, it does not even exist apart from use. It is use itself. In more substantial forms, its use lies in what is absent within itself.

The bowls I make now are intended for a different use: to compel notice; to expose the depth of an everyday object and to embody potential. They ask one to reconsider relationships among the parts of the bowl, and perhaps between ourselves and the objects we so often use without noticing them. They ask one to truly see this form again.

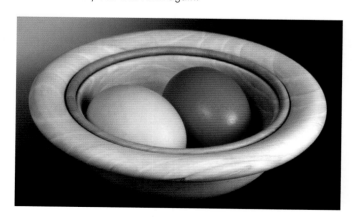

2007: Bowl with bleaching by Judy Ditmer, pear, 6" dia.

Cindy Drozda: my generation's turn to share

It's a new century, and we have a new generation of woodturners on the scene. These turners have had it easy. They haven't had to build their own lathes, forge their own turning tools, or cut down trees themselves to get wood. I put myself in that group. I am following, firmly and confidently, in the footsteps of woodturning's pioneers.

Cindy Drozda at her lathe.

I didn't have to teach myself how to turn. In the mid-1990s, I attended a five-day woodturning workshop and learned good basic techniques for turning and sharpening. I belong to a local AAW chapter and continue to attend classes, exposing myself to different methods and new ideas.

I hone my design skills with the tremendous resource of publications by and about contemporary artists in our field, by sharing ideas at symposiums, and by looking at other turners' work.

2006: Finial Box, narra. Photo by Tim Benko.

A wide range of lathes, tools, and beautiful wood, targeted just for the woodturning market, is now available. I have had total freedom to create the work that inspires me, from whatever material takes my fancy.

Through the innovations of woodturning's pioneers, we all know how to make thin-walled bowls, and hollowing a vessel through a small opening is not a mystery. As 21st century woodturners, we are free to use our energy to create artwork. Form and composition, rather than technical mystery, now define our work. Our turnings are judged as art, with their artistic merit being as important as their technical excellence.

That our turnings are referred to as "art" is a result of those pioneers having spent their working lives getting their work accepted into museums, galleries, and art shows. The pioneers have brought woodturning to a new level of excellence. They have pushed our field as far as they could in one generation. Now it is my generation's turn to push it further.

I didn't invent woodturning, but I give it my own style. My style of work proudly reflects the teachings of all who have shared

their knowledge with the turning community. I pass on to the next generation all of the pioneers' knowledge, along with everything that I have added to it.

Experiencing firsthand the benefits of starting where others have left off, I encourage new turners to use what I have to offer and incorporate it into their own style. As a new generation woodturner, I will pass on a new way to look at our field. I advise my students to embrace innovation and take advantage of technology. To me, woodturning isn't a traditional craft done the "old way," it is a new, creative art form where the sky's the limit. I encourage all of us to participate in the many opportunities for learning and sharing that exist in today's world of woodturning Our willingness to share is the best asset that we have and have always had. I hope that the next generation will value that as much as I do and will work hard to keep our collective ideas flowing and growing. When we share all, we all grow.

Onward, fellow woodturners, into the 21st century!

Maurice Clabaugh: revealing natural beauty

Once I had mastered the basics, I became inspired to focus on looking at the raw materials as closely as I had once observed my students. What was extraordinary in each one? What exactly was nature's handiwork that I could, through my skills, enhance and bring to attention, such features as knotholes, bark inclusions, colorations, and figures. Ultimately, I discovered a way to spotlight the beauty within each piece, and that satisfied my need to express myself.

My new turning style used only wood in its natural raw form, with all the blemishes included. I believed that wood remained a living object even after it is cut, so I attuned myself with its spirit. I dedicated vast amounts of time to harmonize with the spirit of the wood and visualized the basic form of each piece before I even turned on the lathe. I did not demand that the wood become what I patterned it to be, but rather, I tried to allow it to evolve as I worked with it. This metamorphosis helped me to reveal, to the world, the beauty that was naturally there, but hidden to the eye. I became passionate to highlight the blemishes rather than make them disappear. The opportunity to reveal the beauty in each piece and to preserve it so others might enjoy it became a sacred and contemplative experience. Through preserving the beauty of nature in my art form, I renew myself and hopefully those who observe my work.

Maurice Clabaugh, a retired business professor living in Tuscaloosa, AL, caught the bug in 1991 watching Knut Oland turn wood at an outdoor art fair.

Maurice Clabaugh strives to reveal the natural beauty in wood.

Lynda Smith-Bugge: sculpture for the soul

In 1975, right after college graduation, I accepted a dream job of teaching woodworking to New York City young people, who came for one week or more to experience nature, a small working farm, and woodworking in the beautiful Catskill mountains at Goddard-Riverside Camp. There was a lathe and shop in a stone-hewn barn by the pond. I had just graduated from Hunter College in New York City, where I majored in sculpture, fell in love with the college's woodshop, and with Henry Moore's designs and work with wood.

This dream job took me by surprise. Creativity flowed through me in a way that I had never experienced. I helped build the shop and set up work stations to explore the properties of wood. Over the next three years, I discovered lore and poetry about the trees around us. I also discovered burning qualities of specific woods for our 50 gallon heating barrel set up to heat the shop during cold winters.

My intense research with our surrounding trees led me to develop a multi-sensory program for city kids. I set up workstations for the kids to use all their senses to explore the properties of wood: hearing, sight, smell, taste, and touch. Hearing—how woods made different sounds in simple musical instruments; sight—how colors and textures are richly different in the abundant cherry, juniper, hemlock, maple, nut trees of the local area; smell and taste—how sassafras and sweet birch were used for food and medicine; and touch—how turned woods of the same size weighed differently according to the species.

One of the favorite stations in the woodshop was the lathe, where students turned a baseball bat from a local ash tree for their school back in New York City.

After three glorious years, the funding was cut. I went on to earn a degree in museum education at Bank Street College of Education. The forest was my museum, and the trees were part of the museum collection upon which I based much of my museum education program. Succeeding museum jobs continued in natural history and outdoor education. From directing a children's museum in Florida, I eventually brought my museum skills to various contracts at the Smithsonian, the Library of Congress, and Society of Woman Geographers.

In 1998, I came back to trees. It is as if I never left my first love. My first sculptures were juried into exhibitions in the Washington D.C. area. J. Carter Brown's (former director of the National Gallery of Art,) "Sculpture/Mixed Media" award for my sculpture "Mending," inspired me to continue creating sculptures. Along the way, I joined the Capital Area Woodturners (CAW), where I constantly learn new skills and receive much support. In 2003, CAW offered me a grant to Arrowmont, where I took a class with Christian Burchard. I am astounded by the creativity and excellence being done in the American Association of Woodturners. Although I consider myself more of a sculptor than a woodturner, I continue to use turned elements to balance or juxtapose an organic natural form.

After ten years of returning to my love for trees and my sculpture roots, I am ready to offer my sculptures to the world.

Mending, 32" x 16" x 16", cherry, walnut, copper, and plywood base.

Shirley Phillips: turning is a serious art form

My interest in woodturning is close and personal, for my spouse has retired into a workshop where wood shavings sail through the air as he holds a chisel to a huge chunk of wood just sawn from a tree. Sometimes he turns green wood, which sprinkles everyone within six feet with its fine sap, and again he may turn dry wood. The aroma in his workshop is always different, depending on the type of wood he turns. The aromatic cedar is wonderful, but the poplar seems to suggest old manure and straw in an earthy balm.

Bob can be found in his workshop from 7:30 in the morning till 5 or 6 in the evening. He can be recognized in his apron covered with sawdust, his red-neck cap pulled low over his eyes, and his pipe filled with aromatic tobacco. He is not a man of many words, but his woodwork speaks volumes. His turnings can be found in galleries throughout the eastern United States, in local art shows, and in his own workshop tucked away in the mountains of western North Carolina.

If you want to get to know Bob Phillips, just talk about woodturning, but be prepared to listen. Woodturning is his life!

Some of his favorite meetings have been the symposiums sponsored by the American Association of Woodturners (AAW) in various settings throughout the United States. These symposiums provide opportunities for all woodturners to enter their art work in the Instant Gallery, to purchase exotic wood and useful tools from vendors, to hear motivational speakers, to see exceptional demonstrators, to meet and talk with the crème de la crème woodturners, and to purchase the wood art of fellow members in the gallery or at the auction. These symposiums are so popular that many members apply a whole year in advance, and then add an extra week for vacation time to see and experience all the sites and activities that the new setting offers.

Bob Phillips is only one person who has taken woodturning as a serious art form; there are hundreds of others who are either turners or collectors. They love the shape, the feel, the color, the texture. Woodturnings seem to catch an emotion or an experience. Perhaps one day you, too, will catch the spirit of the wood lover.

Cherry burl, found metal, #467, 11.5" dia.

Maple burl, found metal, #437, 14.5" high.

Al Rabold: turned marquetry

I was an art major in high school. Though I worked as an engineer for 30 years, I always dabbled in various art forms, but none really stuck. I did some fairly serious home remodeling and cabinetry, but they where more out of necessity than inspiration. In the summer of 1997, I saw an ad for a woodworking show at Southern Lumber in San Jose, CA. My wife and I decided to attend. Little did I suspect that it, combined with my travels, would ultimately lead to my current life as a professional woodturner and sculptor on the beautiful island of Maui.

On entering the show, I was struck by a huge redwood sculpture. It was perhaps 18 feet tall and six feet in diameter. The base was a natural redwood log. The remainder was a male and female nude, each wielding a hammer and chisel, carving each other from the log. It was magnificent! I could feel the creative energy that gave it life.

Immediately inside, a gentleman was demonstrating spindle turning. I walked over just as he turned on his lathe. Fascinated, I watched as long ribbons of wood flew off his gouge, and a tapered cylinder grew from center to end. Variations in shape, beads and coves magically appeared as though opening in time-lapse photography. And the smell of the airborne shavings intoxicated me!

Next to him, another guy worked tagua nuts on a tiny homemade lathe. He was making a minute cocktail shaker about an inch tall. Next to him was a tray about two inches in diameter with eight minuscule martini glasses—get this—with captive rings around the stems! His gouges were fashioned from the miniature screwdrivers you buy to work on watches. He used an LED on the end of a wire to see inside his work and estimate wall thickness.

The ultimate experience awaited me in the courtyard—a turner making elegant bowls and fascinating boxes with lids so precise they popped when you slid them off. I returned to him during the day, and each time he patiently explained what he was doing and why. Finally, he asked me to try a few cuts—that was it!

Grace and beauty satisfied my artistic senses. Extreme precision mated nicely with 30 years of engineering. And, unlike furniture making that took loads of planning, jigs, fixtures, and forever to reveal the final product, turning provided near-immediate satisfaction. I was hooked. I had found the perfect hobby.

It took six months to find a lathe and tools that I could afford. Armed with those, a book by Richard Raffan, and whatever suitable chunks of wood I could find, I slowly taught myself to turn. My skills took a quantum leap after I met Linda Salter at

Al 'Alapaki' Rabold turns marquetry bowls in Kula, HI.

a neighborhood craft fair, and she hooked me up with the local AAW chapter.

In 1999, I moved to Maui and fell in love with its magnificent tropical flowers. I experimented with sculpting them in wood and soon combined them with my turning. I entered my first juried competition with a floral arrangement in a turned vase in 2001 and received an honorable mention. I started selling soon after. 2003 saw my first Best of Show for Laua'e, a sculptured vase. In 2005, I developed turned marquetry, a technique that has since become my signature work. Turning has become a part of who I am and brings me great joy.

Thanks to the AAW and all its members, both known and unknown, who shared their skills and enthusiasm. The only problem is, it takes loads of planning, jigs, fixtures, and forever...!

Steve Sherman: Bob Opdahl, patron of the art

After retiring from our jobs in New York City, my wife and I moved to the mid-Hudson valley in upstate New York. I was a graphic designer and she a biology teacher. My father was a cabinetmaker, and I inherited the love of wood from him. I spent many after-hours in a community workshop in the city, building furniture and musical instruments, and turning bowls on an old Sears lathe.

A hundred miles from the big city, I needed to find new, creative friends who would not mind sharing their love of wood art with me. I was soon to be overwhelmed by the generosity and love of a large group of passionate artisans squirreled away in the mountains of the Catskills.

I met Robert C. Opdahl back in the spring of 2001. Bob Opdahl was recommended to me as a woodturning guru by a woodworker I met at the hardware store. He said Mr. Opdahl taught a number of people how to use a lathe to produce wonderful pieces of artwork. I called the next day and introduced myself and asked if I might monitor a class. His response was to qualify me by asking what I had accomplished as a city boy. I said I had made some furniture and a banjo. He asked if it was built from scratch, and I said it was. His response was, "Be here by 9 a.m. tomorrow, and bring your banjo."

I arrived at 9:00 sharp at the woodturning shop and introduced myself to Bob. He asked if I had the banjo, I said it was out in the car. He introduced me to four people one at a time with background information about each one, Gary, Lois, Jerry, and Lee. They all smiled and welcomed me. Bob then showed me work by his students, proudly displayed on shelves, and discussed the merits of each piece.

"So, where's your banjo?" he asked.

"It's out in the car," I said.

"So get it," he said.

I brought in the case and put it down on a table and gestured for him to open it. He stepped back and told me to open it, he looked inside and immediately turned to Gary and said, "Tell this guy to get out of here, we can't teach him anything he doesn't know already."

I was not used to his sense of humor and asked once more if I could please just monitor a class and I would not bother him anymore. His response was, "You start tomorrow, bring your apron."

Viola and Bob Opdahl, Hudson Valley patrons of the woodturning arts.

Bob and his charming wife, Viola, live in an old stone and wood frame farm house in Hurley, New York. The estate was made famous in 1982 when it was the site for the farm scenes of the movie "Tootsie." The 345-year-old farm has been kept in pristine condition since 1971, when Bob and Viola acquired it.

Bob is a former IBM engineer and Viola a retired history teacher. The couple have many passionate interests, including raising exotic free-range chickens, egg sculpting and decorating, cooking, woodturning, and publishing a comprehensive book on the life and music of the Shakers in America.

A true country gentleman, "Saint Bob" as Matt Clarke, president of the Kaatskill Wood Turners Association, fondly calls him, is revered by more than 100 members for his knowledge and experience. A few years ago, Bob and Viola generously offered an outbuilding to the group to develop an "Institute of Higher Turning." The only caveat was to keep the exterior of the old barn as it had been for ages, but to alter the interior as we saw fit.

The members accepted the gift and proceeded to make plans for the new interior. The talent and exuberance of the membership reminded me of worker bees, each performing intricate tasks that shortly transformed the farm building into a modern workspace, teaching facility, and lecture hall. The program of workshops and informative lectures developed by the club have led to wonderful artistic experiences and personal growth. Bob and Viola's generosity and sharing will long be appreciated by a group of very grateful people.

Mike Kornblum: I made a living turning

I had always piddled around in my garage with a few hand tools making small projects around the house. I subscribed to *Popular Woodworking* and in 1990 there was an issue with an article on how to turn weed pots from logs. I had no lathe and had never used one, but the Air Force (I'm retired AF) in Southern California where I had lived at the time had a wood hobby shop with a lathe. After finding an oak log, I headed to the hobby shop with my *Popular Woodworking* book and my log.

The shop manager helped me get started on what turned out to be a really bad lathe. Only one speed worked, and it was the high speed, and the tailstock required a stick in the wheel to keep it from backing out. I mounted the log on a faceplate and turned on the lathe. It started walking across the room. I had to stop the lathe and try and recenter it. After about three times, I was able to take a tool to it. I had no idea how to use any tools, so the shop person handed me a scraper and off I went with my book above the lathe. After about an hour of scraping off wood in the same direction, I was told it was time to start shaping. When I finished on the lathe, I band sawed off the bottom above the screws, drilled a hole in the top, put three coats of shellac, and I was done, and also hooked on turning. I remember thinking how cool turning was. A week later, I was back with an English walnut log that I had got from a friend. I still used a scraper, but it didn't take quite as long. I had found a hobby!

Not long after that I was at a major tool show, and at this tool show there was a woman (Brenda Behrens) who had a table with her turnings and some brochures about the Inland Woodturners. I didn't know her at the time, and she was busy talking with someone. I remember telling my wife that if I could ever turn half as well as the work I saw, I would be very happy. It was the fine detailing that really impressed me. I was at their next club meeting and joined the club. Brenda was the president, and we met at her home studio. I soon found someone selling a lathe with a few tools, and I was up and running.

I always found lots of help and instruction from fellow turners. A club is the best thing for anyone interested in learning the art of turning. I took one-on-one lessons from Brenda to improve my turning. I would have to say she was the biggest influence on my turning. I went to annual seminars and on a grant to Arrowmont, where John Jordan was teaching.

I had been working in an office for 20 years in the Air Force and, after retirement, again at a Community College and thought that turning was a lot more fun than an office. In 1993, I convinced my wife to sell our home in California and move back to her home state of Arkansas to turn full time and supplement our income from turning. We moved to Mountain Home, Arkansas, a beautiful area of the Ozarks. I set up shop and turned full time. I treated turning as a job and turned about 40 hours a week. After about a year, I started doing shows around the country. As time went on and my work got better, I was able to get into much better shows and make a living from turning. I did shows for ten years and met hundreds of artist friends from around the country. I wouldn't say it was easy, but we enjoyed traveling and meeting many people.

I stopped doing shows in 2003 after my wife of 39 years passed away. Traveling alone was not much fun. I continued to turn and build up a few wholesale accounts. I have since remarried another wonderful woman and moved to Springfield, Missouri. I still have my studio and turn, but not as much as before. I have always felt very fortunate to be able to do what I love and make a living at it. I was really fortunate to have a wife that went along with some of my nutty ideas and helped with the hundreds of shows we did. I always looked forward to Monday and getting back in my shop to get things made for my next show. I would have to say that woodturning has made my life much richer.

Natural edge burl bowl by Mike Kornblum.

Anthony Napoli: why I joined the AAW

I have worked with wood for my whole adult life, but never tried woodturning. In 2000, Harbor Freight offered their cast-iron bed lathe and eight-piece tool set on sale. I tried turning a file handle out of oak as my first project. Because I have worked with tools all my life and watched several professionals on television turn various pieces, I felt comfortable that the outcome would be acceptable. Unfortunately, it was less than what I expected. The design was good, but there was tear-out and I did not know if I had the speed set wrong, used the wrong tool, etcetera. As a result, the lathe sat unused until 2005 when a Woodcraft store opened near my home. I started with the basics and found that it came relatively easy for me. One of the instructors invited me to a meeting of the Carolina Mountain Woodturners in Asheville, North Carolina. I enjoyed the demonstrator and watching his technique. The instant gallery showed me many variations in turning and the group's willingness to share their knowledge. As a result, I joined the club at the next meeting, and not long after that I joined the AAW.

Woodturning has opened a new door to my artistic and creative side. I was an art major in high school, but drifted away from art for many years. For a number of years during my mid- to late twenties, I was involved in photography but I never felt truly satisfied. Woodturning allows me to do simple to complex projects, ranging from useful pieces to strictly-artwork style pieces. Woodturning also came into my life when work was getting especially stressful, and the time spent at the lathe took me completely out of that world and even helped my staff

Anthony Napoli proudly displays his work.

as they were able to witness my increased skill levels with each piece I brought in to show them. I also enjoy learning new techniques and have participated in a number of workshops offered by the club. I have found that even if a particular style of tool does not fit what I am working on, it does offer other options that I may not have thought about.

Ronald P. Durr: shows drew me in

Since junior high school I have been intrigued with woodwork, with a special interest in the lathe. As the years passed, I built mostly furniture, but did not exercise my interest in the lathe. Then, around 1986 I bought a 12 x 36 bench-type unit. That piece sat on a table without being used until the year 2001.

A friend and I attended a show where a fellow was carving walking sticks. My friend decided that was a hobby he wanted, as he was about to retire. I thought that I did not have enough talent to pursue carving, but said that I did have a lathe and that is what I would pursue.

That year, I studied some woodworking magazines and began turning. Having joined the Bucks County PA woodturners club, I was able to learn what tools I needed and how to use them.

The first time I submitted some pieces in a show, I was awarded 2nd and 3rd prizes in the novice class. The next two years after that I received the same prizes in the intermediate class. The following year, I received a blue ribbon as first prize in the intermediate class.

About this time, I had become a member of the American Association of Woodturners, which was suggested to me

Ronald Durr at his lathe.

by our club leaders, and I am so glad, because the information in the magazine is invaluable. Each issue improves my education in this wonderful hobby by reviewing the products shown and the techniques illustrated. Thanks, AAW, for your influence in my life.

John Lucas: turning gives me friends everywhere

After college, I took a job as photographer at Tennessee Tech University, which had taken over the Joe L. Evans Appalachian Center for Crafts. We started doing photography for the craft artists from the center and through this I met Joe Looper. Joe was introduced to woodturning by David Ellsworth, who had taught a workshop at the craft center. Joe was into it deep. The

John Lucas at the lathe.

Tennessee Association of Woodturners (TAW) had their annual symposium there in the early 90s and Joe suggested I attend as the photographer for the event. What a way to be introduced to the American Association of Woodturners! The demonstrators were John Jordan, Rude Osolnik, Betty Scarpino, and Paul Fennell. As always, the Instant Gallery just blew me away.

I remember it so well because Betty critiqued one of my segmented bowls. She said it was well assembled with clean joints and a good finish, but the rim was too large and the feet didn't fit the shape of the vessel. At first I was put off, but I soon I realized that she was right. I had not thought of turning in the whole sense. Every part of the piece has to work together. Rude was also very gracious and pulled me out of the crowd to try the skew. I joined the TAW and the AAW that week.

I have this need to be creative, but I was never able to really say what's in my mind. When I started seeing the work of artists like Stephen Hogbin, Christian Burchard, Stoney Lamar, John Jordan, and others, I knew this was a direction I had to pursue.

It's not just about being creative. I currently belong to three turning clubs and would not pass up all the friends I've made. Learning from them and in turn learning to teach, so I can share with others has been an incredible ride. Turning has given me respect in the local community. I demo for schools and other organizations. It has given me a creative outlet with pieces accepted into national shows. It has given me friends all over the world. Could you ask for more?

2007: Hand mirrors, various woods, photo by John Lucas.

Dennis Elliott: we're a fraternity

I was living with my wife, Iona, in England when she gave me for Christmas in 1972 a lathe attachment for my Black & Decker power drill. I began making toothpicks and graduated to making candlesticks, napkin rings, and holders. I was a professional musician and didn't have a lot of time to devote to woodturning, but enjoyed it immensely and found it to be very relaxing.

I was basically self-taught, but had read a book by Peter Child. At that time, there wasn't much around to read on the subject, and making things on the lathe was much more fun than reading about it.

After moving to New York in 1975, I saw an exhibit at the American Craft Museum of Edward Jacobson's collection, and that was very enlightening. I bought the accompanying book and marveled at what the turners like Bob Stocksdale, Dale Nish, Mel and Mark Lindquist, David Ellsworth, Giles Gilson, and others were doing in this country.

In 1986 or '87 there was an AAW Symposium in Kentucky, and I had a couple of pieces in the Instant Gallery. I met Ray Leier, co-owner of del Mano Gallery, and he was very interested in my work and gave me a lot of positive feedback and encouragement. Del Mano Gallery is still representing me even after all of these years.

It was also great to meet and talk to other woodturners and people who shared my love and hobby, woodturning. That experience was very positive. Looking back at that event now, I can see how that made a very big difference in my future involvement with woodturning. I also made many friends who I continue to keep in touch with. Friends who I know are always there for me! It's like being part of a fraternity—we're all brothers.

2009: Framed Wall Sculpture, 60" wide. Photo by Iona S. Elliott.

Alina Niemi: a time for every turner

After my mother's unexpected death, I was worried that my father, then 79, would plunge into another deep depression. Prevention meant involving him in something enjoyable that he would continue, so I signed both of us up as members of our local American Association of Woodturners club.

He had always wanted to turn and had acquired a set of tools 60 years earlier as a teenager. He bought a lathe, but had made no further progress. I figured that since I was likely to inherit the lathe and tools, I might as well learn to use them. Besides, my attendance encouraged his, and turning seemed like the ultimate in green art: reduce the number of trees going into landfills, and re-use unwanted and discarded wood to create functional, beautiful pieces.

At our first meeting, we were awed by the turnings in the instant gallery. There were sets of bowls of increasing size with bark edges, clearly cut from the same enormous piece of tree, urn-like vessels with finials that tapered to needle-thin points, a dark poi pounder and base so heavy and shiny that they looked as though made from stone, and pens with intricate geometric designs. This was possible? This is what we were going to do? Amazing.

I was happy to see there was no "Do Not Touch" rule—everyone was picking pieces up, turning them over, running their hands across the surfaces, admiring the quality of work and the beauty of the woods. When the meeting was over, we helped ourselves to free wood from the backs of other members' trucks. We left exhilarated and excited to have stumbled into such a world of wonder.

My father began turning immediately, and I jumped on the Internet to print out articles to help him, which was all I dared to do. I was too scared to pick up one of those sharp tools. It's a good thing I didn't. I repeatedly heard loud bangs and swearing coming from the garage as he forayed this new interest. The slamming sounds kept me far away—hearing them was stressful enough, I couldn't bear to watch them happen.

Our persistence paid off. My father completed his first bowl soon after he began his reckless experimentation, and he spent evening hours reading the information I had printed from the web. We discovered this was a hobby where you could easily try out all sorts of gadgets and tools and still want more.

Two years later, I've taken a week-long class with Alan Lacer, which gave me a solid foundation of basic skills. My father gouges, scrapes, and sands for hours every day, sometimes until late at night, much to our neighbors' dismay. But his turnings get increasingly spectacular. He has progressed to

Alina Niemi in the workshop.

Peacock Bowl, turned by Ed Niemi, colored by Alina Niemi Reclaimed wood from Bulky Pickup furniture.

vessels made from tiny pieces of wood glued together to form designs. I struggle to find turning time, but still try to participate in club challenges whenever possible. I know that only by forcing myself will I step out of my comfort zone and learn new things.

We've met generous, helpful, creative people who share materials, time, ideas, and energy. We are continually inspired by the work of other turners both at our club and in the *AW Journal*. We are blessed to live in Hawaii, where we marvel at the beauty of the tropical woods Nature provides: orangey Norfolk pine, with eye-like knots; creamy pinkish kamani, whose marbled, iridescent patterns change in the light; aptly-spotted pheasant wood; and milo, with browns from beige to dark chocolate.

My father has no time to be depressed these days. He's too busy turning!

Bill Tilson, 1945–2009

Bill Tilson was active in the Gulf Coast Woodturners (Houston), the AAW, and the World of Woodturners. Tilson was known for his enthusiasm, creativity, and positive outlook on life.

2007: Flower Vase #180, elm burl and hickory, 7" dia. In the conservationist spirit of the AAW *Turning Green* exhibition, Tilson tried to use as little wood as possible for this piece: veneer seconds for the petals, beaver-felled hickory for the base.

2008: Flower Bowl, birdseye maple, cocobolo, 7" dia. "I turned a shape to form the petals into a vessel with repetitive matching grain patterns to enhance the visual experience."

2009: Lone Flower on the Mesa, birdseye maple, cherry, black palm, copper; turned, bent, carved, formed, dyed, and assembled, 10" tall. "This piece represents the hard times and aloneness when trying to survive in the often harsh southwest. Desert flowers that survive are strong, beautiful, and graceful when they bloom."

American Association of Woodturners
Officers and Directors, 1986–2011

first name	last name	position	from	to
Jack	Aarsvold	Director	1995	1995
Daniel	Ackerman	Director	1991	1993
		Treasurer	1993	1994
		Director	1995	1995
		Advisor	1996	1997
Steve	Ainsworth	Director	2004	2004
Ron	Alexander	Director	2004	2005
		Advisor	2006	2007
Charles	Alvis	Director	1994	1994
		President	1995	1997
		Vice-president	1995	1995
		Director	1997	1999
Jeanne	Alvis	Director	1999	1999
Frank	Amigo	Director	2007	2009
		Advisor	2010	
Corey	Anderson	Director	2008	2008
		Advisor	2009	2009
Roger	Austin	Director	1999	1999
		Vice-president	1999	2000
Andy	Barnum	Director	2006	2006
Dave	Barriger	Director	1996	1999
		President	1999	2001
		Director	2001	2001
		Advisor	2002	2003
		Director	2004	2005
		Vice-president	2006	2006
		Advisor	2007	2010
Willard	Baxter	Director	2001	2001
		Treasurer	2001	2002
		Secretary	2002	2003
		Director	2003	2003
Phil	Brennion	Director	2002	2002
		Vice-president	2002	2003
		President	2003	2005
		Advisor	2006	2010
Warren	Carpenter	Director	2010	2010
		Treasurer	2010	
Lee	Carter	Director	2001	2003
		Advisor	2004	2005
Bobby	Clemons	Director	2000	2000
		Treasurer	2000	2001
		President	2001	2003
		Director	2003	2004
Ernie	Conover	Treasurer	1986	1990
		Director	1991	1991
		Advisor	1991	1993

first name	last name	position	from	to
Nick	Cook	Secretary	1991	1994
		Vice-president	1995	1996
		Director	1995	1996
		Advisor	1997	1998
Tony	Cortese	Director	2006	2006
		Secretary	2007	2007
		Advisor	2008	2009
Leo	Doyle	Vice-president	1986	1989
		Director	1986	1986
		Advisor	1990	1992
Susan	Ellison	Director	1996	1996
David	Ellsworth	President	1986	1990
		Director	1991	1993
		Advisor	1994	1994
		Advisor	2004	2007
Linda	Everett	Director	2002	2002
		Treasurer	2002	2004
		Advisor	2005	2005
J. Paul	Fennell	Director	2010	
Clay	Foster	Director	1997	1997
		Vice-president	1997	1999
		Advisor	2000	2001
Charlie	Gabriel	Treasurer	1995	1995
Stephen R.	Garavatti	Treasurer	1995	1997
		Advisor	1998	1999
Larry	Genender	Director	2007	2008
Dick	Gerard	Director	1986	1990
		Treasurer	1991	1993
		Advisor	1993	1994
Casimer (Cas)	Grabowski	Director	1993	1995
		Advisor	1996	1997
Larry	Hasiak	Director	1996	1996
		Vice-president	1996	1997
		Director	1997	1997
		Treasurer	1998	2000
		Director	2000	2000
		Advisor	2001	2003
Bill	Haskell	Secretary	2005	2005
		Treasurer	2006	2008
		President	2009	2009
		Director	2010	2010
Kurt	Hertzog	Director	2010	
John	Hill	Director	2004	2004
		Treasurer	2005	2005
		Director	2006	2006
		Advisor	2007	2011

first name	last name	position	from	to
Norman	**Hinman**	Secretary	1998	2002
		Director	2002	
		Advisor	2003	2006
Al	**Hockenbery**	Director	2006	2009
		Advisor	2009	2011
Alex	**Holsinger**	Director	1992	1993
Dave	**Hout**	Director	1991	1994
		Advisor	1995	1995
		Vice-president	2003	2003
		Director	2003	2003
Bill	**Hunter**	Director	1986	1988
		Advisor	1990	1991
Rus	**Hurt**	Secretary	1986	1990
		Director	1991	
		Advisor	1991	1993
Peter	**Hutchinson**	Director	1991	1994
		Advisor	1994	1995
Angelo	**Iafrate**	Director	2004	2004
		Vice-president	2005	2005
		President	2006	2008
		Advisor	2009	2010
Edward (Bud)	**Jacobson**	Advisor	1986	1991
Jeff	**Jilg**	Director	2005	2005
		Secretary	2006	2006
Bonnie	**Klein**	Director	1989	1990
		Vice-president	1991	1994
		Advisor	1995	1996
		Director	2001	2001
		Advisor	2002	2003
Alan	**Lacer**	Director	1989	1989
		Vice-president	1990	1990
		President	1991	1994
		Advisor	1995	1996
Gary	**Lansinger**	Director	2004	2005
Dale	**Larson**	Director	2009	
Albert	**LeCoff**	Vice-president	1986	1986
		Advisor	1986	1991
Jean	**LeGwin**	Director	2007	2007
		Secretary	2008	
Ray	**Leier**	Advisor	1987	1991
David	**Lipscomb**	Director	1986	1987
Arthur	**Mason**	Advisor	1987	1991
Karen	**Moody**	Director	1995	1997
		Advisor	1998	1999
Sandy	**Moreno**	Director	2005	2005
Dale	**Nish**	Vice-president	1986	1986
		Advisor	1986	1991
Rude	**Osolnik**	Advisor	1986	1987
		Director	1987	1991
		Advisor	1991	1993

first name	last name	position	from	to
Binh	**Pho**	Director	2009	
Phil	**Pratt**	Secretary	1995	1997
		Director	1998	1998
		Advisor	1999	2000
Mary	**Redig**	Director	1990	1990
S. Gary	**Roberts**	Director	1993	1994
		Advisor	1995	1996
Robert	**Rosand**	Director	1998	2000
		Vice-president	2000	2002
		Director	2002	2003
		Advisor	2004	2005
Merryll	**Saylan**	Director	1993	1994
		President	1995	1995
Palmer	**Sharpless**	Director	1986	1992
		Secretary	1991	1991
		Advisor	1992	1994
Cassandra	**Speier**	Director	2009	2009
		Treasurer	2010	2010
		Vice-president	2010	
Mark	**St. Leger**	Director	2000	2004
		Vice-president	2004	2004
		Advisor	2005	2006
William L.	**Stephenson**	Director	1996	1999
		Advisor	1999	2000
Al	**Stirt**	Director	1986	1988
		Advisor	1990	1991
Adrian	**Sturdivant**	Director	1999	2000
Malcolm	**Tibbetts**	Director	2005	2006
		Vice-president	2007	2010
Sean	**Troy**	Director	2006	2007
		Advisor	2008	2008
Linda	**Van Gehuchten**	Director	2000	2003
		Secretary	2003	2004
		Director	2005	2005
		Advisor	2006	2008
		Director	2008	2009
Botho	**von Hampeln**	Director	2011	
David	**Wahl**	Director	1997	1997
		President	1997	1999
		Director	1999	2000
Stan	**Wellborn**	Director	2011	
Tom	**Wirsing**	Director	2008	2008
		Treasurer	2009	2009
		President	2010	
Malcolm	**Zander**	Director	2010	

Index of Names

Acker, Bob: 46
Adams, Brad: 209
Adamson, Glenn: 93
Ainsworth, Steve: 91
Allen, Patricia: 191
Allen, Ray: 141, 192, 193
Alvis, Charles: 82, 84
Anderson, Arnold: 233
Angelino, Gianfranco: 152
Anstaett, Floyd: 190
Avisera, Eli: 76, 114, 200
Baldwin, J: 48
Barriger, David: 82, 91, 93
Bates, Marston: 112
Batty, Alan: 169
Baum, L. Frank: 98
Bayer, Herbert: 32
Behrens, Brenda: 241
Belser, David: 159
Bennett, Garry Knox: 102, 165, 171
Berera, Marco: 111
Betley, Walt: 228
Biggs, Dixie: 98, 116
Bird, Kurt: 178
Bird, Leonard: 149
Blaine, Sandra: 56, 63
Blanc, Jérôme: 205
Blank, Pat: 209
Bloch, Peter: 162
Blumer, Jacques: 209, 210
Borer, Howard: 77
Bosch, Trent: 225
Bostick, Matthew: 102
Bowers, Dave: 190, 215
Braniff, Dan: 89
Brennion, Phil: 90, 92, 93, 100, 182
Brennion, Susan: 90, 178
Brolly, Michael: 43, 44
Brown, Cyril: 192
Brown, Doug: 77
Brown, Emmett: 192
Brown, J. Carter: 237
Brown, Phil: 119, 194
Burchard, Christian: 138, 151, 182, 210, 211, 237, 244
Burki, Glenn: 77
Burris, Kevin: 149
Burrows, Dick: 176
Butler, Steven: 218
Campbell, Marilyn: 171
Carpenter, Art: 127
Carter, Jimmy: 43
Castle, Wendell: 70
Chase, Dale: 146
Child, Peter: 49, 245
Christiansen, Kip: 10, 87, 198
Clabaugh, Maurice: 236

Clancy, Bob: 87
Clarke, Matt: 240
Clay, Tim: 189
Clemons, Bobby: 93
Cloutier, Hank: 188
Codding, Dick: 95
Conover, Ernie: 10, 26, 50, 58, 68, 70
Cook, Nick: 66, 167, 212, 215
Cooke, Edward S.: 93
Copeland, Darrell: 197
Cox, Jack: 193
Crabb, Tom: 106, 111
Crawford, Rick: 229
Crockett, Barbara: 17
Cummings, Frank: 76, 139, 198
Curtis, Dana: 63
Darlow, Mike: 100, 143
Davidson, Ed: 178, 186
Day, Monica: 10
Deakins, Chelsea: 106
Delahay, Terry: 178
Derry, Don: 87, 164
Dickerman, Wally: 186
DiPietro, Andy: 118
Ditmer, Judy: 59, 234
Ditto, Cindy: 77
Ditto, Don: 77
Dodge, Robert: 74, 132, 133
Donovan, Neil: 123
Dotson, Virginia: 124, 153, 193
Doughtie, Sharon: 109
Doyle, Leo: 57, 58, 68, 69, 70, 86
Draper, Addie: 151, 192
Drozda, Cindy: 116, 235
Duhl, Florence: 42
Duncan, Kathlen: 77
Dunlap, Ken: 229
Duplessis, Gorst: 103
Durr, Ronald P.: 243
Dutton, Freddy: 190
Eames, Charles: 161
Eames, Ray: 161
Elliott, Dennis: 245
Ellsworth, David: 2, 10, 40, 41, 42, 44, 45, 56, 58, 59, 60, 62, 64, 65, 68, 73, 74, 81, 85, 91, 92, 104, 138, 165, 182, 198, 204, 244, 245
Elvig, Glenn: 142
Erez, Manny: 46
Escoulen, Jean-François: 85, 145, 200
Ewell, Gordon L.: 188
Exton, Peter: 95, 158, 161
Fawver, Melinda: 88
Fein, Harvey: 96, 99, 103, 169
Feltz, Ray: 117
Fennell, J. Paul: 49, 104, 244
Ferber, Linda: 175, 179

Ferguson, Ray: 85
Firmager, Melvin: 100
Fischman, Irving: 192
Fisher, Douglas J.: 115
Fleming, Ron: 76, 125, 142
Foster, Clay: 105, 109
Fruchter, Tina: 10
Gafert, Irene: 109
Gandy, Brian: 212
Garrett, Dewey: 103, 127, 152
Garrison, Tucker: 197
Gehman, Jordan: 160
Gerard, Dick: 10, 56, 58, 59, 69, 73, 93
Giagnocavo, Alan: 10
Gilson, Giles: 39, 41, 42, 100, 101, 102, 105, 141, 165, 183, 230, 245
Glaser, Jerry: 18, 65, 102
Gott, Jim: 222
Graham, Michael: 155
Greaves, Scott: 186
Gross, Barry: 187
Grunke, Ken: 178
Grunwager, Al: 68
Hadley, Bob: 17
Hamilton, Richard: 188
Hansonn, Bobby: 62
Hartline, Leonard (Fletcher): 224
Haskell, Bill: 10, 89, 92, 102, 110, 118
Hatcher, Stephen: 17
Heryet, Julie: 114, 117
Hertzog, Kurt: 172, 186, 187
Heryet, Julie: 114, 117
Hibbert, Louise: 200
Hibdon, Bill: 53
Hill, John: 91, 92, 169, 172, 182, 212
Hill, Matthew: 94
Hinshaw, Bob: 96
Hoadley, Bruce: 231
Hockenbery, Al: 110, 184, 215
Hockenbery, Sherry: 215
Hodgetts, Ted: 193
Hogbin, Stephen: 39, 43, 45, 64, 70, 102, 105, 154, 160, 165, 183, 192, 244
Hogue, Richard: 171
Holland, Harvey: 40
Holtus, Pete: 221
Holzapfel, Michelle: 14, 105, 143
Hooper, Richard: 151
Hormann, Dennis: 70
Horn, Robyn: 64, 85
Horn, Sam: 85
Hosaluk, Michael: 64, 81, 84, 105, 117, 132, 155, 157, 224, 230
Hoyer, Todd: 85, 150
Hromek, Peter: 145
Hrytzak, Bernie: 169
Hudgens, Jeffrey: 188

Hughes, Ray: 113
Hunter, William: 40, 41, 43, 58, 68, 69, 140
Hurt, Rus: 58, 68, 69
Hutchinson, Peter J.: 176
Iafrate, Angelo: 10, 100, 101, 102, 113, 182, 186
Ingram, Bob: 189
Ireland, Beth: 118
Jackofsky, Mike: 118
Jackson, Stonewall: 173
Jacobson, Edward (Bud): 45, 58, 62, 68, 70, 81, 245
Jensen, Allen: 156
Jewell, Bill: 173
Jilg, Jeff: 91, 178
Johnson, Eric: 206
Johnson, Skip: 127
Jonas, Douglas W.: 115
Jones, Bill: 199
Jones, Ray: 155
Jordan, John: 50, 64, 128, 182, 224, 241, 244
Kagan, Neil: 119
Kaplan, Deena: 184
Kaplan, Jerome: 184
Keller, Jim: 99
Kelsey, John: 10, 25
Key, Ray: 93, 137, 229
Klap, Fred: 99
Klein, Bonnie: 50, 51, 58, 91, 93, 146, 173, 174, 182, 212, 215, 216
Kleinhenz, Rich: 187
Kline, Fred: 77
Kornblum, Mike: 241
Kramer, Pat: 197
Krenov, James: 127
Kuc, Carol: 100
Kvitka, Dan: 176
Lacer, Alan: 10, 78, 81, 85, 89, 104, 111, 115, 169, 246
Lacer, Mary: 58, 70, 77, 83, 90, 91, 102, 174, 175, 194, 244
Lamar, Stoney: 63, 64, 150
Lambert, Jim: 186
Lansinger, Gary: 212
Larson, Dale: 76, 77
Latven, Bud: 147, 148, 192
Lawson, Patricia: 186
Layport, Ron: 130
LeCoff, Alan: 47, 60, 103, 198
LeCoff, Albert: 10, 45, 46, 49, 57, 58, 60, 62, 64, 68, 69, 74, 93, 102, 103, 192, 194, 198, 230, 231
LeCoff, Tina: 231
Lee, Mike: 95
LeGwin, Jean: 10

Index of Subjects

More Information about Woodturning

USA
American Association of Woodturners
The AAW is an international, non-profit organization dedicated to the advancement of woodturning. Our mission is to provide education, information, and organization to those interested in turning wood. Includes many Canadian clubs.

222 Landmark Center, 75 W Fifth St, St Paul, MN 55102-1431
(651)484-9094
www.woodturner.org

The Wood Turning Center
...our International Turning Exchange (ITE) residency program has involved over 60 international residents; the Community Outreach program brings hands-on wood turning experience to students throughout the region; the permanent collection contains over 1,000 turned objects from around the world

www.woodturningcenter.org

Australia
Woodturners Society of Queensland
...promote, practice and present the art and craft of woodturning to our members -promote public awareness, knowledge and appreciation of woodturning and the art and artefacts produced.

www.woodturnerssocietyofqld.com

Brazil
A.B.T.M. - Associação Brasileira de Torneiros em Madeira
www.torneirosdemadeira.com.br/forum/

Canada
No national chapter, contact AAW for local affiliated clubs.

France
French Association for Artistic Woodturning
AFTAB's aim is the promotion of artistic woodturning.

www.aftab-asso.com/html/anglais.html

Iceland
Guild of Iceland Woodturners
www.trerennismidi.is

Ireland
The Irish Woodturners Guild
...a national non-profit making organisation dedicated to the advancement and promotion of woodturning. We consist of individual members and affiliated local chapters throughout the whole island of Ireland.
www.irishwoodturnersguild.com

Irish Woodturners Guild, Dublin Chapter
www.dublinwoodturners.com

Israel
Israel Association of Woodturners
www.israelwood.org

Italy
Culturalegno (Wood Culture Association)
www.culturalegno.org

New Zealand
The National Association of Woodworkers New Zealand
Non profit fostering a wide understanding and appreciation of woodturning and woodworking.

www.naw.org.nz

Portugal and Spain
Asociación Iberica Torneros Artesanos de Madera (AITAM)
www.aitam.foroactivo.com/

Quebec
Assocation des Tourneurs sur Bois du Quebec
www.atbq.qc.ca/

South Africa
Association of Woodturners of South Africa
www.awsa.org.za/

United Kingdom
The Association of Woodturners of Great Britain
...an international non-profit making organisation dedicated to the advancement and promotion of woodturning.

www.woodturners.co.uk/

Association of Polelathe Turners and Greenwood Workers
... to promote green woodworking and all its associated crafts so that once again the woodlands of the world are nurtured and valued as a source of employment and enjoyment.

www.bodgers.org.uk

The Society of Ornamental Turners
Providing information on the subject of ornamental turning both to society members and to newcomers to the craft.

www.the-sot.com

Register of Professional Turners
Sponsored by The Worshipful Company of Turners of London, this site is to enable interested parties to find a competent turner.

www.rpturners.co.uk

Websites

American Association of Woodturners
www.woodturner.org
www.galleryofwoodart.org

Collectors of Wood Art
www.collectorsofwoodart.org

Sawmill Creek
www.sawmillcreek.org

Wood Turning Center
www.woodturningcenter.org

WoodCentral
www.woodcentral.com

WoodturningOnline
www.woodturningonline.com

Magazines

American Woodturner
www.woodturner.org

More Woodturning
www.morewoodturning.net

Woodturning
www.thegmcgroup.com

Woodturning Design
www.woodturningdesign.com

Education

Anderson Ranch Arts Center
Snowmass Village, Colorado
970-923-3181
www.andersonranch.org

Appalachian Center for Craft
Smithville, Tennessee
615-597-6803
www.tntech.edu/craftcenter

Arrowmont School of Arts and Crafts
Gatlinburg, Tennessee
865-436-5860
www.arrowmont.org

Canyon Studios
Copper Canyon, Texas
940-455-2344
www.canyonstudios.org

Center for Furniture Craftsmanship
Rockport, Maine
207-594-5611
www.woodschool.org

John C. Campbell Folk School
Brasstown, North Carolina
800-365-5724
www.folkschool.org

Maine Woodturning School
Damariscotta, Maine
207-563-2345
www.woodturningschool.org

Marc Adams School of Woodworking
Franklin, Indiana
317-535-4013
www.marcadams.com

Peters Valley Craft Center
Layton, New Jersey
973-948-5200
www.petersvalley.org

Center for Turning and Furniture Design
Indiana University of Pennsylvania
724-357-2530
www.iup.edu

American Association of Woodturners
Periodicals, Publications and Catalogs

American Woodturner

American Woodturner (*AW Journal*) subscriptions
American Woodturner (*AW Journal*) back issues
American Woodturner (*AW Journal*) back issues on CD

Now bimonthly and in full color.

American Woodturner Techniques & Projects
Books One through Five

These 8½ x 11" books are treasuries of ideas, inspirations, and projects compiled from American Woodturner.

AAW Symposium Instant Gallery videos 2000 through 2010

This video series offers you a slow walk through the amazing Instant Gallery, with the ability to pause and study everything that interests you.

AAW Symposium Techniques videos

These videos capture educational sessions at past AAW symposiums. A treasure-trove of technical demonstration and explanation.

Exhibition catalogs

East Meets West, 1999
From Sea to Odyssey, 2004
A Gathering of Spoons, 2010
Growth through Sharing, 1996
Japanese Bowls, 2007
Maple Medley, 2010
Nature Takes a Turn, 2001
Put a Lid on It, 2002
reTurn to the Land of Oz, 2005
The Sphere, 2008
Step Up to the Plate, 2006
Turned for Use
Turned for Use II
Turning 20, Still Evolving, 2006
Turning Green, 2007
Sprit of the Southwest, 2009
The Spindle, 2009
The Teapot, 2010
Twirlings, 2009

AAW Gallery and online store

American Association of Woodturners
222 Landmark Center,
75 W Fifth St.
Saint Paul, MN 55102
(877) 595-9094
www.woodturner.org
www.galleryofwoodart.org

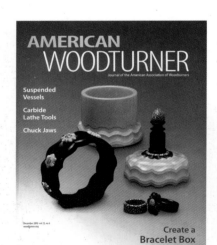

Create a
Bracelet Box

The Teapot